Waiting for Justice

Moving Young Offenders Through the Juvenile Court Process

Jeffrey A. Butts
Gregory J. Halemba

710 Fifth Avenue, Pittsburgh, Pennsylvania 15219 (412) 227-6950

This document was prepared by the National Center for Juvenile Justice, the research division of the National Council of Juvenile and Family Court Judges, and was supported by grant #92-JN-CX-0002 from the Office of Juvenile Justice and Delinquency Prevention, Office of Justice Programs, U.S. Department of Justice.

Library of Congress Catalog Card Number 96-071256
ISBN 0-910099-16-2
Printed in the United States of America

The National Center for Juvenile Justice is a private, non-profit organization and the research division of the National Council of Juvenile and Family Court Judges. The Center's mission is to aid in the prevention of juvenile delinquency, child abuse, and child neglect by conducting research on a broad range of juvenile justice topics.

Price: $18 (U.S.)

Table of Contents

Chapter 3:
NATIONAL SURVEY OF DELINQUENCY DELAYS
by Jeffrey A. Butts and Gregory J. Halemba

Chapter 4:
CASE PROCESSING IN THREE JUVENILE COURTS
by Gregory J. Halemba and Jeffrey A. Butts

Chapter 5:
NATIONAL TRENDS IN CASE PROCESSING TIME
by Jeffrey A. Butts

Tables and Figures

CHAPTER 1

CHAPTER 3

CHAPTER 4

CHAPTER 5

CHAPTER 6

Acknowledgments

This study was supported by funds provided to the National Center for Juvenile Justice (NCJJ), the research division of the National Council of Juvenile and Family Court Judges, by the U.S. Department of Justice's Office of Juvenile Justice and Delinquency Prevention (OJJDP) through grant number 92-JN-CX-0002. The OJJDP program manager was Mr. Jeffrey Slowikowski.

The research described in this report was developed in consultation with the members of a national advisory committee. Members of this committee included:

Ms. Eleanor Austin—Director of Court Services (Retired), Wayne County Probate Court, Detroit, Michigan

Dr. Carol Burgess—Former Deputy Director, Maricopa County Juvenile Court, Phoenix, Arizona

Hon. Cheryl Allen Craig—Family Division, Allegheny County Court of Common Pleas, Pittsburgh, Pennsylvania

Mr. David Fishkin—Chief, Juvenile Division, Baltimore City Office of the Public Defender, Baltimore, Maryland

Mr. John Howley—Assignment Services Manager, Cuyahoga County Court of Common Pleas, Cleveland, Ohio

Ms. Kim Kelly—Juvenile Court Administrator, Maricopa County Juvenile Court, Phoenix, Arizona

Hon. Sharon McCully—Third Judicial District Court, Salt Lake City, Utah

Dr. Edward Mulvey—Law and Psychiatry Program, Western Psychiatric Institute and Clinic, University of Pittsburgh School of Medicine

Ms. Joyce Wright—Chief, Juvenile Division, State's Attorney's Office for Baltimore City, Baltimore, Maryland

Assistance was provided by staff members at the National Center for Juvenile Justice, including Imogene Montgomery, Hunter Hurst IV, Diane Malloy, Lori Hoag, Gail Rico, and Angela Sanders. Legal research was performed by Linda Szymanski. Comments and suggestions were provided by Hunter Hurst III, Melissa Sickmund, and Howard Snyder of NCJJ. The authors also appreciate the comments and suggestions of Barry Feld of the University of Minnesota, William Barton of Indiana University, Bart Lubow of the Annie E. Casey Foundation, Edmund McGarrell of Indiana University, Joseph Sanborn, Jr. of the University of Central Florida, Janet Shapiro of Bryn Mawr University, Hon. John Steketee of the Kent County (Michigan) Juvenile Court, and the Board of Fellows of the National Center for Juvenile Justice, Hon. Maurice B. Cohill, Jr., Chairman.

Finally, this work would not have been possible without the cooperation of the juvenile justice professionals who were interviewed by the project staff, those who took the time to complete the project's mailed survey, as well as those who regularly contribute data to NCJJ's National Juvenile Court Data Archive. Their efforts are gratefully acknowledged.

Foreword

Wedged squarely between the mandate to assure due process, the compelling State interest in protecting and rehabilitating minor children, geometrically expanding caseloads, rapidly eroding resources, and an unprecedented escalation in public demands for "pounds of flesh" to assuage our fears of juvenile crime, the Nation's juvenile courts are finding it increasingly difficult to move young offenders through the legal process with dispatch.

This unique volume is the first major study of processing delays in the history of U.S. juvenile courts. Funded by a grant from the U.S. Department of Justice's Office of Juvenile Justice and Delinquency Prevention, the *Delays in Juvenile Justice Sanctions Project* was conducted at the National Center for Juvenile Justice, the research division of the National Council of Juvenile and Family Court Judges.

Like all virtues, efficiency in the juvenile justice system is easy to embrace but difficult to realize. A variety of legal, organizational, and budgetary problems conspire against the court's efforts to respond quickly to young offenders. Probation investigators have disabling caseloads, judges have numbing schedules, family members cannot be located or fail to show for hearings, and prosecutors and defense attorneys are asked to be in several places at once. When all parties finally come together to agree on the best disposition for a young drug dealer or armed robber, finding an appropriate and available program consumes still more valuable time.

The speed of the juvenile justice process is a crucial element in its fairness and effectiveness. Nobody benefits when the juvenile justice system takes six months to respond to the first suspected burglary of a 14-year-old youth. If innocent, the juvenile lives unjustly under suspicion for six months. If not innocent, the juvenile is allowed to continue behavior that could eventually lead to more serious social harm and result in more severe legal sanctions. Six months of waiting may mean that the juvenile justice system misses an opportunity to intervene swiftly in the early stages of a budding criminal career and the community continues to lose confidence in an essential public institution charged with protecting the public safety and the public welfare.

Despite its obvious importance, the speed of the juvenile justice process has been virtually ignored by researchers. This study begins to fill this void by documenting the extent of processing delays in juvenile and family courts, identifying the correlates of delay, and evaluating the methods currently used to control delay. The study's findings offer a benchmark for court administration and provide a valuable baseline for future research. As important as they are, however, the authors' contributions to empirical knowledge about delay may be overshadowed by their imaginative proposals for rethinking the use of time standards in the juvenile court and for establishing a policy focus on the timing of the court's decision making in cases involving young offenders.

Hunter Hurst III, Director
National Center for Juvenile Justice
Pittsburgh, Pennsylvania

Preface

The *Delays in Juvenile Justice Sanctions Project*, was conducted between 1992 and 1996 at the National Center for Juvenile Justice (NCJJ). Funded by the Office of Juvenile Justice and Delinquency Prevention (OJJDP), the goals of the project were: 1) to determine the extent of delays in the processing of delinquency cases in U.S. juvenile courts; 2) to analyze the causes of delay and their effects on juveniles and the administration of the juvenile justice system—including whether current levels of delay exceed accepted professional standards; and 3) to make recommendations to OJJDP regarding the need for additional standards or policy initiatives related to juvenile justice delays. The report that follows identifies the extent of delay problems in juvenile and family courts, describes the most common problems associated with juvenile justice delays and the methods used to control delay, and suggests a course of action for juvenile justice policy makers.

The number of delinquent youth and dependent children handled by juvenile and family courts in the United States has grown considerably in recent years. According to *Juvenile Court Statistics*, the national delinquency caseload increased 23% between 1989 and 1993 (Butts et al., 1996). During the same period of time, agency reports of child maltreatment grew more than 20% (Snyder, Sickmund, and Poe-Yamagata, 1996). Timely handling of abuse and neglect matters has been a cornerstone of Federal child welfare policy for several decades, perhaps best represented by the *Adoption Assistance and Child Welfare Act of 1980* (P.L. 96–272). In addition, national practitioner organizations have disseminated principles of effective juvenile court practice in an effort to increase the efficiency of dispositions for abuse and neglect cases (National Council of Juvenile and Family Court Judges, 1995).

Timeliness in the processing of delinquency cases has received much less attention from policy makers, practitioners, and researchers. This lack of interest may stem from an untested assumption that the juvenile justice system is always swifter than the adult courts. Or, it may be associated with a generalized disregard for juvenile law within the legal profession. Just as many judges and attorneys have viewed practice in juvenile and family courts as training for later appearances in "real" courts, policy makers and researchers may believe the timing of the juvenile justice process is of little consequence.

Indeed, the juvenile justice process may appear to be relatively unimportant if the number of delinquency cases is compared with the volume of cases seen in the criminal courts, or if the length of the juvenile court process is compared with the duration of the longest criminal trials. However, it would be a serious mistake to dismiss the issue of juvenile justice delay simply because it seems less problematic when compared with criminal court delay. To do so would be similar to disregarding the problem of youth violence because juveniles account for only 10% of homicides or 13% of serious assaults (Snyder, Sickmund, and Poe-Yamagata, 1996:13).

In fact, processing delays in the juvenile justice system may be uniquely harmful. Adolescents are known to be socially, emotionally, and even cognitively different from adults. Particularly in stressful circumstances, adolescents have been found to exhibit a sense of "futurelessness" in evaluating the possible gains and risks associated with personal behavior and choices (Grisso, 1996:234). The nature of adolescence itself may reduce the perceived immediacy of even slightly delayed sanctions. As a result, the juvenile court's impact on youthful offenders may be seriously compromised by processing delays that would be merely routine in the adult justice system.

Most of the reasons for case processing delays in the juvenile justice system are similar to those faced by the criminal and civil courts. Delays have been associated with the seriousness of the offense involved in a case, the prior record of the offender, the pre-trial custody status of the offender (whether confined or not), the size of court caseloads, the ratio of cases per judge, the number and complexity of attorney motions, and court policies regarding continuances. Some studies have suggested that case processing time is affected by a court's choice of docket management systems (master or individual calendar). Others have noted that an underlying cause of delay may be a lack of adequate caseflow information, or an attitude among court employees that delay is normal.

Some aspects of juvenile court delay, however, are unique to the juvenile justice system. Compared with the adult courts, the juvenile justice process is highly individualized and extends beyond legal fact-finding. The juvenile court must consider the social and psychological development of juveniles, their relationships with family members, and the role of other social institutions involved with the youth or family, especially the schools and the child welfare system. Unlike criminal courts, juvenile courts sometimes provide services directly to juveniles and their families. Two factors that especially distinguish juvenile courts from higher trial courts are that more of the juvenile court's caseload is handled without official action, and more of the juvenile court's work takes place after adjudication or even after disposition. Understanding the causes of delay as well as the methods of reducing delay in delinquency case processing requires an understanding of the juvenile justice system. Research on juvenile court delay must consider the diverse goals of the juvenile justice system and account for the unique characteristics of the juvenile court environment.

More than a decade ago, one of the few researchers to investigate delays in the juvenile justice system proposed a number of important questions that had yet to be answered by studies on juvenile court case processing time. Anne Rankin Mahoney (1985) called for future analyses of juvenile justice delays to address issues such as:

- Is there a range of case processing times in juvenile and family courts?
- Do juvenile court processing times vary more or less than adult courts?
- What case or court characteristics are associated with long versus short processing times in juvenile courts?
- What special issues are involved in juvenile court case processing time?
- By whose interests should ideal processing times be determined: the youth, the court, or the community?

The *Delays in Juvenile Justice Sanctions Project* was designed to address these and other questions. The major goal of the project was to identify the extent of processing delays in U.S. juvenile courts and to explore the effects of delay on the juvenile justice system as well as the most effective methods of controlling delay. Hopefully, the results of the study will ensure that future discussions about the juvenile court and the effectiveness of the juvenile justice system will extend beyond traditional debates on the role of diversion programs or the rehabilitative impact of correctional sanctions. The findings of this study should encourage policy makers to place greater importance on early intervention and to consider the effect of processing delays on the juvenile justice system's ability to prevent and reduce juvenile crime.

Chapter 1 of this volume discusses the social, legal, and organizational issues related to delays in the juvenile justice system. Chapter 2 presents findings from the research literature on the causes of delay in both the juvenile court and the adult justice system. Chapter 3 summarizes findings from a survey of judges, attorneys, and administrators from 123 local juvenile justice systems. Chapter 4 presents three case studies of delinquency processing practices and delay problems in urban juvenile courts. Chapter 5 analyzes national patterns in delinquency case processing time using delinquency case records contributed to the *National Juvenile Court Data Archive* by jurisdictions across the country. Chapter 6 presents the project's conclusions and recommendations for juvenile justice professionals and policy makers.

Chapter 1
Delay in the Juvenile Justice System

INTRODUCTION [1]

Among the many social reform movements that swept the United States during the late 1800s and early 1900s, one resulted in the formation of separate courts to handle young law violators. Juvenile courts were founded at least partly on the belief that young people accused of crimes should be handled differently than adult offenders, with less formality and in non-adversarial proceedings (Rothman, 1980). As a result, many juvenile courts had more in common with social agencies than with trial courts, at least for the first 50 to 60 years of their existence. In keeping with this less formal atmosphere, juvenile courts provided very few procedural protections for youths accused of delinquent acts.

By the 1960s, however, it was apparent that juvenile courts were becoming very similar to criminal courts, with an emphasis on culpability and punishment rather than treatment and rehabilitation. In a series of important cases beginning in 1966, the U.S. Supreme Court ruled that the just deserts orientation of some juvenile courts merited greater legal rights for all juveniles. The Supreme Court acted to increase the standard of evidence used in delinquency proceedings, and to require States to provide juveniles with a number of due process rights, including the right to counsel, the right to confront and to cross-examine witnesses, the right to formal notice of charges, and the protection against self-incrimination.[2]

The Supreme Court stopped short of applying all Fifth and Sixth Amendment rights to juvenile court proceedings. For example, a right to jury trial in juvenile courts was explicitly rejected by the Supreme Court (*McKeiver v. Pennsylvania*, 1971). Individual States were free to grant such rights to juveniles, and 16 States allowed jury trials in juvenile court in at least some circumstances as of 1992 (Szymanski, 1993). Some critics argue that all juveniles should be provided with the right to jury trial, or at least those charged with the most serious offenses since they are more likely to be exposed to the court's punitive tendencies (Sanborn, 1993).

The question of speedy trial rights for accused juveniles has never been addressed by the Supreme Court. Concern about the speed of the juvenile court's dispositional process, however, has been growing among legislators, judges, practicing attorneys, court administrators, and law enforcement personnel. Some of these concerns may be related to a new emphasis on due process rights for juveniles. Others may stem from an interest in accelerating the imposition of sanctions on juvenile law violators under the assumption that swift sanctions are more effective sanctions.

Policy makers have also been calling for the juvenile justice system to provide more timely sanctions for young law violators. A keystone of the Federal government's program strategy for dealing with serious, violent, and chronic juvenile offenders is the use of "immediate interventions" that "stop the juvenile's further penetration into the system by inducing law-abiding behavior as early as possible through the combination of appropriate intervention and treatment sanctions" (Wilson and Howell, 1993:19). In order to implement this agenda fully, policy makers, researchers, and juvenile justice professionals need to understand the scope and nature of processing delays in the juvenile justice system.

COURT DELAY

The phenomenon of court delay has a "long and notorious history" (Church et al., 1978:2). Researchers have noted references to the "law's delay" by literary figures from Shakespeare and Moliere to Chekhov and Dickens (Fleming, 1973; Haynes, 1973; Luskin, 1978; Neubauer and Ryan, 1982; Trotter and Cooper, 1982; Luskin and Luskin, 1986). Government officials have been concerned about court delay for decades. Chief Justice Earl Warren advised that "interminable and unjustifiable delays in our courts" could compromise the "basic legal rights" of Americans and eventually erode "the very foundations of constitutional government in the United States" (as quoted in Haynes, 1973:46-47). William Howard Taft once asserted that the efficiency of the courts was a critical component in the effectiveness of the entire government:

> If one were asked in what respect we have fallen furthermost short of ideal conditions in our government, I think we would be justified in answering, in spite of the glaring defects of our system of municipal government, that it is our failure to secure expedition and thoroughness in the enforcement of public and private rights in our courts (as quoted in Haynes, 1973:46).

Dire warnings such as these have been issued periodically throughout the past century and have prompted many research investigations into the causes and effects of court delay, some dating to the 1920s (Pound and Frankfurter, 1922; Morse and Beattie, 1932). During the 1950s and 1960s, researchers examined delays in the handling of personal injury litigation (Rosenberg and Sovern, 1959), in the processing of civil court caseloads (Zeisel et al., 1959; Levin and Woolley, 1961), and in criminal prosecutions (Banfield and Anderson, 1968). Despite this lengthy history, the problem of court delay continues to generate concern and debate. Court delay appears to be a very stubborn problem. Numerous solutions have been advanced to deal with it, but none have been overwhelmingly successful. Some researchers have argued that court delay is uniquely resistant to intervention because the two most influential groups of court professionals tend to view delay in vastly different terms. Court administrators seek order, rationality and predictability in the courtroom, while judges and other attorneys are trained to think non-bureaucratically and to place primary importance on the quality of the legal process rather than on efficiency (Saari, 1982). While administrators, judges, and attorneys share the common goal of providing justice and due process, their relative concern over the timeliness of court procedures often varies.

The fact that court delay continues to cause problems despite extensive efforts to control it may also reflect a desirable tension between the conflicting goals of justice. Packer described two competing models that influence our thinking about the justice system—*crime control* and *due process* (Packer, 1968). Under the *crime control* model, the most important function of the justice system is to repress criminal conduct. The effectiveness of the system, therefore, depends on uniformity, speed, and finality (i.e., low rates of appeal). Under the *due process* model, the central function of the justice system is to regulate governmental intrusions in individual rights and to mediate disputes among citizens and the State. The *due process* model stresses quality and thoroughness, and places much less importance on efficiency or speed. While the *crime control* model is affirmative, emphasizing the exercise of official power and the authority of the legislative and executive branches of government, the *due process* model is negative, stressing limits on official power and emphasizing the authority of the judiciary and the Constitution.

Packer noted that the criminal justice system has tremendous destructive potential for civil liberties and social freedoms. Thus, society must prevent the justice system from achieving maximum efficiency. In other words, courts should be encouraged to pursue the crime-control values of uniformity, finality, and speed, but they should never be permitted to reach perfection. Thus, a reasonable level of court delay benefits society by providing a check upon the destructive powers of the State. Pervasive and chronic delays, however, impede due process which is also an important check upon State power.

A certain magnitude of delay may be necessary for a court to function as an organization. The word "delay" is a pejorative term suggesting that faster is always better. Yet, the parties involved in a court case do not always desire a speedy resolution. Judges, attorneys, witnesses, and defendants often have competing interests which at times may be satisfied by slower rather than faster dispositions (Luskin, 1978; Sarat, 1978). If court administrators were to become too successful in reducing delays, prosecutors and defense attorneys would most likely take actions to restore delay, such as filing more motions or seeking additional continuances (Levin, 1975; Posner, 1973).

Speed of case processing may be one of the more easily measured standards with which to evaluate the performance of the court system, but equating speed with effectiveness would be inappropriate. The task of court administration is not to eliminate all delays, but to control *unnecessary* delays. Of course, it is far easier to profess one's opposition to unnecessary court delays than it is to specify which delays are unnecessary and then to reduce them. Cases that seem to take forever are easily identified, and delays in their resolution have few defenders. Most of the inefficiencies of justice, however, are generated by routine delays in routine cases.

Effects of Delay

Delay can have severely negative consequences for society, for the courts, and for the accused. Posner described the costs that accrue to defendants when backlogs and congestion generate a long "court queue" (Posner, 1973). These costs include the temporary loss of income, perhaps the loss of employment altogether, and ultimately the effective loss of due process (Levin, 1975:121). Defendants may spend months in crowded jails waiting for their cases to be resolved. In some pretrial facilities, relatively minor offenders may be mixed with serious offenders for extended periods. Feeley concluded that the court process itself often serves as a form of punishment for those accused of crimes (Feeley, 1992).

Of course, defendants may benefit from delay. For those released to await trial, delay brings at least temporary liberty. Even for jailed defendants, delay may be beneficial if it weakens the prosecution's case by causing witnesses to lose memory of an incident or to drop out of the court process from frustration. In his study of criminal case processing in the New Haven Court of Common Pleas, Feeley found a shared belief among defense attorneys that delay was usually in the interests of their clients rather than those of the prosecution. In fact, the defense attorneys told Feeley of an ironic courthouse adage, "speedy trial is a denial of due process" (Feeley, 1992:134).

In addition to its impact on defendants, delay may interfere with the general effectiveness of the courts. Some researchers have warned that excessive delay may increase a court's willingness to grant lenient case dispositions, thereby reducing the overall deterrent effect of the process (Banfield and Anderson, 1968). According to this argument, long processing delays and case backlogs make courts reluctant to engage in full-length trials, more tolerant of plea bargaining, and more receptive to the delaying tactics of attorneys. Delays may also weaken the certainty and finality of sanctions if the appellate process is prolonged unnecessarily (Levin, 1975:128; Chapper and Hanson, 1988:7). In Posner's cost-benefit framework, excessive court delays increase both the "direct costs" and "error costs" of the legal process (Posner, 1973). Direct costs increase as court participants expend considerable time and resources on tangential matters that do not lead directly to case dispositions. Error costs increase as witnesses drop out or other evidence becomes unavailable or less useful to the prosecution due to the passage of time (Cannavale and Falcon, 1976; Rosett and Cressey, 1976).

Other researchers have noted that slow case handling is essentially a bureaucratic bottleneck, similar to the obstacles afflicting all human service organizations (Blumberg, 1967; Mather, 1979; Heumann, 1978; Eisenstein and Jacob, 1977; Jacob, 1983). Mohr observed that sluggish court procedures may be inevitable since the courts serve a primarily impoverished clientele (Mohr, 1976:621). Any large organization that must move people and their problems through a complicated decision-making process will confront frequent operational failures. When the people served by the organization are mostly from poor, low-status communities, there is an increased tendency for the processing organization to be under-staffed, under-funded, and overwhelmed by its workload. For the poor and disadvantaged, therefore, court delay may be just another encounter with bureaucratic disrespect.

Time and the Effectiveness of Juvenile Court Sanctions

The importance of early intervention is an underlying theme throughout the juvenile justice literature. Almost by definition, early intervention implies the timely processing of cases by the juvenile court. Research has shown that while most juveniles referred to the juvenile court are referred only once, a substantial number (roughly 40%) will recidivate prior to reaching the age of majority (Snyder, 1988). Snyder found that the probability of subsequent recidivism was related to the juvenile's age at the time of court referral and the number of times the juvenile had been previously referred to the court. Juveniles referred to court twice before the age of 16 had recidivism rates comparable to chronic or persistent offenders (Snyder, 1988:66). Snyder concluded that the juvenile court has a better opportunity of reducing recidivism if it intervenes early in the delinquency "careers" of juveniles that exhibit indicators of future recidivism.

If the juvenile court is more effective when it intervenes as soon as possible after a youth's initial arrest, case processing within the court must proceed as expeditiously as possible. Unnecessary delays in case processing may increase the likelihood of a juvenile's subsequent involvement with the court as well as the likelihood that the juvenile's involvement in law-violating behavior will continue to escalate. The juvenile court's ability to intervene is already "time bound" since the court relinquishes authority over a case once the juvenile reaches a specified age (Mahoney, 1987). These time constraints are made even more acute by the fact that unless it intervenes shortly after the occurrence of the initial offense, there is a considerable chance that first-offenders will be referred to the court again before the court has had the opportunity to deal with their first offense. In a 1982 study of 1,505 first-time offenders in Phoenix, a majority (57%) of youths recidivated at least once following their first offense, and 33% of those that recidivated did so within three months of their initial arrest (Burgess, 1982). Thus, a court process which typically takes 90 days or more to bring cases to disposition is virtually guaranteeing that up to a third of all juvenile offenders will not receive any court attention or any sanctions until after their second offense.

Adolescents as Defendants

Minimizing delay in juvenile delinquency cases may be especially critical because of the nature of adolescence. The imposition of legal sanctions is essentially an attempt to teach offenders that illegal behavior has consequences and that anyone who violates the law will be held accountable. In order to deliver this message effectively, the juvenile court process must fit the unique learning style of adolescents. During the years of adolescence, young people experience many developmental changes, and the passage of time is often distorted—i.e., three months of summer vacation seems like an eternity to a 14-year-old. If the juvenile court takes too long to respond to youthful misbehavior, the corrective impact of the court process may be greatly curtailed.

Adolescence refers to a time of transition between childhood and adulthood. It is a period characterized by rapid physical growth and emotional changes. In Western societies, adolescence is generally thought to begin at approximately 11 or 12 years of age and to continue through the late teen years. In addition to developing adult physical and sexual characteristics, it is during adolescence that individuals develop the psychological, emotional, and social skills of adulthood. Although the developmental tasks of adolescence are similar for all youths, the rate at which they are completed may be very different. Some milestones may never be reached if an individual's social environment is particularly disadvantaged.

Cognitive development is a critical task of adolescence and is thought to occur in four stages (Inhelder and Piaget, 1958; Elkind, 1966; Piaget and Inhelder, 1969). "Sensorimotor" cognition focuses on objects rather than on social interaction, and characterizes the thinking of infants under two years of age. "Preoperational" cognition usually develops between the ages of two and seven. During this stage, a child's understanding of complex ideas is reduced to simple principles. Children between the ages of seven and eleven develop "concrete operational" cognition, acquiring a more sophisticated understanding of complex ideas. However, they operate in the present reality, do not think abstractly, and do not fully comprehend probability and distant consequences. These abilities emerge with the development of "formal operational" cognition, the fourth and final stage of cognitive development.

Formal operational thinking allows individuals to understand probabilities, analogies, and abstract principles. They can think beyond the present reality and can imagine or deduce future conditions. Formal operational thought is usually acquired by age 16, but this achievement is not assured and is not universal. Cognitive development in general is dependent on adequate environmental stimulation, but the development of formal operational thought has been found to be especially dependent on environmental support (Piaget, 1972; Berzensky, 1978). Without the support of a safe and nurturing social environment, cognitive structures may continue in the concrete operational stage well into the late teens and twenties. If the social environment is especially disadvantageous, a substantial portion of the population may never develop formal operational thought (Piaget, 1971; Gallagher and Moppe, 1976; Berzensky, 1978).

The delinquency caseloads of most juvenile courts include a disproportionate number of young people from poor and disadvantaged communities. Thus, it is likely that many youths appearing before the court do not have fully developed cognitive abilities. Delayed cognitive development could decrease their understanding of the juvenile court process and reduce their ability to alter their behavior in expectation of sanctions. In order to maximize the effectiveness of juvenile justice sanctions, the juvenile court process should be conducted in a manner that is consistent with an adolescent's ability to learn. At the very least, it should be clear and direct, involve a minimum number of hearings and court appearances, and be concluded as soon as possible.

CONTROLLING DELAY

Like any court reform, an effort to control court delays must contend with a range of legal, organizational, psychological, and political factors. Two approaches are generally used to control case processing delays: 1) direct inducements (legal or professional), and 2) management interventions. These approaches are designed to ensure speedy case handling by either mandating efficiency or re-engineering the court process to encourage efficiency. The following section reviews various approaches to controlling delay.

Direct Inducements to Control Delay

The assumption behind direct inducements is that processing delays are ultimately within the control of people who work in the court system *and* that they will work faster once they are instructed to do so in sufficiently forceful terms. The research literature on court delay indicates that the effectiveness of legal or professional inducements may be limited. No prescriptive sanction will eliminate court delays if long processing times are necessary for the stability of the court. Legislation, case law, and professional standards may be useful, however, as a means of establishing the basic expectation that cases will move as quickly as possible through the court process.

Constitutional Provisions and Case Law

The most basic expression of a direct inducement to control delay is the Sixth Amendment to the Constitution, which guarantees any American citizen involved in a criminal prosecution the right to a "speedy and public trial" (Constitution of the United States, Amendment VI). The U.S. Supreme Court has held that the right to a speedy trial is as "fundamental as any of the rights secured by the Sixth Amendment" (*Klopfer v. North Carolina*, 1967).

The Supreme Court first attempted to establish a standard for the implementation of the Sixth Amendment's speedy trial guarantee in *Barker v. Wingo* (1972). The *Barker* case involved a Kentucky prisoner who petitioned for *habeas corpus* as a result of a 5-year delay between arrest and trial. The Court found that the defendant's right to speedy trial had *not* been violated because: 1) the defendant had not been seriously prejudiced by delay; and 2) the defendant had apparently not desired a speedy trial. The *Barker* Court also asserted that the right to speedy trial was "generically different" than any of the other rights of due process (*Barker v. Wingo*, 1972:519). Society has an interest in both the quality of the court process *and* the effectiveness of the outcome—i.e., adequate protection from crime. In some cases, society's desire for an effective outcome will come into conflict with a defendant's desire for high-quality process. Thus, evaluating the speediness of the legal process requires a "balancing" of the rights of the defendant with those of society. The Court proposed four factors that should be considered in assessing Sixth Amendment violations (*Barker v. Wingo*, 1972:530). Known as the "*Barker* balancing test," the four factors to be considered were:

1) the length of delay;
2) the reason for delay;
3) the defendant's assertion of due process rights; and
4) the existence of prejudice to the defendant.

The Court acknowledged that some parties would favor an explicit standard to identify violations of Sixth Amendment rights. It asserted, however, that there was "no constitutional basis for holding that the speedy trial right can be quantified into a specified number of days or months" (*Barker v. Wingo*, 1972:523). The Court argued that to establish a quantitative standard would be to engage in "legislative or rulemaking activity," which was outside the proper scope of its authority (*Barker v. Wingo*, 1972:523). As a result of the Court's reasoning in *Barker*, legislation and court rules have remained the predominant methods of controlling court delay through direct inducements.[3]

Legislation and Court Rules

The most widely used delay reduction techniques are the administrative rules issued by courts, and statutes enacted by local, State, and Federal legislators. Statutes and rules have been used to limit the time courts may take to file charges, complete trials, and reach final case dispositions. Statutory time limits are seen as having more authority than court rules and often include dismissal sanctions for cases which are not disposed within the required deadlines. Elected officials, however, are often reluctant to implement mandatory dismissal sanctions and have usually granted courts considerable discretion in defining violations of case processing statutes.

Two well-known efforts to reduce delay through legislation and administrative rules were implemented in the Federal court system during the 1970s: Rule 50(b) of the *Federal Rules of Criminal Procedure*, (406 U.S. 979, 1972) and the *Federal Speedy Trial Act of 1974* (§§3161–74, 1974). Both measures established national goals for reducing delays in the handling of criminal cases, encouraged local district courts to plan specific delay reduction strategies, devised procedures to monitor compliance by the local courts, and provided incentives for the courts to establish quantitative objectives for increasing the speed of their criminal case dispositions (Frase, 1976; Garner, 1987).

Rule 50(b) was developed by the Federal judiciary. It provided incentives for Federal courts to reduce case delays but allowed considerable discretion in the time standards that individual courts could adopt. The Rule was to be fully implemented following a planning process that began in 1973 in each of the Federal district courts. The planning process was negated, however, by the passage of the *Federal Speedy Trial Act of 1974*, which was passed by Congress despite the opposition of the Federal judiciary and the Department of Justice (Garner, 1987:230).

The Speedy Trial Act mandated a single time standard for all Federal courts—criminal cases were to reach final disposition within 100 days of arrest. The most contentious aspect of the Act was the provision that failure to meet the 100-day time limit would result in case dismissal. Faced with widespread concern about dismissals, Congress later allowed the courts to exclude certain periods from the calculation of disposition time, gave them authority to waive the standards when necessary to meet the "ends of justice," and permitted dismissal *without prejudice* thereby allowing defendants to be re-indicted on the same charges. The extent of the exceptions led one observer to describe the Speedy Trial Act as a "flexible restraint" on case processing time in the Federal courts (Partridge, 1980:34). Speedy trial controls have also been widely used in state courts, either through legislation, administrative rules, or both (Trotter and Cooper, 1982).

Some researchers have expressed skepticism about the long-term impact of these approaches to delay reduction. Researchers have found mixed support for the effectiveness of administrative and legislative controls, both in the Federal system (Bridges, 1982; Garner, 1987) and in State courts (Grau and Sheskin, 1982; Marvell and Luskin, 1991). Legislation and court rules can be insensitive to the reality that participants in the court process may "need" a certain degree of delay (Misner, 1979). Some observers have cautioned that the efforts of courts to comply with speedy trial legislation in criminal cases may result in even greater delays for civil cases, while others have argued that the administrative burdens of speedy trial laws create more processing delays than they reduce (Holten and Lamar, 1991:255). Like most research findings on court delay, the effectiveness of legislative and administrative rules is best viewed in context. They can be a useful part of a delay-reduction strategy as long as they are not seen as a substitute for all other efforts.

Professional Standards and Guidelines

Another common method of controlling case processing delays is the adoption of professional standards and guidelines. Issued by organizations such as the American Bar Association and the Conference of State Court Administrators, professional standards derive their authority from consensus and voluntary compliance rather than the threat of legal sanctions. By themselves, professional standards may not influence the behavior of court actors to a great extent. Standards can be effective, however, in establishing administrative goals. By comparing their case handling time with nationally recognized standards, State and local courts can assess the adequacy of their case processing system and identify areas in need of improvement.

The standards most familiar to U.S. court professionals are the guidelines developed by the American Bar Association's National Conference of State Trial Judges (National Conference, 1985; Lawyers Conference Task Force, 1986). The ABA standards include separate provisions for civil and criminal cases, as well as separate standards for felonies and misdemeanors. In Standard 2.52, the ABA recommended that courts conclude 90% of all felony cases within 120 days of arrest, 98% within 180 days, and 100% within one year.

Researchers from the National Center for State Courts (NCSC) compared the relative success of 17 State trial courts in meeting these standards. Based upon felony cases handled from 1983 to 1985, *none* of the courts in the NCSC sample met the ABA standards in full (Mahoney et al., 1988:33–38). Multnomah County (Portland), Oregon came the closest, processing 85% of its felony caseload within 120 days, 91% within 180 days, and 96% in one year or less. Most courts were able to conclude only between 45% and 75% of their felony cases within 120 days, far short of the 90% figure recommended by Standard 2.52. Several courts in the study completed fewer than 85% of their cases within one year.

The NCSC researchers noted that while professional standards are obviously not a panacea, they still play an important role in reducing processing delays. Standards, rules, and legislation help to express and reinforce judicial commitment to reducing unnecessary case delays, provide clear goals for courts wishing to reduce delays, and often lead to the development of administrative systems for monitoring caseload status and tracking the progress of individual cases through the system (Mahoney et al., 1988:63; Goerdt et al., 1989:78). Other researchers have suggested that the adoption of explicit time goals may be indirectly associated with reductions in case delays because in the close, personal culture of a local court system, the existence of formal goals may encourage some court participants to place a higher value on administrative conformity (Luskin and Luskin, 1987:215).

Management Interventions to Control Delay

Direct inducements such as case law, statutes, rules, and standards cannot be expected to eliminate delay in every court case. In order to control delay more effectively, it is necessary to confront the organizational arrangements that perpetuate delay.

The research literature generally supports an organizational approach to delay reduction. In their 1988 study, Mahoney and his colleagues found that State trial courts varied considerably in their ability to improve efficiency and speed (Mahoney et al., 1988:6). Some courts in the study were able to improve their case processing speed significantly, while others were unable to change. Importantly, these courts were not differentiated by the factors typically thought to cause delay, such as caseload size, offense severity, or court resources. The successful courts did, however, share a number of characteristics. In general, they:

- had strong judicial leadership with active participation of State and local court officials;
- had clear and widely shared goals for keeping case processing times to a reasonable minimum;
- organized to generate and use timely and accurate information about the speed of case processing;
- maintained open channels of communication among major court actors; and
- made use of effective management techniques.

Researchers are quick to caution that reducing court delays through management interventions sounds much easier than it is. Management research has sometimes failed to understand the essentially non-bureaucratic nature of courts and the implications that this has for traditional management techniques (Sarat, 1978). Courts are not even organizations in the conventional sense. Most importantly, courts lack a clear, unitary, hierarchical structure (Eisenstein and Jacob, 1977; Sarat, 1978). Rather, they are composed of a number of relatively equal and competing clusters of actors—judges, prosecutors, defense attorneys, etc. Each cluster of actors has its own reward structure and chain of authority. Often, there is not even a framework of shared goals or values. The only value shared by all participants in the court process may be that all of them would prefer not to appear in court if at all possible (Sarat, 1978).

Judges, administrators, prosecutors, defense attorneys, and clerks should be seen as "stake holders" with an abiding interest in the court process but with different goals and varying investments in processing efficiency. In some cases, delay may frustrate their interests. In other cases, delay may be essential for them to achieve other important goals, such as controlling the timing of particular case events or managing the volume of their total workload. At times, these other goals may be far more critical to various actors than whether an individual case is delayed.

Procedural reforms that address court functions in isolation (continuances, pretrial diversion, calendaring systems, etc.) will inevitably fail if they are not implemented with an acute awareness of how each of the actors in the court system will respond. In order to address the true origins of delay, therefore, it is often necessary to approach case processing from an inter-organizational perspective.

Caseflow Management

Beginning in the 1970s, judges and court administrators came to believe that the best method of reducing delay was to implement aggressive "caseflow management" systems that could reverse the inter-organizational incentives maintaining delay. Caseflow management refers to:

> [The] supervision or management of the time and events involved in the movement of a case through the court system from the point of initiation to disposition, regardless of the type of disposition (Solomon and Somerlot, 1987:3).

The word "caseflow" does not suggest that court cases are expected to flow smoothly through the dispositional process. Cases still move intermittently through a series of events, separated by various intervals of time involving little to no activity. Caseflow management is simply a method of making the occurrence of these events and the intervals between them more predictable and regulated.

Prior to the development of caseflow management systems, the progress of a court case was governed by the independent efforts of various individuals, each seeking to meet his or her own organizational and personal needs by influencing the timing of continuances, pretrial conferences, hearings, etc. Reducing delay was not in the self-interest of any single person or group, and it was often not a part of anyone's formal job responsibilities (Flanders, 1980).

Caseflow management represents a shift in thinking about the responsibility for case progress. It relies on the active oversight of each case event by a judge and/or court administrator, as well as frequent and direct consultation between court managers, judges, and lawyers. An effective caseflow management system essentially re-designs the entire case handling process to facilitate speedy dispositions and to make efficiency a part of everyone's job.

Many students of court delay believe that judicial leadership and supervision are essential to effective caseflow management. Fleming argued two decades ago that the individual efforts of judges are far more likely to reduce delay than are rules and legislation, "whose long-term impact is about as effective as legislation outlawing sin" (Fleming, 1973:23). He advocated an approach that later came to be known as caseflow management:

> The first step in any effective campaign against court delay in the routine criminal case is to enable the judge, the one person in the courtroom who represents the general public interest, to regain control over the [the court process] (Fleming, 1973:25).

One of the strongest findings of the National Center for State Courts' *Pretrial Delay Project* was that a court is less likely to experience backlogs and delay if it has an effective caseflow management system in place (Church et al., 1978). This finding applied to both civil and criminal courts, although caseflow management systems were more common in criminal courts when the *Pretrial Delay Project* was conducted. At that time, court control over the pace of litigation was a relatively new concept for civil courts. In most of the courts studied by the project, attorneys controlled the pace of civil case processing. Criminal courts, on the other hand, almost always had formal time limits and a system for monitoring compliance. Prosecutors may have played a role in the timing of case filing, but no criminal court in the study gave attorneys as much discretion over the speed of case processing as did the civil courts. The *Pretrial Delay* researchers believed that this difference was at least partly responsible for the fact that delays were nearly always more extensive in the civil courts.

Financial Incentives

Another approach to controlling court delays is the use of monetary incentives to encourage more efficient case handling. One such effort, known as the *Speedy Disposition Program* (SDP), was implemented in New York City during the early 1980s (Heumann and Church, 1990; Church and Heumann, 1992). The SDP provided prosecutors' offices in four New York boroughs with an opportunity to share several million dollars of "incentive" funds if they acted successfully to reduce the average age of their pending criminal cases.

The evaluation of the SDP suggested that the use of financial incentives had little long-term effects on the average length of time that cases awaited disposition. Results were mixed, however, and the researchers saw enough impact in some sites to indicate that the approach was worth further experimentation. The SDP effort may have fallen short of expectations because New York prosecutors were provided with more than adequate resources by the City and did not respond strongly to the promise of new funds. In more appropriate contexts, however, the use of direct financial incentives to improve efficiency may be an effective method of controlling delay.

CONTROLLING DELAY IN THE JUVENILE COURT

> Speedy processing of all juvenile cases is important for two reasons. First, in order to maximize the impact upon the juvenile that he has been caught in a criminal act, that he will be held accountable for what he has done, and that there will be consequences for his actions, it is important that the case be resolved quickly. If the case drags on for too long, the impact of the message is diluted, either because the juvenile has been subsequently arrested for other offenses and 'loses track' of just what it is that he is being prosecuted for or because the juvenile has not engaged in any further delinquent acts and feels that any consequences for the past offense are unfair. Speedy processing is also important because excessive delay is obviously unfair and damaging to victims (Shine and Price, 1992:115).

Efforts to reduce court delay have been widespread for several decades in the form of legislation, case law, administrative rules, organizational change, and policy interventions. Yet, research about these efforts has been conducted entirely in criminal and civil courts. Juvenile court delays have not been a prominent concern among researchers, court professionals, or policy makers. Very little systematic knowledge is available on the causes and consequences of delayed delinquency cases, and virtually no literature exists on the relative effectiveness of the various delay reduction techniques in juvenile courts. The following section reviews the extent of administrative, legislative, and judicial efforts to affect the timing of delinquency case processing in juvenile courts.

Constitutional Provisions

Juveniles have no federal constitutional right to a speedy trial. Before the 1960s, a youth appearing before a juvenile court had few rights in general. Since the official purpose of juvenile court proceedings was to "help" juveniles and not to establish guilt and administer punishment, juvenile courts were not considered to be trial courts. Thus, a youth involved in a delinquency proceeding was not considered to be at risk of criminal prosecution and did not require formal due process protections. These assumptions began to change during the 1960s as juvenile courts were required to provide procedural protections for juveniles.

The U.S. Supreme Court first granted limited procedural rights to juveniles in *Kent v. United States* (1966). Ruling against the District of Columbia's arbitrary and poorly documented procedures for transferring juveniles to the criminal court, the Supreme Court required transfer hearings to incorporate basic standards of due process, orderliness, and fair treatment. *Kent* challenged the fundamental premise that juvenile court proceedings were outside the sphere of criminal prosecution. The Supreme Court had previously interpreted the Equal Protection Clause to suggest that classes of people could receive lesser due process *if* a "compensating benefit" came with this diminished protection (Bernard, 1992:113). In theory, the juvenile court provided such a compensating benefit since its concern was for the best interests of juveniles rather than guilt or innocence. The *Kent* decision referred to evidence that this compensating benefit did not exist in reality, and while the Court did not equate juvenile court hearings with criminal trials, it did suggest that juvenile court proceedings had to provide at least the "essentials" of due process. These essentials were enumerated by the Court in its next important juvenile procedure case.

The case most responsible for changing the American juvenile justice system was *In re Gault* (1967). Gerald Gault was an Arizona youth who had been incarcerated for placing an obscene telephone call. His appeal asked the Supreme Court to consider whether the juvenile court process had violated several of his Fifth and Sixth Amendment rights—counsel, notice of charges, confrontation of witnesses, the privilege against self- incrimination, and the right to a transcript and appellate review. The *Gault* Court ruled that in any juvenile court proceeding where commitment to an institution is a possible outcome, juveniles should have the right to notice and to counsel, to confront and cross-examine witnesses, and to the privilege against self-incrimination. The Court did not rule on a juvenile's right to appellate review or transcripts, but it encouraged States to provide those rights.

The Supreme Court based its ruling on the fact that Gault had been punished by the juvenile court rather than helped. The Court also rejected the doctrine of *parens patriae* as the founding principle of juvenile justice, describing the concept as "murky" and of "dubious" historical relevance, and concluded that the process used to incarcerate Gault violated the Due Process Clause of the Fourteenth Amendment. Extending the reasoning that first appeared in *Kent*, the Supreme Court asserted that juveniles need not give up their Fourteenth Amendment rights in order to derive the benefits of their status as juveniles—i.e., the greater concern for the well-being supposedly inherent in juvenile court proceedings. Furthermore, the Court suggested the aspects of due process it considered essential for juvenile court proceedings: "fairness, impartiality and orderliness" (*In re Gault*, 1967:19).

The Supreme Court soon demanded more of juvenile court proceedings. In a 1970 decision, *In re Winship*, the Court ruled that the "preponderance of evidence" standard used for delinquency adjudications in New York violated the due process promised in the *Kent* and *Gault* cases (*In re Winship*, 1970). The *Winship* case involved an adjudication based upon evidence that the juvenile court judge openly admitted would not have met a "reasonable doubt" standard. Upon appeal, the Supreme Court ruled that the reasonable doubt standard should be required in all delinquency adjudications. The Court rejected the opinion of the New York appellate court which had upheld the adjudication arguing that juvenile courts were not required to operate on the same standards as adult courts because they were designed to save rather than punish.

Limiting Due Process for Juveniles

The *Winship* decision appeared to signal the end of the Supreme Court's expansion of procedural rights for juveniles. In fact, Justices Stewart and Burger offered a dissent to the *Winship* decision that foreshadowed the future direction of the Court in matters of juvenile due process rights (Bernard, 1992). They re-asserted that the intent of juvenile court proceedings was still to help juveniles rather than to punish. They conceded that while actual practices were sometimes inconsistent with this rehabilitative intention, the solution to such failures was not to be found in *Kent* and *Gault*, which they believed would eventually undermine the legal and philosophical bases of juvenile justice. Stewart and Burger favored a continued distinction between adult and juvenile court procedures so as to preserve the special treatment accorded young people.

In its next significant juvenile law case, the Supreme Court ruled that the Due Process Clause did not require jury trials in juvenile court (*McKeiver v. Pennsylvania*, 1971). In the Court's view, *Gault* and *Winship* had already enhanced the accuracy of the juvenile court fact finding process. Juries would add little to the factual quality of the process and would be disruptive to the informal atmosphere of the juvenile court, tending to make it more adversarial. *McKeiver* appeared to signal the Court's retreat from the direction established by *Gault*, *Kent*, and *Winship*. Thus, after several dramatic cases that granted juveniles greater due process protections, the Supreme Court stopped short, refusing to grant juveniles the right to jury trial, appellate review, or transcripts of court proceedings.

The Supreme Court was never asked for an explicit opinion regarding juvenile rights to speedy trial. However, the *Gault* Court was careful to characterize juvenile court proceedings as being accountable only to the Due Process Clause of the Fourteenth Amendment and specifically not within the purview of the Sixth Amendment (Sanborn, 1993:232). Furthermore, during the 1970s and 1980s, the Court continued its attempts to resuscitate the *parens patriae* philosophy of juvenile justice (see, for example, *Schall v. Martin*, 1984). To date, the Supreme Court has not indicated any new willingness to expand due process for juveniles, including the right to speedy trial.

Legislation and Rules in the Juvenile Court

Approximately half of the States use legislation and court rules to control delinquency case processing time in the juvenile court. The extent of these controls, however, varies greatly (Szymanski, 1994). In 31 States, there are formal deadlines for adjudication hearings (table 1.1).[4] Several States set maximum allowable times between the initial case referral and the adjudication hearing (30 days in California, 60 days in Massachusetts, and 56 days in Oregon). More commonly, States set a maximum number of days allowed between the filing of the delinquency charges and the adjudication hearing. For example, in cases where a youth is being held in detention, Georgia establishes a limit of 10 days between the filing of charges and the adjudication hearing. In non-custody cases, Georgia requires the adjudication hearing to be held within 60 days of charges being filed.

There are time limits for juvenile court dispositional hearings in 25 States. In Nebraska and Wisconsin, for instance, the deadline for dispositional hearings is set relative to the filing of the delinquency petition. Nebraska sets a maximum of 180 days between the petition and the dispositional hearing, regardless of the youth's detention status. Wisconsin limits the time between the plea hearing and the final disposition to 10 days if the youth is being held in detention, and 30 days if the youth is released awaiting disposition.

Twenty-four States limit the time between the adjudicatory and dispositional hearing. Arizona, for example, allows no more than 30 days between adjudication and disposition for detained juveniles—45 days for non-detained juveniles. A number of States restrict the time between adjudication and disposition for detained juveniles only (e.g., 14 days in Arkansas, 15 days in Florida, 30 days in Georgia). Washington is one of the most aggressive States in controlling pre-dispositional delays. Dispositional hearings in Washington are required within 14 days of adjudication for detained juveniles and 21 days for non-detained juveniles.

A few States limit the time for handling cases being considered for transfer to the criminal court. While judicially transferred cases account for a very small portion of all juvenile delinquency cases, they represent a highly visible and contentious area of the juvenile court caseload (*cf.* Feld, 1993a; McCarthy, 1994; Zimring, 1991). Nine States regulate the timing of juvenile transfer cases, either through statute or court rules (table 1.2). Indiana, for example, requires the court to hold transfer hearings within 60 days of referral (20 days for youth held in detention).

Case Law and Juvenile Court Processing Time

Although the U.S. Supreme Court has not applied all constitutional due process protections to juvenile court proceedings, some States have interpreted the Court's use of the Fourteenth Amendment in *Gault* and *Winship* to suggest at least the possibility of other rights for juveniles—including the right to speedy trial (Choper, 1984). Courts in Arkansas, Florida, Illinois, Minnesota, New Hampshire, New York, and Washington have extended some form of speedy trial rights to juveniles.

- The New Hampshire Supreme Court ruled in a 1983 case that juvenile court adjudications should be dismissed if the court failed to meet the statutory deadline for adjudication and the delay was not due to actions of defense counsel (*In re Eric C.*, 1983).
- In a 1985 case, the Appellate Court of Illinois (First District, Second Division) vacated the adjudications of four juveniles whose due process rights were found to have been violated by a delay of more than 700 days between their arraignment and adjudicatory hearing (*Illinois v. A.J., T.M., L.R. and J.R.*, 1985).
- In 1987, the adjudication of a Minnesota juvenile was reversed and the delinquency petition dismissed *with prejudice* by the State Court of Appeals (*In re J.D.P.*, 1987). The court held that the juvenile's right to speedy trial had been violated when prosecutors failed to bring the case to trial within 60 days as required by Minnesota statute.

TABLE 1.1
Time limits (in days) for juvenile court adjudication and disposition hearings in cases not involving proceedings for transfer to criminal court.

	Start of Adjudication Deadline				Start of Disposition Deadline	
State	Court referral	Filing of Charges (det / release)	Prelim. hearing (det / release)	Detention Admission	Filing of Charges (det / release)	Adjudication (det / release)
Alaska						immed.[c]
Arizona			30 / 60			30 / 45
Arkansas				14[g]		14 / –
California	30	30[c]		15		
Delaware				30[a]		
Florida		21 / 90[a]				15 / –
Georgia		10 / 60				30 / –
Illinois		120[ac]		10[a]		
Iowa		60[bc]				a.s.a.p.[c]
Louisiana			30 / 90			30[c]
Maryland		60[c]		30		30[c]
Massachusetts	60					
Michigan		180[c]		63		35 / –
Minnesota		30 / 60				15[a] / 45[a]
Mississippi		90 / –		21		14 / –
Montana						a.s.a.p.[c]
Nebraska		180 / –			180[c]	
New Hampshire		21 / 30				21 / 30
New Jersey				30		30 / 60
New Mexico						20 / –
New York			14 / 60			10 / 50
North Dakota		30[c]		14		
Ohio		10 / –				immed.[c]
Oregon	56			28		28[cf]
Pennsylvania		10 / –				20 / –
Rhode Island				7		
South Carolina		40[c]				
Tennessee		– / 90		30		15 / 90
Texas		10 / –				
Vermont		15 / –				30[c]
Virginia		– / 120		21		30 / –
Washington		30[e] / 60[e]				14 / 21
Wisconsin			20[d] / 30[d]		10[d] / 30[d]	10 / 30
Wyoming				60[g]		

a = Extensions are possible.
b = If statutory right to speedy trial is waived.
c = Statute did not distinguish detention status.
d = Statute specified time from "plea hearing."
e = Statute specified time from "arraignment."
f = Statute specified time from assumption of jurisdiction.
g = Statute referred to time of detention hearing rather than admission.

Note: Twenty States did not have adjudication time limits as of 1993: AL, AK, CO, CT, DC, HI, ID, IN, KS, KY, ME, MO, MT, NV, NM, NC, OK, SD, UT, and WV.
Twenty-six States did not have time limits for dispositions: AL, CA, CO, CT, DE, DC, HI, ID, IL, IN, KS, KY, ME, MA, MO, NV, NC, ND, OK, RI, SC, SD, TX, UT, WV, and WY.

Source: Based on analysis by the National Center for Juvenile Justice (Szymanski, 1994).

TABLE 1.2
Time limits on juvenile court handling of delinquency cases considered for transfer to criminal court.

State	Time limits
Arizona	■ 30 day maximum between motion for transfer and transfer hearing ■ 30 day maximum between denial of transfer and juvenile court adjudication
Indiana	■ 20 day maximum between case referral and transfer hearing if youth is detained (otherwise 60 days maximum)
Iowa	■ 40 day maximum between case referral and transfer hearing
Maryland	■ 30 day maximum between time of detention and transfer hearing ■ 30 day maximum between denial of transfer and juvenile court adjudication
Massachusetts	■ 30 day maximum between case referral and Part A of transfer hearing ■ 45 day maximum between Part A and Part B of transfer hearing ■ 21 day maximum between denial of transfer and juvenile court adjudication if youth is detained (otherwise, 30 days maximum)
Michigan	■ 28 day maximum between case referral and Phase 1 of transfer hearing ■ 35 day maximum between case referral and Phase 2 of transfer hearing ■ 28 day maximum between Phase 1 and Phase 2 of transfer hearing ■ 28 day maximum between denial of transfer and juvenile court adjudication if detained
Minnesota	■ 1 day maximum between placement of youth in adult jail and filing of transfer motion
New Mexico	■ 30 day maximum between motion to transfer and transfer hearing if youth is detained (otherwise, 90 days) ■ 30 day maximum between denial of transfer and juvenile court adjudication if youth is detained (otherwise, 90 days)
Virginia	■ 21 day maximum between time of detention and *either* transfer hearing or adjudication ■ 30 day maximum between denial of transfer and juvenile court disposition if detained

Note: 42 States (and the District of Columbia) did not have time limits for transfer cases as of 1993.

Source: Summary table based on analysis by the National Center for Juvenile Justice (Szymanski, 1994).

- The Arkansas Supreme Court recently affirmed the dismissal of burglary and theft charges against a juvenile because the State failed to prosecute the case for more than one year. The court's opinion in the case was based on the speedy trial rules for juveniles provided in Arkansas statute (*Arkansas v. McCann*, 1993).

Appellate courts have dismissed other delinquency proceedings due to violations of speedy trial statutes in Washington (*State of Washington v. Smith*, 1987); *State of Washington v. Day*, 1987; *State of Washington v. Adamski*, 1988) and New York (*In re Oranchank*, 1983; *In re J.V.*, 1985; *In re Steven C.*, 1985; *In re Juan V.*, 1990; *In re Robert S.*, 1991; *In re Jessie C.*, 1992; *In re Lydell J. and Taseem D.*, 1992; *In re Nicole D.*, 1992; *In re James H.*, 1993; *In re Shannon FF*, 1993; *In re Jose R.*, 1993).

In the State of Florida, appellate courts have dismissed delinquency proceedings against juveniles for a large number of reasons related to speedy trial. Among these reasons are:

- a delay of more than one year between arrest and adjudication (*Shanks v. Cianca*, 1986);
- failure to properly state the reasons for extending the statutory deadline for speedy trial (*J.J.S. v. Florida*, 1983);
- failure to provide proper notice of a hearing, which resulted in an adjudicatory hearing being delayed for more than 90 days after arrest (*In re M.A.*, 1986);
- filing motions to extend a speedy trial period after the expiration of the speedy trial deadline (*D.A.L. v. Florida*, 1984; *J.T. v. Florida*, 1992);
- misplacement of a case file by the clerk's office, which did not constitute an "exceptional circumstance" for extending a statutory speedy trial period (*T.C. v. Florida*, 1989); and
- failure to respond for more than 21 days to a juvenile's motion for dismissal due to a violation of speedy trial rights (*E.R. v. Florida*, 1993).

Yet, other courts have either explicitly denied speedy trial rights to juveniles or severely limited their application. In 1985, the Appellate Court of Illinois (First District, Fifth Division) denied the appeal of a delinquent juvenile who claimed that the Cook County Juvenile Court violated his Sixth Amendment rights when an adjudicatory hearing was not held within 30 days as required by statute (*Illinois v. M.A.*, 1985). The appellate court found that while the lower court had refused to comply with an Illinois statute that called for the dismissal of delayed cases, this refusal did <u>not</u> violate the juvenile's rights because juvenile court proceedings were thought to be *separate and distinct* from criminal court proceedings. Thus, although the juvenile court had in fact violated the statutory requirement that a fact-finding hearing be held within 30 days, the court did not interpret this violation as granting the juvenile an absolute right to dismissal of the proceedings.

The right to a speedy trial was clearly denied to juveniles in the State of Kansas. In a 1987 case, the Court of Appeals of Kansas heard the case of a delinquent minor whose adjudication by a magistrate court had been upheld by a County District Court

(*In re T.K.*, 1987). The minor appealed for dismissal on the grounds that the District Court had not held *de novo* review in a timely manner (i.e., within 30 days as specified in the Kansas statute). In affirming the lower court's decision, the Court of Appeals held that juveniles did not have a constitutional right to speedy trial in proceedings conducted under the Kansas juvenile offenders code, and that the statutory requirement of *de novo* review within 30 days was not intended as a codification of the right to speedy trial. Thus, the 30-day requirement was not mandatory and juveniles were not entitled to a speedy-trial dismissal based upon failure to meet this standard.

Another case before the Florida Supreme Court involved the question of whether a juvenile would be denied a speedy trial if his or her adjudication occurred after the 90-day period mandated by Florida statute (*R.J.A. v. Foster*, 1992). Florida statute required that juvenile court adjudications taking more than 90 days be dismissed *with prejudice*. State court rules, however, provided an additional 10-day "grace period" for holding adjudication hearings. The Florida Supreme Court ruled narrowly that a juvenile court's use of the 10-day grace period did not violate juveniles' right to speedy trial because speedy-trial rights were procedural rather than substantive and fell within the court's discretion. The opinion was based on the Sixth Amendment "balancing" analysis contained in *Barker v. Wingo* in which courts were given the discretion to determine the amount of delay that constitutes a violation of speedy trial (Dale, 1992). The Florida court did affirm, however, that the State's juvenile courts have an obligation to process delinquency cases in a timely fashion or face the risk of dismissal.

During the past decade, courts in a few States have supported time limitations for juvenile court proceedings. Speedy trial mandates have been endorsed by courts in the States of Arkansas, Florida, Minnesota, New Hampshire, New York, and Washington. In some cases, however, a juvenile's right to speedy trial has been defined rather narrowly. Speedy trial rights have been explicitly denied to juveniles in other cases (e.g., Illinois, and Kansas). It would appear that non-legal inducements will continue to be a common mechanism for ensuring speedy case handling in the Nation's juvenile courts.

Time Standards in the Juvenile Court

Since the 1970s, several sets of juvenile justice standards have been issued by groups representing federal agencies or national professional associations. One of the earliest of these standard-setting groups was the Joint Commission on Juvenile Justice Standards, an effort by the Institute of Judicial Administration and the American Bar Association (IJA/ABA, 1980).[5] The IJA/ABA project began its work in 1971 and issued its final recommendations in 23 separate volumes published between 1977 and 1980. Each volume of the IJA/ABA standards addressed a separate topic of interest (e.g., court administration, prosecution, probation, adjudication, disposition, and appeal).

Other prominent juvenile justice standards include those of the National Advisory Committee for Juvenile Justice and Delinquency Prevention (NAC), which was established in 1974 by the *Juvenile Justice and Delinquency Prevention Act* (§207,

P.L. 93-415). Congress directed the NAC to develop general standards for the administration of juvenile justice. The NAC's final report was published in 1980 and contained standards for a wide range of juvenile justice functions, including prevention programs, court administration, adjudication, and supervision (OJJDP, 1980).

The standards developed by these groups addressed case processing time and juvenile court delay in a number of ways. For example, the IJA/ABA Joint Commission asserted that time limits on juvenile court case handling were necessary to combat the negative effects of unwanted court delays:

> Delay in the processing, adjudication, and disposition of criminal and juvenile cases compounds the disadvantages of detention, increases the risks of nonappearance and antisocial conduct if the juvenile is released, and is harmful to the interests both of the accused and the community (IJA/ABA, 1980a:11).

In Standard 7.1, the IJA/ABA Commission declared that "juvenile court cases should always be processed without unnecessary delay" in order to "effectuate the right of juveniles to a speedy resolution of disputes involving them" and to be consistent with the "public interest in prompt disposition of such disputes" (IJA/ABA, 1980b:21). Case processing time should be monitored especially closely, according to the IJA/ABA, in cases involving "young, immature, and emotionally troubled juveniles," "juveniles who are detained or otherwise removed from their usual home environment," and "juveniles whose pretrial liberty appears to present unusual risks to themselves or the community" (IJA/ABA, 1980b:21). The IJA/ABA standards advanced the following time limits for specific stages of the juvenile justice process and recommended that delinquency cases be dismissed *with prejudice* when these time limits were exceeded (IJA/ABA, 1980a:13):

- 2 hours between police referral and the decision to detain;
- 24 hours between detention and a petition justifying further detention;
- 24 hours between a detention petition and the detention hearing;
- 15 days between police referral and adjudication (if youth is detained);
- 30 days between police referral and adjudication (if youth is not detained);
- 15 days between adjudication and final disposition (if youth is detained); and
- 30 days between adjudication and final disposition (if youth is not detained).

In effect, the IJA/ABA standards suggested a maximum of 60 days from referral to disposition for non-detained cases, and 30 days in the case of detained juveniles. In Standard 3.3, the Joint Commission clarified that the time standard for adjudicatory hearings should apply to transfer hearings also (IJA/ABA, 1980c:32). Juvenile courts were to hold *either* adjudicatory or transfer hearings within 15 days for detained youth, and within 30 days for non-detained youth.

Similar time limits were recommended by the National Advisory Committee for Juvenile Justice and Delinquency Prevention. The NAC recommended that in all "matters subject to the jurisdiction of the family court over delinquency, the following time limits should apply" (OJJDP, 1980:311):

- 24 hours between police referral and the report of an intake decision (if youth is detained);
- 30 days between police referral and the report of an intake decision (if youth is not detained);
- 24 hours between detention and the detention hearing;
- 2 days between the intake report and the filing of a petition by the prosecutor (if detained);
- 5 days between the intake report and the filing of a petition by the prosecutor (if not detained);
- 5 days between filing of the petition and the initial arraignment hearing;
- 15 days between filing of the petition and the adjudication hearing (if detained);
- 30 days between filing of the petition and the adjudication hearing (if not detained); and
- 15 days between adjudication and the final disposition hearing.

The NAC standards suggested that the total time between police referral and court disposition should not exceed 80 days in cases of non-detained juveniles, and 33 days for detained cases. As recommended in the IJA/ABA standards, the NAC called for dismissal of the case if court processing extended beyond these maximums. However, the NAC permitted dismissal *without prejudice*, allowing prosecutors to re-file for adjudication on the same case. The NAC also suggested the use of sanctions for court officials when cases were delayed beyond the recommended time limits:

> When these time limits are not met, there should be authority to release a detained juvenile, to impose sanctions against the persons within the juvenile justice system responsible for the delay, and to dismiss the case with or without prejudice (OJJDP, 1980:311).

The decision to impose sanctions, according to the NAC, should account for the possibility that excessive delays may have been caused by a "lack of sufficient resources" rather than "individual failures" (OJJDP, 1980:312). The NAC standards also recognized that there were situations when exceptions to the time limits could be granted. Extensions could be authorized in the following circumstances: 1) when important evidence or witnesses are unavailable to the prosecuting attorney during the prescribed time period even after reasonable efforts to secure them; and 2) when a continuance is requested by any party to the case and the judge finds that the "ends of justice" would be better served by a continuance than by "a speedy resolution of the case" (OJJDP, 1980:313). Even when necessary, extensions were not to exceed 30 days in cases involving detained juveniles, or 60 days in non-custody cases.

The NAC standards also listed a number of circumstances in which it would be appropriate to exclude certain periods of time in calculating elapsed processing time:

> Any period of delay caused by the absence, incompetency, or physical incapacity of the respondent; consideration of a motion for change of venue, a motion for transfer to a court of general jurisdiction pursuant to Standard 3.116, or an extradition request; a diagnostic examination ordered by the family court and completed within the time specified in the order; or an interlocutory appeal; and a reasonable period of delay caused by joinder of the case with that of another person for whom the time limits have not expired, should not be included in the computation of the prescribed time periods (OJJDP, 1980:313).

Following the release of the IJA/ABA and NAC standards, other national groups issued juvenile justice standards. In their standards for State trial courts, the ABA's National Conference of State Trial Judges included Standards 2.50 through 2.56, known as the "Standards Relating to Court Delay Reduction" (National Conference, 1985; Lawyers Conference Task Force, 1986). In Standard 2.52 on "timely disposition," the ABA explicitly addressed the issue of time standards for delinquency cases (National Conference, 1985:12). The ABA standards recommended that:

- Detention hearings should be held within 24 hours of a juvenile's admission to a detention facility.
- Adjudicatory (or transfer) hearings should be held within 15 days of admission to detention for juveniles in custody, and within 30 days following the filing of a delinquency petition for non-custody cases.
- Disposition hearings should be held no later than 15 days following the adjudicatory hearing.

The National District Attorneys Association (NDAA) also issued standards for the handling of delinquency cases. In 1987, the Juvenile Justice Committee of the NDAA began an effort to revise Prosecution Standard 19.2, which had been originally adopted by the NDAA in 1977 (Shine and Price, 1992). The revised standards were issued in 1989 and addressed a wide range of issues related to the prosecution of juvenile cases—e.g., case screening, criteria for diversion, determining legal sufficiency, uncontested cases and the use of plea agreements, transfer or certification to adult court, adjudication, and disposition (Shine and Price, 1992:120–132). The NDAA recommended the following time limits for the processing of juvenile delinquency cases:

- Prosecutors should screen cases for legal sufficiency within 24 hours of police referral if the youth is in detention, and within 7 days if the youth is not detained.
- Intake decisions (whether to divert, file a formal petition, or transfer) should be made within 3 days of police referral if a youth is detained, and within 10 days if not detained.

- Adjudicatory hearings should be held within 30 days of police referral for detained juveniles, and within 60 days for non-detained juveniles.
- Disposition hearings should be held within 30 days of the adjudicatory hearing.

Altogether, the NDAA standards suggested a maximum time of 60 days between police referral and disposition in cases where a youth is detained, or 90 days in non-detained cases. The NDAA recognized that these time limits may be exceeded in particularly complex cases, such as when the discovery process requires more time, or the prosecutor must review a lengthy social history or psychological evaluation before making a decision to transfer a case for criminal prosecution. In the commentary accompanying Standard 19.2, the NDAA issued the following caution:

> The time limits suggested are model ones. It is recognized that some jurisdictions by law or practice make even more prompt determinations, and that other jurisdictions, due to limitations in resources or the environment, have been unable to make such timely decisions. The point is that prompt determinations generally promote confidence in the system and fairness to the victim, the community, and the juvenile. Further, prompt decisions are more likely to result in rehabilitation of the juvenile by providing more immediate attention (Shine and Price, 1992:126).

In general, the provisions of NDAA's Standard 19.2 mirrored the juvenile justice guidelines developed by the earlier standard-setting associations. The time limits recommended in the NDAA standards, however, were more lenient than those published earlier by the IJA/ABA, NAC, and ABA. The NDAA's maximum of 60 days between referral and disposition in detention cases was twice the 30-day maximum recommended by the IJA/ABA standards and the ABA's Standard 252, and nearly double the limit of 33 days recommended in the NAC standards. The NDAA's time limit for non-custody cases (90 days from referral to disposition) was also the longest of all the standard-setting groups (table 1.3).

The development of these standards and guidelines reflects a growing awareness of juvenile court delay among legal professionals and policy makers. Of course, the impact of standards on actual case processing may be limited. This is especially true if the time frames suggested by the standards are considerably faster than the pace at which many juvenile courts are currently able to process their delinquency caseloads. According to the analyses in Chapter 5 of this report, the *median* time between case referral and final disposition for petitioned delinquency cases often exceeds 60 days. In large jurisdictions, nearly half of formally petitioned cases have disposition times in excess of 90 days. Thus, actual case processing time in many jurisdictions may often exceed the time limits recommended by professional standards. Whether juvenile courts are overloaded and poorly managed or the standards themselves are out-of-date and unrealistic, remains to be determined by research.

TABLE 1.3
Time limitations provided by various juvenile justice standards.

	Maximum days from referral to adjudication	Maximum days from adjudication to disposition	Total maximum days from referral to disposition
Detained Juveniles			
IJA/ABA (1977–80)	15	15	30
NAC/OJJDP (1980)	18	15	33
ABA Std. 252 (1984)	15[a]	15	30[a]
NDAA Std. 19.2 (1989)	30	30	60
Released Juveniles			
IJA/ABA (1977–80)	30	30	60
NAC/OJJDP (1980)	65	15	80
ABA Std. 252 (1984)	30[b]	15	45[b]
NDAA Std. 19.2 (1989)	60	30	90

a. Time limit begins at point of detention admission rather than police referral.
b. Time limit begins at filing of delinquency petition rather than police referral.

Management Interventions in the Juvenile Court

Research on the criminal and civil courts has suggested that legislation, case law, court rules, and professional standards may encourage an organizational climate that is supportive of efficient case handling. However, they tend to have little empirical association with actual patterns in the timing of case dispositions. Instead of relying on such inducements, many judges and administrators in the criminal and civil courts advocate caseflow management systems to ensure speedy case handling.

Caseflow management has been applied just as effectively in the juvenile justice system. The Cuyahoga County (Cleveland) Juvenile Court implemented a caseflow management system in 1991 after an internal study found that the average disposition time for delinquency cases was 226 days. Following consultation with a variety of court personnel and outside experts, a new system was designed to move delinquency cases through the court process more quickly. The system was designed to provide continual monitoring and oversight of case progress and to increase the use of caseflow data within all areas of the court. The results were promising. In six months, the court realized a 61% reduction in the average time to disposition—from 226 to 88 days (Graham and Howley, 1992:6).

It is likely that juvenile courts will continue to turn to caseflow management systems in order to control delinquency delays. Most problems encountered by such efforts will be similar to the issues typically faced in the criminal and civil courts. Studies on court delay have found that slow processing time is often associated with inefficient courtroom procedures, indifferent staff attitudes, lack of consistent caseflow data, and poor organizational arrangements that limit the court's ability to control continuances and other critical events (see Chapter 2). These factors are likely to be just as problematic in juvenile courts as they have been in the adult justice system.

Other factors, however, may be unique to the juvenile court and may present special problems for future case management systems. Compared to the adult courts, the juvenile court process is more diverse and often extends beyond fact-finding and case disposition. Juvenile courts must consider the social and psychological development of juveniles, their relationships with family members, and the role of other social agencies involved with the youth and family. Processing delays caused by investigations and reports on such issues are often considerable in the juvenile court.

Compared to adult courts, more of the juvenile court's work takes place after disposition. Delays at this stage are thought to be highly problematic. In a recent national survey, juvenile court judges, administrators, and attorneys were asked to indicate their degree of concern about various types of delay in the juvenile justice system (Chapter 3). The survey respondents expressed more concern about delays following disposition than about any other stage of the court process. Respondents were most concerned about obstacles encountered in arranging probation or in securing placements. Such delays are difficult to control since they involve agencies beyond the immediate influence of the court (private providers, State corrections departments, etc.). They have also been largely ignored by prior research on delay. Studies of the criminal courts tend to view sentencing as the logical conclusion of the court's responsibility.

Caseflow management systems in juvenile justice will also have to contend with the unique characteristics of adolescents. One method of accomplishing this may be to modify the factors incorporated in caseflow management decisions. The criminal and civil courts have found that "differentiated case management" can be an effective tool in controlling court delays (Bureau of Justice Assistance, 1993). Differentiated case management systems acknowledge that not all cases are alike. Rather than simply push all cases through the court process in the order in which they are received, different kinds of cases are placed on different processing "tracks." Case processing tracks in criminal courts are based on factors such as the nature of the offense, the number of hearings required, the defendant's bail status, evidentiary complexities, etc. Delinquency case management systems will have to account for these items, as well as other factors related to juvenile court case processing time such as the developmental status of juveniles or the role of counsel (Feld, 1993b:151).

Finally, while judicial involvement is critical in any delay reduction effort, it should be a major focus of attempts to improve caseflow in juvenile courts. Juvenile courts tend to be more dependent on judicial leadership than the criminal courts. The juvenile court process is more subjective than the adult justice system since it is bound by fewer constitutional requirements and is less likely to operate under strict legislative controls. By design, a juvenile court judge has more control over the dispositional process. The extent of this judicial authority led one historian to refer to the juvenile court as a "cult of personality" in which case outcomes are strongly influenced by the attitudes, beliefs, and morals of judges (Rothman, 1980:236). In addition to their influence on outcomes, juvenile court judges may also have greater control over the timing of the court process.

CONCLUSION

Generally accepted theories of cognitive development suggest that the effectiveness of the juvenile court process may depend in part on its timeliness. Adolescent offenders are likely to have less ability to anticipate the long-term consequences of their actions, and the behavioral impact of court sanctions may be greatly diminished if the dispositional process drags on for long periods of time.

Yet, nearly half of the States place no formal time limits on the juvenile court's processing of delinquency cases, either through State court rules or legislation. Only a handful of State courts have recognized some form of speedy trial rights for accused juveniles. Some States have explicitly denied juveniles this right.

Since the 1970s, several national commissions have promulgated standards and guidelines for the handling of juvenile delinquency cases. The impact of these efforts, however, is uncertain. Organizational interventions such as coordinated caseflow management systems may offer a more productive approach to dealing with juvenile justice delays, but their use is not yet widespread and little evidence exists about their effectiveness.

Currently, the principal factor that determines whether an individual youth is afforded any protection against unreasonable juvenile court delay is where that youth happens to reside within the United States. Similar inconsistencies in juvenile rights have been described as providing "justice by geography" (Feld, 1991).

Researchers and policy makers should examine the efficacy of various methods to reduce juvenile court delay. Studies are especially needed to measure the impact of the current patchwork of rules, statutes, and standards throughout the country. The importance of time for the overall effectiveness of the juvenile justice system suggests that policy makers should consider whether a more coherent approach to controlling the pace of juvenile court case processing is needed.

Chapter 1 Notes

1. Much of this chapter was published previously in the *American Journal of Criminal Law*. See "Speedy Trial in the Juvenile Court," by J. Butts, Vol. 23, 1996.

2. The U.S. Supreme Court's juvenile justice decisions are summarized in Snyder and Sickmund (1995:80).

3. Prior to Barker, several important cases helped to define the right to speedy trial in State and Federal courts. In Smith v. United States (1959), the U.S. Supreme Court explicitly affirmed a defendant's right to speedy trial but did not specify what would constitute a violation of that right. In 1966, the U.S. Court of Appeals (D.C. Circuit), affirmed a defendant's conviction on federal narcotics charges despite a delay of 14 months between indictment and trial (Hedgepeth v. United States, 1966). The ruling was based in part on the fact that much of the delay was caused by the defendant's requests for continuances and that the resulting delay was not shown to be "prejudicial" to the defendant. In Solomon v. Mancusi (1969), the U.S. Court of Appeals (2nd Circuit) denied a habeas corpus petition from a New York appellant who claimed that his Sixth Amendment rights had been violated by a wait of nine months between arraignment and trial. The court concluded that a delay of nine months did not necessarily violate the defendant's speedy trial rights because the defendant was unable to show prejudice from the delay, or to prove that the delay was caused by purposeful or "oppressive" actions of the district attorney.

4. The analysis portrayed in Table 1.1 summarizes the use of legislation and State court rules only. In some jurisdictions, local court rules may be used to set case processing standards.

5. The Institute of Judicial Administration began the project in 1971. The American Bar Association joined as co-sponsor in 1973. For a review of the standards and the process used to develop them, see Flicker (1982).

Chapter 2
The Causes of Delay

INTRODUCTION

In order to understand the sources of juvenile justice delay, it is useful to identify the general factors thought to cause delay. Some aspects of juvenile justice delay may be unique to the juvenile system, but most of the factors behind delay in the juvenile justice system are likely to be the same forces that hinder case processing in the adult justice system.

Since the *Gault* decision in 1967, juvenile courts have been required to incorporate more of the due process protections traditionally afforded adult defendants. As the juvenile court environment has become more similar to that of the criminal courts, the causes of juvenile justice delay and criminal justice delay may have become more alike as well. Thus, it is instructive for those concerned with delay in the juvenile justice system to understand court delay in general.

THE CONCEPT OF DELAY

One of the first tasks in any study of court delay is to define the concept of delay. What is an excessive length of time for the disposition of a court case? What is a normal length of time? Should the definition of "normal" and "excessive" vary according to the characteristics of the case, the court, or the community? Assuming exceptions will be necessary, how much longer than the normal time is acceptable for some cases, or for most cases?

One method of establishing the definition of unacceptable delay is simply to assert a range of maximum allowable processing times for various types of cases. This is often done by professional associations (e.g., American Bar Association, Conference of State Court Administrators). Another means of establishing the dividing line between acceptable processing time and unnecessary delay is to rely on the statues and court rules written by State and Federal lawmakers and judges. Any trial time in excess of these defined maximums would then constitute unwanted delay. In all instances, definitions of delay must rest on some consensus about what is a reasonable time for processing cases. Still, it is not easy to specify an exact threshold for what constitutes excessive delay.

Many researchers do not use the concept of delay at all, choosing instead to analyze "case processing time." Some analysts have argued that research on case processing time encourages better research strategies and is likely to produce more useful insights for administrators and policy makers. Neubauer and Ryan (1982), for example, preferred the term "pace of case disposition" rather than court delay as the latter was thought to be "inherently subjective." Grossman and his colleagues (1981:87) rejected the term delay as "vague, inherently subjective, and hopelessly weighted down by speculative normative assumptions." Ryan et al. (1981:75) observed that research "focusing narrowly on delay is not very helpful" and that delay was better seen as a "symptom of substantive, equitable, and managerial problems that exist within a particular court system."

Luskin (1978:116) argued that use of the term delay could limit the range of causal variables considered by researchers since it seems to suggest that the "causes of abnormal case processing time are distinct from those that produce normal processing time." Case processing time was offered as a more accurate term for empirical investigation since it encourages researchers to view the time required to process cases as consisting of "normal plus abnormal time lapse, and not delay alone" (Luskin, 1978:116). Throughout the 1980s and 1990s, while researchers, policy makers, and elected officials continued to speak and write about "delay" in the courts, most empirical studies were focused on the factors related to case processing time.

Measuring Delay

Whether a study investigates *court delay* or *case processing time*, it is still necessary to operationalize these concepts. To operationalize a concept is to define it in such a way as to render it measurable. For example, to research the topic of "economic growth" one must first create a measurable definition of growth—a specific increase in the number of new jobs created, percentage change in the stock market, etc. Researchers have had to cope with a number of issues in operationalizing delay.

Non-Standard Terms

Research on delay must first clarify the terms to be used in gathering and analyzing data from the justice system. This can be difficult when the data come from multiple jurisdictions. In the widely cited *Pretrial Delay Project*, researchers from the National Center for State Courts had to resolve a number of definitional issues in measuring case processing time using data from courts throughout the country (Church et al., 1978).[1] The basic events of case processing differed greatly between jurisdictions. Terms such as "case filing" and "final disposition" meant different things in different court systems. The researchers had to study the nomenclature of each jurisdiction in order to arrive at their own standard definitions of case processing events and then adjust the local data accordingly. This solution to non-standard definitions was seen as preferable to the methodology used by earlier studies in which data were collected from one jurisdiction only. While single-jurisdiction studies reduced definitional complications, their findings had limited usefulness since the researchers could not generalize the findings to all courts (Church et al., 1978:2). The problem of non-standard terminology may be particularly acute in juvenile courts which often incorporate concepts and language from the social services in addition to the legal system (Snyder and Sickmund, 1995).

Processing Stages

As Mahoney and his colleagues have pointed out, still other issues must be resolved before case processing time can be operationalized in a standard fashion (Mahoney et al., 1988:28–29). For example, should case processing time include only the time following the filing of a case in court, or should it include the time between arrest and case filing? Should measures of delay include time lapses that are no fault of the court? For instance, should a defendant's failure to appear for a hearing count against the court in measuring processing delay? What about the time spent awaiting a psychiatric examination to determine the defendant's competence to stand trial? Also, how should case disposition be defined? Should it be when the court issues its dispositional order, or when the ordered sentence is actually imposed? Particularly for out-of-home placement cases in the juvenile justice system, there may be significant delay between a dispositional order and a youth's actual placement (see Chapter 3).

In their study of case processing in 18 criminal courts, Mahoney and his colleagues chose to measure case processing time in several ways depending on the particular analysis that was needed.[2] Their primary measure was "total disposition time," or the time between arrest and final court disposition. The researchers indicated that this measure was preferred since it was consistent with a "consumer's perspective"— a focus on how long the entire criminal court process takes, rather than on the relative efficiency of a single bureaucratically defined component of the system (Mahoney et al., 1988:30). Other measures included the "upper court disposition time" (time between filing in the general jurisdiction trial court and that court's disposition) and "upper court time in jury trial case" which applied only to cases involving jury trials and measured the time elapsed between the filing of an indictment and the issuing of a final verdict.

Multiple Measures

Most researchers advocate the use of more than one measure of court delay. In a study of congestion in civil courts, Rosenberg (1965) noted that researchers should use multiple measures of case processing time because the potential for mistaken conclusions increases if one relies on a single measure. Levin (1975) identified two separate components of case processing time: the "age" of a case at final disposition (time since arrest), and the actual court time devoted to the case by the time of final disposition (trial days). Depending on which aspect of processing time one is measuring, courts can look very different.

Levin studied case processing times in five criminal courts: the Minneapolis District Court, Pittsburgh Common Pleas Court, the district court of the District of Columbia, and two courts in Chicago (the preliminary hearing court and criminal division court). He compared various structural aspects of the courts with their median case processing times for criminal cases. His results showed that the median *age* of criminal cases at final disposition ranged from 14 to 160 days, while median *court times* were all under three days (Levin, 1975:85). The age of criminal cases at disposition depended primarily upon the general case handling characteristics of the court, while court time was largely a function of the procedures used to process each particular case. When courts are criticized for excessive delays, it is likely that the perceived problems are with the age of cases at final disposition rather than with the amount of court time required to bring cases to disposition:

> While it is commonly thought that it takes a long time to settle most criminal cases, in fact we shall see that in most of the cases in most courts, the defense attorneys and judges take actions that lead to fast settlements. But first everyone waits (Levin, 1975:85).

Gordon (1978:323–324) described three measurements of delay:

1) "experienced delay" is retrospective and measures the actual time elapsed between case initiation and disposition;
2) "expected delay" is prospective, measuring the "amount of delay that a case being initiated during the current month should expect to experience, assuming continuation of the current disposition rate"; and
3) the "age of pending cases" measures the "length of time cases [currently] pending have spent on court calendars since initiation."

Gordon (1978:327) recommended that researchers analyze expected delay since it was thought to be more convenient—requiring less data and fewer calculations. The increasing availability of automated information systems, however, has changed this assessment. Calculation of "experienced delay" is now within easy reach of many court systems.

Summary Measures

Church (1982:409–410) noted that a number of "nuts and bolts" questions are left unresolved by simply directing research at the time elapsed between stages of case processing. One question is how to measure the time lapses. What "summary measures" of processing speed should be used? The use of "crude" measures such as the median or mean days between two events may be misleading for some analyses. In an evaluation of Federal efforts to reduce court delay, Garner (1987) found that a study's conclusions would be very different if only median days to disposition was used to assess the effectiveness of a delay reduction effort, rather than combining analyses of the mean, the median, and the 90th percentile.

The *Pretrial Delay Project* found that aggregate caseload statistics sometimes distort case processing differences between courts. Some courts handle large numbers of minor, uncontested cases (traffic, misdemeanors, etc.) that do not consume much of the court's time but can greatly affect measures such as the mean and median time to disposition (Church et al., 1978:26). In reporting the results of the *Pretrial Delay Project*, the mean and median number of days between case filing and final disposition were used to analyze processing time for all cases. Other measures were designed to reveal the effect of exceptionally long cases. In each court, the project collected the case processing time (in days) for the lengthiest case in the third quartile (i.e., the case whose processing time was longer than 75% of all the court's cases). The researchers also measured the proportion of cases that required more than a specific period of time for processing (6, 18, and 24 months). In this way, the project was able to measure both average case processing as well as the nature of processing among unusually lengthy cases (Church et al., 1978:12). These additional measures revealed that in certain cases, two courts with similar median processing times had very different proportions of older cases. For example, while criminal courts in Pittsburgh and Cleveland had equal median case processing times (103 days), Cleveland had more than twice the proportion of cases taking more than 180 days to proceed from case filing to final disposition. In Cleveland, 24% of all cases required more than 180 days to reach final disposition, compared with 9% in Pittsburgh (Church et al., 1978:18–19).

Throughout the 1980s and 1990s, other researchers found similar patterns in case processing time and concluded that analyses of delay should employ several measures of processing time, such as the mean and median time to disposition, the 75th percentile, the 90th percentile, etc. (e.g., Mahoney et al., 1988; Goerdt et al., 1989; Hewitt, Gallas and Mahoney, 1990).

Continuous Measures

Even multiple measures of central tendency are unlikely to provide a complete description of case handling. For this reason, some researchers have advocated using continuous measures of case processing time. In the study by Grossman and his colleagues (1981), case processing times were analyzed using data on criminal cases handled by State and Federal courts in five Federal judicial districts. The researchers compared the courts using graphical techniques rather than reporting aggregate measures of case processing time. Similar to "life tables" or a rudimentary "survival" analysis, the technique involves plotting the cumulative termination of cases within each court by particular case characteristics. The researchers asserted that graphical analysis is superior to the more common approach of reporting measures of central tendency and dispersion, since case processing occurs in stages and the distribution of processing time is always highly skewed:

> All courts dispose of some cases very quickly; and even the fastest courts have cases which drag on well beyond the median for that court. There is no *a priori* criterion by which to determine when survival length becomes "delay" (Grossman et al., 1981:100).

Rather than imposing a definition of when delay occurs, graphical analysis allows researchers to consider case processing time as a whole and to compare courts on the basis of the time required to handle their entire caseload.

Other researchers have advocated the use of longitudinal methodologies to analyze court processing time (see Zatz and Lizotte, 1985; Hagan and Zatz, 1985). Traditional research methods such as correlation and regression assume that the phenomenon being measured is static, or in a state of equilibrium. In other words, the relationships between case processing time and other variables (such as court or offender characteristics) are assumed to be stable over time. Longitudinal models include the passage of time as a variable. For example, while many studies have pointed to jail status as a predictor of the time between arrest and disposition, a longitudinal model of case processing time could account for when defendants were actually in jail on a day-to-day basis as well as any differences in the processing of defendants jailed for 7 days, 30 days, 90 days, etc.

Backlog

Another approach to studying case processing time is to measure a court's "backlog," or the number of pending cases at the end of a year in relation to the volume of the court's workload. One method of measuring "backlog" is to divide the number of cases pending at the end of a year by the total number of dispositions in that year. Some researchers have called this measure "statistical delay" or the "inventory control index" (Church et al., 1978:25). Backlog measures allow researchers to track the outcome of court delays while greatly simplifying data collection tasks. Backlog studies eliminate the need to collect time measures for every case handled by a court. Using this measure has limitations in comparative studies, however, since no standard method exists for weighting the severity of pending caseloads (Clarke and Merryman, 1976; Doyle, 1978).

CAUSAL FACTORS IN DELAY

Although court delay has existed for centuries, empirical exploration of its causes is more recent. Few studies of delay were published prior to 1960. The vast majority of the existing research was published after 1980. In recent decades, studies have investigated the correlation between delays and offender-specific factors such as the seriousness of offenses involved in a case, the prior record of the offender, and the pre-trial custody status of the offender. Other studies have looked at the size of court caseloads, judicial workloads, the number and complexity of attorney motions, and policies governing the granting of continuances. Some studies have suggested that case processing time is affected by docket management systems (e.g., master versus individual docket) or the impact of informal norms and attitudes about case processing time.

Most of the available studies on delay have focused on the adult justice system (civil and criminal). There are very few studies on the timing of the juvenile justice process. One researcher found that as of the early-1980s there was "essentially no literature on the delay of juvenile justice" (Mahoney, 1985:37). Although recent studies may indicate growing interest in juvenile court processing time (Mahoney, 1987; Feld, 1993b; Butts, 1996b), most empirical understanding of delay continues to originate in research on the criminal and civil courts.

During the past four decades, researchers have proposed a wide range of factors to explain the timing of court processing. Studies have attempted to identify the various influences on court delay and to specify how, when, and why they reduce a court's ability to handle its workload in a timely manner. The following sections review the causal factors that have most often been investigated by previous research on court delay.

Resources / Workload

In the first comprehensive study of court delay, Zeisel, Kalven and Buchholz (1959) attributed delay to an imbalance of supply and demand—cases move too slowly when the demand for court time overwhelms the potential supply of judges. Given this perspective, the obvious solution to excessive court delay would be to add more judges. Zeisel and his colleagues wrote confidently that "it takes no ghost come from the grave to tell us that delay can be cured by adding more judges" (Zeisel, Kalven and Buchholz, 1959:8).

Other studies have promoted similar views of delay. In 1967, the President's Commission on Law Enforcement and Administration of Justice issued a task force report on the operation of U.S. courts that described the problem of court delay and listed various causes for it, including a lack of resources and increasing caseloads (President's Commission, 1967:82). Rosenberg (1965) characterized court delay as an outcome of inadequate court management that allowed the demand for services to overtake supply.

Gillespie (1977) reviewed the literature on delay and identified a familiar set of factors thought to cause delay: "archaic procedures, judicially mandated changes in criminal procedures to make 'due process' more meticulous and protective of the rights of the accused, lack of court resources to cope with the 'litigation explosion,' a shortage of trial lawyers, or—in the view of an early researcher in the area—simply a lack of administrative will by the courts themselves" (Gillespie, 1977:1).

Twenty years after Zeisel's study, Church and his colleagues noted that an imbalance in court resources and workload was the "most commonly asserted cause of delayed case disposition" (Church et al., 1978:24). Researchers typically focused on staffing shortages, budget limitations, overworked judges, lack of courtrooms, etc. Studies often began with the assumption that increasing a court's resources would enable it to cope better with its workload and thereby reduce the problem of case processing delays (e.g., Miller, 1966; Banfield and Anderson, 1968; Frank, 1969; Katz, Litwin, and Bamberger, 1972).

Yet, the results of many of these studies failed to confirm this widely shared hypothesis. Research that compared trial times in criminal courts with varying levels of judicial resources (or those that examined single courts whose judicial resources varied over time) consistently failed to find an association between delayed case processing and lower levels of judicial resources (Rhodes, 1976; Campbell, 1973; Gillespie, 1977; Goerdt et al., 1989:74).

Still, most observers continued to believe that workload was related to court productivity in some way. It has obvious effects on the time available for handling each case, and at some point a consistently growing caseload will certainly generate processing delays. Some studies suggested that other factors—some of which occur under conditions of high workload—may be more directly responsible for the extent of processing delays.

Levin (1975:97) found that a large workload indirectly brings about delay by creating opportunities for court participants to prolong the dispositional process in particular cases. Defense attorneys may take advantage of the pressures created by a large workload to engage in plea bargaining or "judge shopping," knowing the court will be more willing to grant continuances due to a large backlog. Other dilatory tactics, such as filing multiple motions or requesting a full-length trial in nearly every case, may be used more often by attorneys in courts with large backlogs. However, this does not mean that workload alone will inevitably generate such behavior.

Eventually, the consensus that emerged was that it is overly simplistic to assume that delay is solely a function of workload and that additional court resources will clear up all delay problems. Courts with large caseloads (or those with a high ratio of cases per judge) are not necessarily slower than courts with small caseloads. While resources and workload should be considered in any effort to explain delay, their effect on case processing time is often indirect.

Jurisdiction Size

Many criminal justice professionals assume that only large jurisdictions have court delay problems. Mahoney and his colleagues observed that "one of the most commonly held maxims about court delay" is that large, urban courts are far more likely to have delay problems simply because of their size (Mahoney et al., 1988:46). There may be a grain of truth in this argument. Small, rural courts tend to have fewer problems with delay. However, delays are probably not a simple function of size. Goerdt et al. (1989:71–72) found "little, if any, relationship" between case processing time and the size of a court's jurisdiction, the number of cases handled by the court, or the number of judges. Hagan and Zatz (1985) investigated the same question and found that size was not directly related to court processing time. Size was useful, however, in predicting the case handling style of police and prosecutors (e.g., the likelihood of a case being dismissed at pre-trial), which may be related to the severity of delay problems.

Mahoney and his colleagues also found no relationship between the size of a court's jurisdiction and the speed with which it was able to handle its caseload. Their study compared case processing times in 18 urban trial courts. One of the elements of court structure they examined was the relationship between the size of a court and its ability to bring cases to final disposition in a timely fashion. Their results suggested that smaller courts had no inherent advantage in case processing time when compared with larger courts (Mahoney et al., 1988:46).

Similarly, the *Pretrial Delay Project* found that while there was some association between court size and processing time, the slowest courts in the study were not always the largest. Some of the smaller courts in the study were "substantially slower" than expected given their size (Church et al., 1978:24). The conclusion of most studies seems to be that delay problems are often more prevalent in larger jurisdictions, but significant variation remains among both smaller and larger jurisdictions in the ability to manage court caseloads effectively. Apparently, size alone does not cause case delay.

Case Characteristics

Another common assumption among both researchers and practitioners is that courts with severe processing delays are courts that handle a disproportionate number of "problem" cases. Problem cases may be defined as cases with serious offenses, cases involving defendants with lengthy prior records, cases involving bailed defendants, etc.

Pre-Trial Custody

Many researchers have found that case processing times tend to be longer when defendants are released to await trial (e.g., Swigert and Farrell, 1980). Obviously, when a defendant is out on bail awaiting trial, it is in the defendant's self interest to procrastinate since the final disposition of the case might involve incarceration (Wildhorn et al., 1977). Other court participants may also have reasons to give priority to jailed defendants (Luskin and Luskin, 1987:209). State statutes and court rules often require more speedy handling of cases when a defendant is in jail, and the pressures created by jail over-crowding sometimes prompt courts to focus on resolving the cases of jailed defendants more quickly.

Regardless of the reasons, it is clear that cases involving defendants who are in custody awaiting trial tend, on average, to reach disposition faster than cases involving defendants who were released to await trial. One exception in the juvenile justice system, however, may be juveniles held in secure detention pending a motion for transfer to the criminal court system. Juveniles who are detained awaiting transfer may be in the court system far longer than the typical delinquency case (Butts and Gable, 1992).

Racial Characteristics

Some researchers have found that the racial characteristics of offenders are associated with case processing time. Banfield and Anderson (1968), for example, found that criminal cases with white defendants took longer, although one reason for the difference was that cases involving white defendants involved more continuances. Swigert and Farrell (1980) found evidence to suggest that homicide cases in which the defendant was white were processed more slowly than cases in which the defendant was black.

In the criminal cases of first-time defendants, Zatz and Lizotte (1985:324) found that the defendant's race was related to the time between arrest and disposition for cases resulting in guilty pleas as well as those involving trials. In both guilty plea and trial cases, Latino defendants were processed more quickly than white defendants (8% and 13% more rapidly, respectively). Criminal cases involving black defendants reached disposition at about the same rate as white defendants when the case resulted in trial. In cases involving guilty pleas, however, dispositions were significantly slower if the defendant was black.

On the other hand, Neubauer and Ryan (1982:233) found no significant relationships between case processing time and a defendant's race. The conflicting and inconsistent results of the available research on race suggests that the impact of racial characteristics on processing speed is most likely an artifact of other factors.

Case Severity

Several studies have suggested that the courts with the greatest delay problems are those with the most serious offenders. Hausner and Seidel (1979), for instance, found that the time required to process cases in the D.C. Superior Court increased with the average seriousness of the charges involved in a case. Time to disposition was greater in cases involving violent felonies such as robbery, rape, or homicide.

In their comparison of 26 felony courts, Goerdt and his colleagues (1989) found a significant association between the proportion of cases involving drug sales and the length of case processing time in the court as a whole. However, there was some evidence to suggest that courts which had experienced the greatest increase in drug sale cases during the 1980s were already among the slowest courts in the study's sample (Goerdt et al., 1989:65–66).

Zatz and Lizotte (1985) also found that offense severity was related to case processing time, although not in a uniform way. They speculated that a prosecutor may prefer to share responsibility for the most serious cases with the judge, and that the court's involvement would be naturally greater in such cases, thereby increasing delays (Zatz and Lizotte, 1985:324). Defendants in serious cases may also be more likely to prolong their plea decisions because charge severity increases the likelihood of incarceration (Mather, 1979).

Mahoney and his colleagues (1988) were unable to find evidence that case processing delays were caused by offense severity. They analyzed the proportion of serious cases in a court's caseload and median case disposition time and found "little relationship" between the two (Mahoney et al., 1988:47). The findings of the *Pretrial Delay Project* also showed no relationship between the severity of a criminal court's caseload and the extent of delay. Courts with the most serious caseloads did not seem to have difficulty handling cases efficiently (Church et al., 1978:29–30).

Other researchers have explored whether court delay is a function of the mix of cases seen in a court rather than simply the offense profile of each case. Neubauer and Ryan (1982) analyzed case records and interview data from three criminal courts (Providence, Rhode Island, Dayton, Ohio, and Las Vegas, Nevada). Based upon large samples of cases handled during the late 1970s, they found that length of case processing time was positively correlated with three variables: 1) the number of motions filed in each case, 2) the "mode of disposition" being something other than a guilty plea, and 3) the pretrial custody status of the defendant (i.e., bailed cases were processed more slowly than jailed cases). Some associations that at first appeared to be significant turned out later to be the result of interactions between other independent variables. Neubauer and Ryan's initial analysis showed that cases involving charges of burglary were processed more quickly. Multivariate analysis, however, revealed that burglary charges were more likely than other charges to be disposed by guilty pleas, which reduced the time required to reach to disposition (Neubauer and Ryan, 1982:221).

Other researchers have reached similar conclusions. One reason that case processing time may increase with the severity of charges involved in a case is that courts naturally spend more time and resources in reaching dispositions (e.g., negotiating pleas) when the charges are relatively serious. Cases involving serious charges may also be more likely to be disposed through trial, which leads to longer case processing (Mather, 1979). Luskin and Luskin (1987) found that "case-specific incentives" and case complexity had minor and inconsistent effects on case processing time, while "case events" and structural factors were more consistently predictive of the length of case processing.[3] Among case-specific factors, only the defendant's pretrial custody status had significant and expected effects—cases were processed at least a month faster in all courts when the defendant was jailed during the pretrial period. Other case factors, including severity of offense, may have had significant associations in some courts but not others, leading the researchers to conclude that the effect of these factors was not essential to understanding variations in processing delays.

Offender's Prior Record

While the offenses involved in each particular case may not be strongly related to processing time, some researchers have explored whether a defendant's prior record affects case handling. Zatz and Lizotte (1985:318) tested whether case processing time was related to the defendant's prior experience with the justice system. When a person has been arrested repeatedly, they hypothesized, he or she may become familiar to the prosecutors and judges in the court, and the court may be more comfortable reaching speedy decisions because of this prior knowledge.

Experienced defendants may also exercise their choices about pleas differently than first-time defendants. Their greater experience may lead them to evaluate the prospects of conviction and incarceration differently. For this reason, Zatz (1982) proposed analyzing case processing time separately within "processing shifts," where a shift is defined as an entire sample of cases with the same number of prior arrests (all first-time defendants, all those with one prior arrest, etc.).

In their longitudinal analysis of criminal court processing times in California, Zatz and Lizotte (1985:322) tested whether the speed of case processing was related to the defendant's "offense specialization." In other words, they explored whether cases involving defendants with prior arrests for the same offense were handled slower or faster than defendant's whose prior arrests were for different offenses. Most of the relationships shown in Zatz and Lizotte's analysis of first-time defendants were not found in cases involving experienced defendants, or those with prior arrests. Offense severity, for example, did not consistently affect case processing time for defendants arrested for their second, third, or subsequent charge. However, offense specialization had a consistent and delaying effect on criminal cases going to trial. In other words, defendants arrested repeatedly for the same offense moved more slowly from arrest to disposition by trial (Zatz and Lizotte, 1985:329). The researchers observed that plea negotiations may be more intense and more complex in such cases due to the greater experience of everyone involved, and this prolongs the time before one party eventually demands to go to trial (see also Hagan and Zatz, 1985).

The consensus of the research literature on case characteristics would appear to be that factors such as pre-trial custody status, offense severity, and a defendant's prior record are often related to aggregate patterns of case processing time. Their connection to case processing time, however, may reflect the impact of case complexity on delay rather than straightforward associations between case processing time and each of these variables. In addition, their relationship to case processing time can be non-linear. An extensive prior record may sometimes increase the time to disposition, while other cases involving experienced defendants may reach disposition more quickly. Simply correlating case characteristics and the time to disposition, therefore, may distort or even conceal the true nature of these associations.

The Role of Counsel

Several studies have found that courts with high rates of private defense counsel tend to experience more delay problems. Researchers have suggested that case processing time is increased when a defendant is represented by private as opposed to court-appointed counsel because court-appointed attorneys are more subject to administrative control by the court and may accommodate more readily to the court's pressure to quicken the pace of litigation (Wice, 1978).

Others have found that the effect of counsel on delay is indirect. The relationship between case processing time and legal representation may be an artifact of the association between defendant resources and bail status—defendants who are able to afford private counsel are also more likely to pay bail and more likely to seek delayed dispositions (Skolnick, 1967; Neubauer, 1974; Neubauer and Ryan, 1982).

Type of counsel, or simply the use of counsel has been found to affect the speed of case processing in the juvenile justice system. Researchers have found that the use of counsel is associated with longer times to adjudication and disposition of delinquency cases (Lemert, 1967; Chused, 1973; Mahoney, 1987). Some observers have argued that the presence of counsel may be correlated with juvenile court delays because the use of a defense attorney generally increases the adversarial nature of the traditionally informal juvenile court process, which results in longer processing times (Feld, 1993b).

Excessive delay may also be an indication of a relatively stable courtroom work group in which attorneys have become highly experienced. Experienced attorneys can become very skilled at defeating judicial efforts to control the speed of case processing. Galanter (1974) described how attorneys who appear frequently in a single court develop certain tactical advantages by becoming "repeat players" and "insiders." An experienced attorney can sometimes be more familiar than the judge with the informal norms of a courtroom, and may be able to manipulate procedures to prevent timely dispositions if delay is thought to be of benefit to the client (Rosett and Cressey, 1976). Delay can also be advantageous to attorneys themselves, either from a financial or workload perspective. As observed by Fleming, "a lawyer with a large and increasing backlog is a happy lawyer; a lawyer with a dissolving backlog tends to be an unhappy lawyer" (Fleming, 1973:17).

Others have noted that attorney-related processing delays are not necessarily the result of conscious conspiracies against the court. It is possible that practicing attorneys are simply less concerned with case processing time. Wilson (1972) acknowledged that the legal profession as a whole is sometimes insensitive to the need for efficient courtroom procedures:

> The legal profession has not always been responsive to calls for change in the institutions and procedures it has developed and nurtured. It is said that lawyers are uniformly in favor of progress and uniformly opposed to change (Wilson, 1972:92).

Procedures

Case characteristics such as offense severity, custody status, and type of counsel are related to court delay in some way. Yet, they have not been shown to be the primary causes of delay. Moreover, even if researchers were able to establish clear, empirical relationships between case characteristics and court processing time, this would not offer court administrators much assistance in their efforts to reduce unwanted delays since such factors are often beyond their control. For these reasons, many researchers have studied court operations and courtroom procedures in order to understand court delay.

Obviously, the time a court spends on a case is largely determined by the complexity of the trial procedures required to reach a final disposition in that case. Processing delays, therefore, are a function of courtroom procedures. Several procedural factors have been found by researchers to be associated with delays in the criminal courts— the number of continuances granted per case, the number of substantive motions filed per case, and the proportion of cases involving full-length trials (e.g., Levin, 1975; Luskin and Luskin, 1987). While other factors may sometimes mediate the association between these factors and delay, in the aggregate courtroom procedures determine the nature of court delay.

Continuances

Researchers have often asked why judges would contribute to delay problems by agreeing to repeated continuances. The literature on plea bargaining suggests that judges may sometimes tolerate excessive defense requests for continuances because the defense wields an implicit "threat" of forcing time-consuming trials by maintaining not guilty pleas. In his study of five metropolitan trial courts, however, Levin found that most court participants did not think such "threats" were credible because defense attorneys were just as interested in avoiding trial as any other party (Levin, 1975:115).

Some students of court delay have suggested that judges may grant large numbers of continuances out of concern for appellate reversals if the defense is able to argue it had insufficient time to prepare for trial (Fleming, 1973). In most courts, however, the actual rate of criminal appeals is so low that this argument cannot explain judges' willingness to grant continuances (Banfield and Anderson, 1968; Levin, 1975:115).

Others argue that judges grant continuances out of professional courtesy to attorneys, and because they see a certain amount of delay as expected and normal. Feeley (1992:175) suggested that judges may simply prefer to give "blanket" approval to continuances rather than make the effort in every case to distinguish between legitimate and "concocted" reasons for continuances.

Levin described the sometimes entertaining ways that participants in the court process can collaborate in postponing cases through the use of continuances. In one of the courts he studied, Levin found that continuances were occasionally granted to private defense attorneys who were having difficulty obtaining their client fees. Since it is far more difficult to collect these fees once a case is disposed, courts were lenient in granting continuances to allow defense attorneys an opportunity to persuade their clients to pay. The attorneys used a code phrase in the courtroom, asking for a continuance on the grounds that an important witness, "Mr. Green," had yet to appear (Levin, 1975:107).

Continuances may not always represent a court's failure to handle its cases effectively. Sometimes continuances represent the best, innovative efforts of the court, the prosecutor, and defense counsel to reach a just disposition while minimizing formal court action. In the court studied by Feeley, sometimes all the participants in a case would agree to "prosecutor's probation" or "accelerated rehabilitation" in lieu of trial (Feeley, 1992:175–176). Such "pre-trial diversion" programs are used to give defendants adequate time to demonstrate their sincere desire for rehabilitation or to make restitution before being formally charged and/or adjudicated (Baker and Sadd, 1981). When a case is deemed appropriate (i.e., minor charges, no prior convictions, and a compliant defendant), the court agrees to delay formal adjudication so that the defendant may complete a counseling program, obtain employment, repay a victim, etc. If the defendant successfully completes the court's suggested plan of action, the case is often dismissed, the defendant is spared a criminal record, and the court saves the time and expense of additional filings and hearings. Thus, in some cases the use of continuances may actually increase the efficiency of the court process.

Researchers have debated whether controlling continuances was essential to reducing case processing delay. Zeisel (1959) found that, empirically, the granting of continuances had a relatively minor impact on a court's general ability to process cases in a timely manner. The *Pretrial Delay Project*, on the other hand, concluded that while continuances may have a minor impact on a court's aggregate case processing time, the secondary effects of easily obtained continuances were far more serious. Leniency toward continuances may influence a court's organizational culture in such a way that concern for delay decreases.

Other Procedures

Researchers have examined other aspects of court operations for their association with processing delays, including the relative use of settlements versus full-length trials and the processes used to initiate formal criminal charges. Church and his colleagues confirmed the widely held notion that courts that rely heavily on the grand jury process are more likely to experience case processing delays than courts who use indictment-based systems to bring charges (Church et al., 1978:46–47). On the other hand, the same study did not find evidence to support one of the more logical theories of court delay—the rate of jury trials is expected to increase delay problems while the use of plea bargains is expected to decrease delay. In the courts studied by the *Pretrial Delay Project*, however, no clear relationship existed between the proportion of a court's caseload settled at pre-trial and its overall case processing time (Church et al., 1978:31–36).

Mahoney and his colleagues tested another common assumption—that courts with large backlogs and slow processing times suffer from excessive continuances resulting from defendants failing to appear for scheduled hearings (Mahoney et al., 1988:38–39). They analyzed data on felony cases from their sample of criminal courts and measured the proportion of cases that involved bench warrants issued for defendants' failure to appear. The study found no correlation between the proportion of a court's caseload requiring bench warrants and its typical case processing time. When the researchers removed all cases involving bench warrants from their data base, there were virtually no changes in the rankings of 17 courts according to median case processing time. Delays due to bench warrants apparently did not explain variations in case processing time. Thus, continuances granted for failures to appear were not the primary cause of backlog and court delay.

Procedural factors may be statistically related to case processing delays because courts with high rates of continuances, multiple motions, etc. have lost control over how court participants utilize available procedures. If continuances are granted easily out of professional courtesy, for example, this may reduce the urgency of the entire process. While the use of various courtroom procedures may be empirically associated with prolonged case processing, the existence of this relationship is primarily an indication that the court is failing to manage its case flow properly. It is for this reason that more recent studies of court delay have often focused on organizational and managerial factors.

Management and Organization

Perhaps the most frequent assumption made by delay studies is that case processing delays are caused by poor court management. Occasionally, managerial approaches have been taken to extremes. Nagel and his colleagues suggested that courts could reduce delay by adopting techniques developed in manufacturing settings. Using quantitative models, they analyzed each component of the criminal court process and proposed various methods of maximizing efficiency: "queuing, optimum sequencing, critical path methods, optimum level and mix analysis, optimum choice analysis, and Markov chain analysis" (Nagel, Neef, and Munshaw, 1978:129–130).

Nagel's approach attracted considerable criticism for being too cut-and-dried and not recognizing the special characteristics of the court process—a weakness of which Nagel et al. were not completely unaware (see Ryan, 1978; Good, 1980). Flanders (1980:306) stated flatly that "the effort to apply management science and operations research to court processes has produced hardly any quantitative results that are specifically and directly applicable to reducing court delay." This failure was thought to be due primarily to the nature of court processing, which, unlike manufacturing, is highly individualized, irregular, and often unpredictable.

The negative reaction to overly ambitious uses of operations research, however, does not imply that management techniques are unimportant. Numerous studies have identified organizational and managerial problems as the root of court delay. A study reported at the 1972 Fourth National Symposium on Law Enforcement Science and Technology described criminal court delays as being largely a result of inadequate management (Foschio, 1973). The factors identified by the study were a high use of continuances (usually initiated by defense counsel) and a generalized lack of judicial control over case processing. Foremost among the indicators of a lack of judicial control was the fact that courts seemed always to anticipate the need for case events that in reality occurred infrequently. For instance, some courts provided time in every case to prepare for grand jury procedures, even though most cases were ultimately handled with prosecutor affidavits.[4]

Case Scheduling

A number of management-oriented studies have focused on the case scheduling or "calendaring" systems used by courts. The primary issue in these studies is whether case processing is faster under a "master calendar" or "individual calendar" system. Under a master calendar system, cases are assigned to judges at each stage of processing based upon availability. This means that each phase of case handling could be assigned to a different courtroom and a different judge, with the possible result that no single judge is invested in moving the case along to a quick disposition. In contrast, an individual calendar system assigns a single judge the responsibility for each case, and that judge manages the case from start to finish. Individual calendar systems are thought to enhance a judge's sense of ownership and responsibility for his or her caseload. In practice, of course, there are very few "pure" systems of either individual or master calendars. Most courts use hybrid systems that are more like one or the other to varying degrees (Mahoney et al., 1988).

Some studies have suggested that master calendaring systems facilitate speedy case handling by encouraging more efficient allocation of court resources (Luskin and Luskin, 1987:215). On the other hand, in some courts where master calendar systems were replaced by individual calendars, the result was a substantial increase in the speed and efficiency of case processing (Wilson, 1972:90). Church and his colleagues found a "striking" association between the use of master calendaring systems and longer case processing times in the handling of civil cases (Church et al., 1978:37). In the handling of criminal cases, however, the relationship was not as strong. The researchers concluded that neither the individual or master calendaring system was inherently more efficient for criminal cases (Church et al., 1978:38). However, they believed the individual calendar system had other advantages for case processing that would likely increase court efficiency.

> The individual calendar system does not emerge from this analysis as a panacea, but it is our strong impression that it provides an accountability for individual judges not possible in the master calendar. Stated baldly, individual calendar systems create incentives for judges to work harder, and to expend that effort on activities that increase productivity and decrease individual case delay (Church et al., 1978:72).

Church and his colleagues found that individual calendars tended to instill competition among judges. This competition was never formalized, and its existence was often denied in the study's interviews, but judges using individual calendar systems were more likely to show a keen interest in the comparative statistics produced by court management. The researchers concluded that friendly competition was desirable, and open comparisons between judges might help to increase the level of judicial concern about case processing time. They warned, however, that high productivity should never be "the all-encompassing definition of a good judge" (Church et al., 1978:73–75).

In their 1988 study, Mahoney and his colleagues agreed that while the individual calendar system appeared far more efficient for the handling of civil cases, "neither the [individual calendar] system nor the master calendar system [was] appreciably more effective than the other in minimizing felony case delays" (Mahoney et al., 1988:73). Among their sample of criminal courts, the mean disposition time for courts using individual calendar systems was 84 days, compared to 109 days for those using master calendars. When the slowest master calendar court was omitted from the analysis, however, the mean disposition time for master calendar courts dropped to 71 days.

Mahoney and his colleagues concluded that the type of calendar system used by a court has less impact on the court's overall processing time than whether the court itself begins to manage the movement of cases very early in the dispositional process. Individual calendars may encourage early intervention in the handling of criminal cases, which could be far more important in facilitating timely case processing than simply the choice of calendaring system (Mahoney et al., 1988:80).

Organizational Culture

Most traditional assumptions about the impact of court management on case processing delays were tested by two major research programs in the 1970s—the Federal Judicial Center's *District Court Studies Project* (Flanders, 1977), and the National Center for State Courts' *Pretrial Delay Project* (Church et al., 1978). Each study sampled case records from a number of different courts and compared them using multiple measures of case processing time.

In these studies, speed of case processing seemed to vary independently of the factors that were thought by most researchers to cause delay. Although a court's calendaring system, charging process, and the extent of administrative control over case processing appeared to be important factors in the pace of litigation, the primary influences on court delay were the "informal expectations, attitudes, and practices of attorneys and judges" (Church et al., 1978:5). Both studies helped to foster the development of what Church (1982) later called the "new conventional wisdom" about court delay.

This new perspective identified the primary cause of delay as organizational culture. Although the nature and degree of case delays in a particular court may be partly shaped by resources, procedures, and structure, according to this perspective, delay exists in the first place because the informal norms and expectations of participants in the court process *allow* it to exist. Overtime, informal norms and expectations lead court administrators, judges, and attorneys to believe that a certain amount of delay is "normal."

This new perspective on delay pointed to a completely different set of causal factors for researchers. The new factors included "informal practices" such as when attorneys accommodate each other's scheduling preferences and create endless continuances out of professional courtesy, "practitioner incentives" that encourage lawyers to organize their workload around billing needs rather than the needs of litigants, and "expectations and norms" that allow courts to accept as normal a pace of litigation that would seem excessively slow in other courts (Church, 1982:401–403). Nimmer (1976) described this new set of factors as the "local discretionary system." Others referred to it as "local legal culture" (Church et al., 1978), or "socio-legal culture" (Neubauer et al., 1981).

Researchers found that the roots of socio-legal culture could be very deep. Church (1981:79) described a "common theme" of the *Pretrial Delay Project's* interviews with judges and other court personnel as a "firm belief that the [existing pace of litigation] was really the only proper one, that any significant speeding up or slowing down would almost certainly produce injustice." This aspect of organizational culture had not often been appreciated by researchers. Most research on delay had assumed that slow processing was caused by unwanted inefficiencies.

> The idea that an existing leisurely pace of criminal cases might be considered satisfactory—even desirable—by the judges and attorneys who ultimately control the pace was seldom considered (Church, 1981:85).

The "cultural" approach to court delay dominated research throughout the 1980s and into the 1990s (e.g., Raine and Wilson, 1993). Of course, like all "conventional wisdom," the insight that court delay is caused by organizational culture was occasionally over-emphasized. At best, the cultural school encouraged researchers and practitioners to consider the self-interests of court participants, and to seek reductions in court delay by altering the incentives that promote or inhibit desired behavior. At its worst, however, the concept of local legal culture may have suggested that nothing could be done about court delay, and that courts inevitably develop their own natural pace of case handling and any attempts to modify that pace would be futile.

Luskin and Luskin (1986:212) rejected the "nebulous" answers of local legal culture and recommended instead that researchers focus on determining which factors are empirically related to case processing time in various court settings. They argued that the research literature on court delay had still provided only a "tenuous and partial" understanding of the variations in court processing times.

Other researchers agreed that the cultural approach to court delay could not adequately explain how delay develops and why some courts are able to avoid it while others seem unable to prevent it. Grossman and his colleagues argued that local legal culture was not even an explanation of court delay as much as it was "a convenient restatement of the problem" (Grossman et al., 1981:112). The fundamental assertion of the cultural approach, that "practices and attitudes toward court processing of attorneys and court personnel play a significant role in determining the pace of litigation in a particular court," was, according to Grossman et al., already "generally accepted" by researchers (1981:112). Local legal culture was simply a new label for an established idea. Critics of the cultural approach called for a new approach to research on case processing time.

APPLYING ORGANIZATIONAL THEORY TO COURT DELAY

The development of the cultural approach during the 1970s would have come as no surprise to anyone familiar with organizational theory. As often happens in applied fields that are loosely tied to the social sciences, court administration researchers during the 1970s freely adapted the ideas of organizational psychology and sociology in devising their approach to court delay. Subsequent developments in the study of court delay have continued to parallel the ideas of organizational theorists. Therefore, it is useful to understand how the concepts of organizational theory can be applied to the study of delay.

The Human Relations School

The concept of "local legal culture," "local discretionary systems" or "socio-legal culture" can be traced to a well-known school of organizational theory called "human relations."

Management theorists once assumed that business organizations could be adequately understood by studying their formal structure. Beginning with research conducted during the 1930s, however, organizational scholars began to understand that organizations were more complicated than machines. Organizations were collections of human beings, with emotions, beliefs, superstitions, and ambitions. Management research began to take the "human factor" into account. Studies found that the most effective managers were those who knew how to coordinate the dynamics of "human relations."

One of the most important studies in the development of the human relations school was the "Hawthorne Experiment" (Roethlisberger and Dickson, 1939; Mayo, 1949). Researchers studying the factors related to worker productivity in an industrial plant found that almost any intervention in the workplace increased the productivity of employees. Both lowering and increasing the level of lighting in the factory, for example, had the same positive effect on employee productivity. The Hawthorne researchers concluded that workers sometimes respond to the fact of intervention, rather than to the type of intervention. They found that the perceptions and attitudes of workers were just as important to productivity as management's efforts to manipulate formal procedures and technology. The Hawthorne study also demonstrated the importance of "group affiliation" and "sentiment" in the behavior of individuals in the workplace. It led to new prescriptions for effective management and an emphasis on informal structures and communication in organizations.

Another early study in the human relations tradition analyzed how technological changes in the coal mining industry had significant, negative impacts on the informal relations among workers in coal-mining companies (Trist and Bamforth, 1951). Adjusting to technological changes required conscious intervention by management to maintain previous levels of worker productivity. The focus of the research was on how management could effectively utilize "small group dynamics" to influence the informal aspects of organizational culture. The researchers coined the term "socio-technical system" to describe the interdependency of technical and social factors in organizations. More than two decades later, very similar terms were used by researchers to describe the importance of informal organization in understanding the problem of court delay.

The Environmental School

As studies of court administration continued to parallel theoretical developments in organizational theory, it was appropriate that court delay researchers next turned their attention to the influences of inter-organizational networks and the organizational environment. This has been the dominant trend in the sociology of organizations for more than two decades.

Until the 1960s, management researchers were interested almost exclusively in internal organizational factors, either the coordination of formal operations (Taylor, 1911), informal human relations (Mayo, 1945), or the effectiveness of decision-making methods (March and Simon, 1958). Beginning in the 1960s, a number of organization theorists concluded that internal variables alone would never account for the significant variations found in organizational change, effectiveness, structure, adaptation, and growth (see the review in Aldrich and Pfeffer, 1976). Instead, internal organizational characteristics were thought to be partly shaped by external factors such as the extent of competition and cooperation between related organizations, market characteristics, cultural values, economic conditions, and the overall political climate. Together, these factors were viewed as the "environment" in which organizations exist. Without an awareness of the interactions of the organization with its environment, researchers would be misled by spurious relationships between internal factors and organizational outcomes (Emery and Trist, 1965; Aldrich, 1979).

Although early studies often portrayed the relationship between organizations and the environment as one-way (i.e., organization adapt to the environment), more contemporary theorists recognize that influence flows both ways. Organizations attempt to influence the environment as well. In fact, the operational and structural characteristics present in an organization may be the results of previous "exchanges" and "negotiations" with the environment, both successful and unsuccessful (Meyer and Rowan, 1977; Pfeffer and Salancik, 1978).

Researchers studying court delay also began to be aware of environmental forces. In fact, Mohr (1976:625) argued that the environmental school was the organizational perspective most appropriate for studying courts. Haynes (1973:52–54) asserted that the term "court delay" was actually a misnomer because it suggested that delays were caused by factors within the court itself. He noted that blaming delays entirely on the court ignores the large number of individuals and agencies that come into contact with a typical court case: police, prosecutors, the public (in reporting crimes), witnesses, defense counsel, investigators, judges, etc. At every step in the processing of a case, one or more of these actors can contribute to processing delays, although only some of them are formally a part of the court.

Other researchers have noted that courts cannot be understood adequately without recognizing their place in the larger network of organizations that constitute the justice system. For example, Gillespie (1977) studied judicial productivity in Federal district courts and concluded that most causes of delay were external to the courts themselves. Particularly influential among these external factors were "professional legal inputs," or the actions of the private bar, public defenders, and prosecuting attorneys (Gillespie, 1977:21).

Malcolm Feeley (1992) argued that the court process should be studied within the context of the entire justice system. He suggested that courts are not classic bureaucracies but "open systems" that achieve their goals through interactions among the set of actors making up the justice system.

Jacob (1983:191) defined the court itself as "groups of people engaged in a common task, interacting on a regular basis, performing specialized roles, utilizing specialized knowledge, and responding to some direction and supervision from others." Such a definition encouraged researchers to view the court as a collection of actors with primary ties to other organizations.

Eisenstein and Jacob (1977) proposed that judges, prosecutors, and defense attorneys should be seen as representatives of different organizations working jointly on common goals. They studied "courtroom workgroups" in three cities to determine how the interactions of key actors contributed to organizational problems such as court delay. Each set of court actors (judges, attorneys, clerks) pursue their own interests. At times, they have good reasons for maintaining a pace of litigation that may appear to others as unreasonable delay. Reducing court delay, according to Eisenstein and Jacob, requires an organizational analysis to identify and target the entire system of incentives perpetuating delay.

Classical organizational theorists such as Max Weber viewed a hierarchy of power relations to be the distinguishing characteristic of formal organizations. Courts demonstrate hierarchy and a method of distributing power, but they are far from traditional organizations. For example, while a "weak hierarchy" exists between lower and upper courts, theirs is not a true subordinate-superior relationship (Jacob, 1983:193). Appellate courts may overrule a trail court decision, but this action is initiated by the litigants in a case and not by the policies or procedures of the appellate court. Supreme courts may issue rules of procedure for their lower courts, but they do not supervise the operations of those courts on a day-to-day basis.

Even the task of running a trial court is not organized according to a strict hierarchy of authority. While a judge is the "nominal and formal superior" of a courtroom work group, judges influence only some aspects of courtroom procedure while sharing responsibility for others (Jacob, 1983:194). Judges do not always control the assignment of staff in the courtroom—especially the assignment of attorneys. Judges, therefore, cannot control the flow of cases by themselves. "Work group" members outside the actual court structure have considerable influence over the nature and speed of case processing.

Secondary Goals

Although courts are not the self-contained, bureaucratic structures envisioned by classic organizational theory, much can be learned by viewing courts from an organizational perspective. One of the most basic insights of organizational theory is that organizations have multiple goals, and some of the goals they pursue are not directly related to their stated mission. Primary goals are the formally stated objectives an organization was designed to achieve (e.g., hospitals cure the sick, firefighters put out fires). All organizations, however, devote some of their efforts to secondary goals (e.g., hospitals maximize insurance receipts, firefighters protect their public image).

The primary goal of a court might be described as the production of timely, just, and effective case dispositions. Like all organizations, however, courts pursue a variety of secondary goals that are separate from this stated mission. One of the more essential secondary goals of the courts is to mediate the influence of the external environment. Courts attempt to limit the negative effects of outside forces and to protect their core activities from external manipulation (Jacob, 1983:198–200).

While case processing delays might seem to undermine the court's primary mission, a certain degree of delay could be a rational outcome of the organization's efforts to achieve other environmental goals, such as controlling the volume of the workload in order to prevent more serious organizational failures. Any attempt to explain or control court delay, therefore, should include an analysis of how delay may serve secondary but essential organizational goals. This perspective represents the future direction of research on court delay.

CONCLUSION

After several decades of studying court delay, researchers have found that there is no such thing as a finite set of "causes" which inevitably lead to delay. In any court, one or more features of the case handling process may be inefficient and create backlogs. However, another court sharing these same features may not have problems with delay. In still another court, the existence of delay problems may be traced to a completely different set of precipitating factors. Malcolm Feeley observed that delay is not even one problem, but more of a syndrome of related problems—"delay is a blanket term covering a host of different problems caused by various factors, all requiring different responses" (Feeley, 1983:182).

At times, the speed of case processing has been found to vary independently of most of the factors commonly thought to cause delay—offender characteristics, court resources, and courtroom procedures. Delay may be partly caused by "cultural" elements such as staff attitudes and informal customs. Cultural factors, however, will never fully explain why case delays develop, nor can they help courts to avoid or reduce all delays.

In order to develop a complete understanding of court delay, it is necessary to take account of the range of forces outside the court. Courts are organizations after all, and organizations are partly products of external forces, such as the extent of competition and cooperation between related organizations, market characteristics, cultural values, economic conditions, and the overall political climate. Without an understanding of the relationship between an organization and its environment, researchers may be misled by meaningless empirical relationships between internal management characteristics and organizational outcomes.

Recent studies have located the origins of court delay in the social, political, and organizational contexts within which courts operate. Together, all of these factors can create incentives for a court to operate slowly regardless of its level of resources or managerial acumen. Mays and Taggart (1986:200), for example, grouped the various causes of court delay into three categories:

1) "external socio-political pressures—for example, population increases, increased litigiousness, and underfunding of the courts";
2) "external legal changes—such as increased creation of legal rights and what has been termed 'overcriminalization' "; and
3) "internal behavioral factors—for example, judicial inertia, lack of management or interest in management, and complexity of case scheduling."

Luskin and Luskin (1987:209–217) categorized all potential influences on case processing time into one of five general classes:

1) "Case-specific incentives," such as attorney type, pretrial custody status, offense seriousness, defendant's prior arrest record, and the status of the judge (regular or visiting);

2) "Case complexity," primarily whether a case involves multiple defendants;

3) "Case events," including trial (versus pleas), early dismissals, pretrial motions, psychiatric evaluation delays, defendant's failure to appear, continuances, postponed or repeated preliminary hearings, and mistrials;

4) "Structural incentives and facilitation," including docket type (central or individual), the existence of case tracks or event deadlines, whether the court has official processing time goals, the court's role in case scheduling, the court's ability to produce useful case processing statistics, the role of an administrative judge, the use of centralized or locally managed plea bargaining; and

5) "Caseload" factors, including both the average caseload size of the court in general, and the caseload size of the judge in each case.

In the late 1970s, Luskin found that most studies of court processing advanced relatively simple views of the causes of delay. She called for researchers to be more explicit about their theories of the causes underlying delay in case processing.

> ...we have relatively little understanding of how court delay is related to demand for court services, to available court resources, to procedures used to settle disputes, and to the motivations of participants. To gain this understanding, we need to develop and test a theory of case processing time (Luskin, 1978:116).

Few researchers responded to Luskin with theoretical treatments of case processing time (possible exceptions include Hagan and Zatz, 1985 and Zatz and Lizotte, 1985). However, research on the origins of court delay has since become far more sensitive to the non-traditional nature of courts as organizations.

Researchers seeking to understand court delays or to reduce their impact on court operations should continue to study the incentives and motivations of other organizations in their investigations. Court administrators, judges, prosecutors, defense attorneys, service providers, and victim groups should be seen as "stake holders" with an interest in the court's process and in the speed with which it operates.

While the existence of case processing delays may conflict with the justice system's primary mission to dispense speedy justice, they may be quite functional when viewed in the context of the court's wider interests in stable inter-organizational relations and other environmental goals. True progress in combating court delay will be made by ensuring that speedy case handling is consistent with these larger goal structures.

Chapter 2 Notes

1. The *Pretrial Delay Project* was a collaboration of the National Center for State Courts, the National Conference of Metropolitan Courts, and the Courts Division of the Law Enforcement Assistance Administration (LEAA), formerly within the U.S. Department of Justice. One of the major goals of the project was to formulate a general theory of the pace of litigation in civil and criminal courts. The project collected data in 21 general jurisdiction courts in major cities across the United States. Data were obtained from interviews with court personnel and abstracted from the records of cases disposed during 1976. In each court, the researchers collected data on approximately 500 civil cases and 500 criminal cases (Church et al., 1978:30).

   Intensive evaluations of case processing were also conducted in five criminal courts: the Bronx County Supreme Court (NY), Dade County Circuit Court (FL), Allegheny County Court of Common Pleas (PA), Essex County Superior Court (NJ), Orleans Parish Criminal District Court (LA), and five civil courts: the Bronx and Dade County courts as well as the Hennepin County District Court (MN), the Maricopa County Superior Court (AZ), and the Wayne County Circuit Court (MI). Each intensive evaluation study included on-site interviews conducted over a two-week period with judges, prosecutors, public defenders, private defense counsel, and court staff. Interviews were designed to be informal and to obtain each individual's description and opinions of court operations (Church et al., 1978:4).

2. This 1988 study by the National Center for State Courts had two major objectives: 1) to "provide an up-to-date picture of the pace of civil and criminal litigation in urban trial courts" and 2) to "develop an understanding of the change process in courts—a charting of trends over time, an increased understanding of the dynamics of delay reduction and delay prevention programs" (Mahoney et al., 1988:3). The researchers collected detailed data on random samples of cases from the civil and criminal (felony) dockets in each of the 18 courts. (Criminal case were studied in just 17 courts since one court handled only civil cases.) Systematic random samples were selected from among all cases disposed by each court during 1983, 1984, and 1985. Approximately 500 cases were selected for the study from each docket in each court during each of the three years. Altogether, the study collected information on about 50,000 cases across all sites (Mahoney et al., 1988:5).

   In addition to collecting case specific data, the research team assembled information on the structures, procedures, and workloads of the courts. The researchers also conducted interviews with judges, court administrative staff, and attorneys associated with each court.

   Study sites were selected in a manner that would maximize the ability of the researchers to compare their data to information collected by studies during the 1970s. Thus, of the 18 sites in which new data were collected, 13 had been studied previously in the Pretrial Delay Project conducted by the National Center for State Courts (Church et al., 1978). Three of the other five courts had been the subjects of studies conducted by the American Judicature Society from 1979 to 1981 (Mahoney et al., 1988:5). By comparing the case processing times in the earlier studies to the data collected as part of their study, the researchers were able to analyze whether the 18 courts experienced any substantial changes in their ability to manage their criminal and civil caseloads in the ensuing five to ten years.

3. Luskin and Luskin (1987) analyzed data collected from three criminal courts during a federally funded evaluation of delay reduction programs (see also Neubauer et al., 1981). The researchers tested a variety of case-specific and court-level variables for their relationship to the time between case initiation and final disposition. The effect of the explanatory variables on case processing time was modeled using structural equations (GLS regression). Each hypothesized relationship was tested using data from each of the three courts (Detroit, Dayton, and Providence, Rhode Island).

4. The project collected data on more than 2,500 felony cases handled by Indiana courts in St. Joseph (South Bend) and Marion (Indianapolis) counties between 1963 and 1970. Data collection was limited to cases involving relatively serious offenses. The analysis focused on a wide range of case-handling and court operations variables. The researchers used a factor analysis to test the relationship of these variables with: 1) the time elapsed from arrest to arraignment, 2) the time from arraignment to disposition, and 3) the time from disposition to appeal.

Chapter 3
National Survey of Delinquency Delays

INTRODUCTION [1]

This chapter presents findings from a national survey in which more than 300 juvenile justice professionals from 123 U.S. counties answered questions about processing delays in their juvenile courts. The survey was designed to identify the extent of processing delays in juvenile courts and to explore the perceptions of juvenile court professionals about the origins and impact of delays in their handling of delinquency cases.

METHODOLOGY

Questionnaires were mailed to juvenile court professionals in a representative sample of 127 U.S. counties (see Appendix for sampled counties). The questionnaires measured opinions and attitudes about delays in the handling of juvenile delinquency cases. In addition to collecting data on the attitudes and opinions of respondents, the questionnaires collected information on a variety of organizational, procedural, and legal factors that were thought to affect delinquency case processing. The major purposes of the survey were to develop information on the degree to which juvenile court operations were hindered by the type of organizational problems that are related to case delays, and to obtain preliminary data on the prevalence and impact of delays in the handling of delinquency cases.

Study Sample

A stratified, random sampling technique was used to generate a nationally representative sample of juvenile court jurisdictions. Stratification was based on the size of a jurisdiction's youth population. Each of the Nation's 3,141 counties was placed into one of three strata, based on the number of county residents between the ages of 10 and 17 (inclusive) reported in the 1990 Census of the United States. In 1990 the largest 164 counties in the Nation contained approximately 50% of the youth population. These counties comprised the first sampling stratum. The remaining counties were placed into a second and third stratum so that each stratum contained 25% of the youth population.

Counties were selected at random from within each of the three strata by taking every n^{th} county from lists sorted by population size. The larger jurisdictions in the first stratum were slightly over-sampled since juvenile courts in large urban counties are thought to handle a disproportionate number of the Nation's serious delinquency cases. In all, 127 counties were sampled—77 counties were taken from stratum 1, and 25 counties each were randomly selected from strata 2 and 3. The sampling frame was designed to reflect the jurisdictions that handle the Nation's delinquency cases, rather than representing the range of actors within the juvenile justice system (e.g., judges, prosecutors, etc.).

Data Collection

Between four and five survey forms were mailed to each of the sampled jurisdictions. Published directories and telephone contacts were used to identify several respondents from each jurisdiction, including the administrative (or presiding) judge, the juvenile court administrator, a staff person with responsibility for managing the court calendar or docket (if such a position existed), the chief juvenile prosecutor, and the chief public defender. In jurisdictions without a public defender's office or its equivalent, the researchers asked another respondent to identify a member of the local defense bar thought to have extensive juvenile court experience. In all, 567 questionnaires were mailed to respondents in the 127 sampled jurisdictions.

The response rate was 65%, with 371 surveys returned (table 3.1). At least one survey was returned from 123 of the 127 jurisdictions contacted by the study. Thus, only four jurisdictions failed to respond entirely. More than a third (44) of the jurisdictions returned four or more surveys. A majority (86) returned three or more surveys, while 20 jurisdictions returned just two forms and 17 returned one survey.

TABLE 3.1
Survey response rate by type of respondent.

Type of Respondent	Mailed	Received	Response Rate
Judge	123	82	67%
Administrator or docket manager	199	148	74%
Prosecutor	121	70	58%
Defense Counsel	124	71	57%
All Respondents	**567**	**371**	**65%**

The response rate was satisfactory among all respondent groups (57% or higher). Court administrative staff (administrators and docket managers) were the most likely to return the survey (74%). Analyses of the survey data did not reveal any important differences in the response rate according to several county characteristics that could be expected to affect the operations of the juvenile justice system—i.e., population size, juvenile population as a proportion of the total, percentage of racial and ethnic minorities in the population, and the rate of juvenile arrests for FBI Index Crimes in 1990.

RESULTS

Of the 123 responding courts, 76% described themselves as juvenile or family courts, while 20% were courts of general jurisdiction.[2] By definition, all courts in the study were responsible for handling delinquency cases, while 93% were also responsible for abuse and neglect cases, 77% for juvenile status offense cases, and 53% handled adoptions. Fewer than half (47%) of the responding courts were responsible for guardianship cases, 46% for juvenile traffic cases, and 45% for general domestic relations. Approximately one-fourth of the responding courts (usually the smaller, more rural jurisdictions) were responsible for handling criminal and civil cases.

When asked to rank their various caseloads according to which consumed the most of the court's time, 42% of the courts indicated that their delinquency caseload required the most time overall. The delinquency caseload was the second most time-consuming for another 28% of the responding courts. Thus, for 70% of the responding courts, delinquency cases represented one of the two most time-consuming caseloads handled by the court. The child dependency caseload was the most time-consuming for 22% of the responding courts. Of these 27 courts, two-thirds (18) listed their delinquency caseload as the second most time-consuming.

As would be expected, the courts in larger jurisdictions—those most likely to be juvenile or family courts—were twice as likely as smaller courts to report that their delinquency caseload was the most time-consuming. Among the 77 large jurisdictions in the first sampling stratum, 55% reported that their delinquency caseload required the most overall court time. Just 22% of the smaller jurisdictions believed that their delinquency caseload was the most time-consuming.

Satisfaction with Case Processing Time

The survey included a range of questions about the respondents' satisfaction with case processing time for delinquency cases. For each item, respondents were asked to indicate whether they were "dissatisfied," "somewhat dissatisfied," "somewhat satisfied" or "satisfied" with the time required to process delinquency cases in their jurisdiction. One fifth of all respondents expressed some dissatisfaction with their court's timeliness in processing delinquency cases in general (table 3.2).[3] The greatest degree of dissatisfaction noted by respondents was with the time required to process cases being waived or transferred to criminal court (26%). Transferred cases, however, typically represent a very small proportion (under 1%) of a juvenile court's delinquency caseload (Butts, Snyder, Finnegan et al., 1995).

TABLE 3.2

Proportion of respondents expressing dissatisfaction with the timeliness of case processing, by type of delinquency case, by type of respondent.

		Total	Type of Respondent			
			Judge	Admin.	Prosecutor	Counsel
		(N=371)	(N=82)	(N=148)	(N=70)	(N=71)
	Type of Case					
*	Delinquency cases in general	20%	12%	20%	20%	31%
**	Informally diverted cases	11	9	5	13	21
	Formally charged cases, not detained	21	17	20	20	30
**	Formally charged cases, detained	18	16	11	16	38
*	Cases waived to criminal court	26	20	24	23	41

* Significant difference (χ^2; $p < .05$) in dissatisfaction expressed, according to type of respondent.

** Significant difference (χ^2; $p < .01$) in dissatisfaction expressed, according to type of respondent.

The time required to process informally handled delinquency cases—i.e., cases handled without the filing of a petition—was least likely to generate dissatisfaction among the respondents. Only 11% of the survey respondents expressed dissatisfaction with the timeliness with which informal cases were handled. Informally handled cases usually account for half of all delinquency caseloads nationwide (Butts, Snyder, Finnegan et al., 1995). In cases where juveniles were formally petitioned, 18% of respondents were dissatisfied with the time required to handle cases when juveniles were being held in detention awaiting disposition, while 21% were dissatisfied with the timeliness of cases that did not involve detention.

Considerable variation was found when the analysis examined dissatisfaction with case processing time by respondent group. The respondents least dissatisfied with case processing time in general were judges (12%). Defense attorneys were more dissatisfied with case processing time (31%) than other respondents. Among both administrative staff and prosecutors, 20% expressed dissatisfaction with the speed of delinquency case processing in general. Differences in general dissatisfaction were statistically significant (χ^2; $p < .05$).

Significant differences were also found when the analysis considered specific types of delinquency cases. With one exception (formally charged cases, not involving detention), higher levels of dissatisfaction were expressed by defense counsel respondents. For informally handled cases, 21% of all defense counsel respondents expressed dissatisfaction with the amount of time needed for court processing, compared with 13% of prosecuting attorneys, 9% of judges, and 5% of administrators. Defense counsel respondents were also far more likely to be dissatisfied with the time required to process cases involving detained juveniles—38% of defense attorneys, compared with 16% of prosecuting attorneys, 16% of judges, and 11% of court administrators.

Case Processing Stages

Respondents were asked to rate their satisfaction with the amount of time needed for delinquency cases to proceed through various stages of the court process, including intake screening, petitioning, adjudication, disposition and the implementation of services and sanctions (table 3.3). One-fifth of all respondents expressed dissatisfaction with the timeliness of petitioning (21%), adjudication (20%), and disposition (20%). Just 14% were dissatisfied with the time necessary to complete intake screening. More than a third (35%) of the respondents, however, expressed dissatisfaction with the time required to implement the services and/or sanctions planned for youth involved in delinquency cases.

TABLE 3.3
Proportion of respondents expressing dissatisfaction with the amount of time needed to process delinquency cases, by stage of processing, by type of respondent.

		Type of Respondent			
	Total (N=371)	Judge (N=82)	Admin. (N=148)	Prosecutor (N=70)	Counsel (N=71)
Dissatisfied with Timeliness of...					
** Intake screening	14%	13%	6%	21%	25%
** Filing of charges (petitioning)	21	23	16	14	38
Adjudication	20	16	18	20	27
** Disposition	20	15	17	23	28
** Onset of services or sanctions	35	33	22	43	55

** Significant difference (χ^2; $p < .01$) in dissatisfaction expressed, according to type of respondent.

The respondents' dissatisfaction with the time needed to implement services and sanctions may be an accurate reflection of their concerns about the difficulties involved in fulfilling dispositional orders including placement on probation and arranging other post-dispositional sanctions and services (e.g., residential and other out-of-home placements). On the other hand, their responses may simply reflect an accumulated frustration with delays in general—the time spent waiting to complete the last aspect of case handling may be magnified by all of the waiting that has gone before. Respondent dissatisfaction with the implementation of sanctions and services may also reflect concerns about the quality and adequacy of these rather than merely the timeliness of their implementation.

Defense counsel respondents were more likely than other respondents to express dissatisfaction with the time required for intake screening (25%), petitioning (38%), adjudication (27%), disposition (28%), and the implementation of services or sanctions (55%). Interestingly, the lowest dissatisfaction rates for each processing stage were found within the respondent group that typically would be most directly responsible for completion of this activity.[4] That is, court administrators were least likely to be dissatisfied with the amount of time needed to complete intake screening (6%). Prosecutors were least likely to be dissatisfied with the amount of time needed to file charges (14%). Judges were least likely to express dissatisfaction with the amount of time needed for a case to proceed to adjudication and disposition (16% and 15%, respectively). Court administrators were also least dissatisfied with the time required for the implementation of services or sanctions (22%). Differences in the dissatisfaction of respondent groups were statistically significant in all instances except for adjudication (χ^2; $p < .01$).

ORGANIZATIONAL CHARACTERISTICS

Researchers have often found delay to be associated with increased workloads, inadequate resources, inefficient courtroom procedures, indifferent staff attitudes, and poor organizational arrangements that limit the court's ability to monitor the flow of cases effectively (e.g., Church, 1982; Eisenstein and Jacob, 1977; Luskin and Luskin, 1986; Mahoney et al., 1988; Zatz and Lizotte, 1985). The survey included a range of items about organizational characteristics and courtroom procedures and whether they were thought to cause problems in juvenile courts. For each problem listed, respondents were asked to indicate whether the item was "not a problem," a "minor" problem, a "moderate" problem, or a "serious" problem for their court.[5] In all, 35 items were used to measure respondent perceptions about organizational problems. The selection of these items was based upon their saliency in the research literature, and their potential contribution to understanding delays in a juvenile justice setting.[6]

The analysis that follows is divided into two parts. First, data are presented that indicate the degree to which respondents believed that particular organizational and procedural items were either a moderate or serious problem for their court. Percentages are provided for each respondent group. Comparative rankings of each item are also provided. The presentation is divided into seven subsections, reflecting groups of related items as suggested by the literature:

1. Court workload;
2. Resources;
3. Caseflow management;
4. Calendaring;
5. Procedural issues that affect case flow;
6. Staff attitudes; and
7. Legal environment.

Second, the analysis examines the degree to which the respondents' perceptions of problems in these areas were correlated with their dissatisfaction with the timeliness of delinquency case processing. Correlation statistics are provided along with a rank ordering. Together, these analyses suggest that certain organizational and procedural problems are more likely than other problems to be associated with case processing delays. That is, some items that were considered to be serious court problems by many respondents were only weakly correlated with perceptions of case processing delays. On the other hand, a number of items infrequently cited as moderate or serious problems proved to be highly correlated with case processing delays.

Court Workload

Studies of court delay conducted prior to the 1970's often focused on the size of a court's workload in an attempt to explain case delays (e.g., Zeisel, Kalven and Buchholz, 1959). More recent research suggests that it is simplistic to assume that case processing delays are principally a function of court workload. Still, the volume of cases handled by a court is often a critical starting point in understanding the nature of processing delays in juvenile courts. Four questions on court workload were included in the survey. Two items asked whether increases in the volume and backlog of delinquency cases presented problems for the court. Two other items asked about increases and backlogs of non-delinquency (i.e., dependency) cases.

A large percentage of respondents indicated that their court was experiencing problems in handling a growing number of delinquency case filings and/or coping with a large backlog of delinquency cases. Of the 371 juvenile justice professionals responding to the survey, 178 (or 48%) indicated that their court was experiencing moderate to serious problems in coping with an increasing number of delinquency case filings (table 3.4). This problem ranked second overall on the list of problem areas evaluated by the respondents. More than a third (36%) of survey respondents also indicated that their court was experiencing problems with an increasing number of non-delinquency cases. This item ranked 8th among all problem areas.

Another 30% of the survey respondents noted that a large backlog of delinquency cases presented moderate to serious problems for their court. The response to this item varied by respondent type. Defense counsel respondents and prosecutors were significantly more likely to report problems with delinquency case backlogs (42% and 39%, respectively) than were judges (12%).

Resources

Studies of court delay have traditionally examined the issue of court workloads within the context of available resources. In other words, it is not merely large or increasing workloads that are associated with delays, but an imbalance between workload and resources. Several items in the survey addressed the adequacy of available resources by asking the degree to which respondents perceived problems with:

- insufficient court staff;
- a lack of court staff with specific responsibility for caseflow management;
- not enough hearing officers and judges;
- insufficient court funds;
- a lack of courtroom space; and
- a lack of diversion alternatives.

TABLE 3.4
Proportion of respondents acknowledging a "moderate" or "serious" problem with organizational and procedural characteristics in their juvenile court.

Problem Area	Rank‡	Total	Type of Respondent			
			Judge	Admin.	Pros.	Counsel
		(N=371)	(N=82)	(N=148)	(N=70)	(N=71)
Workload						
Increase in delinquency case filings	*2*	48%	43%	44%	59%	52%
Increase in non-delinquency case filings	*8*	36	40	38	31	34
** Large backlog of delinquency cases	*14*	30	12	30	39	42
Large backlog of non-delinquency cases	*19*	25	21	25	23	32
Resources						
Not enough judges/hearing officers	*12*	30	32	27	29	37
Insufficient court staff	*6*	38	30	40	41	41
Lack of court staff with primary responsibility for monitoring caseflow	*11*	32	26	31	34	38
Insufficient court funds	*1*	54	56	49	61	55
Lack of courtroom space	*5*	40	40	36	41	46
**Lack of diversion alternatives	*3*	46	52	34	47	61
Caseflow Management						
Case processing is unnecessarily complex	*33*	13	10	14	13	13
Lack of established case processing methods	*30*	17	12	16	14	27
Lack of automated caseflow reports	*15*	30	34	32	30	18
** Inability to identify time-consuming cases early in the court process	*28*	17	12	11	20	32
Lack of internal accountability regarding caseflow management	*21*	23	22	20	23	32
Inadequate communication within court regarding processing delays	*26*	19	13	20	21	24
Calendaring						
** Inefficient calendar/assignment system	*22*	22	10	17	34	37
Too many court continuances granted	*7*	38	38	42	34	32
* Lack of guidelines governing continuances	*16*	29	16	30	36	34
Hearing schedule is not regarded as "certain" by participants	*20*	24	20	27	20	25
Other Procedures						
Delays in police filing of initial complaint	*25*	20	12	20	24	27
** Quality of evidence in police investigations	*4*	42	34	24	56	73
Time consuming jury trials	*35*	6	5	6	7	6
Slow service of process (hearing notification)	*26*	19	22	14	24	24
* Delays in distribution of court orders	*31*	16	6	16	19	23
** Delays in court-ordered investigations	*10*	32	27	22	40	51
Counsel assignment is slow or inefficient	*29*	17	15	17	21	15
Counsel reimbursement method encourages protracted case processing	*33*	13	9	12	10	21

(Continued)

TABLE 3.4 (Cont.)

Problem Area	Rank‡	Total (N=371)	Judge (N=82)	Admin. (N=148)	Pros. (N=70)	Counsel (N=71)
			Type of Respondent			
Staff Attitudes						
Timely case processing is not of sufficient concern to judges	*32*	15%	6%	20%	14%	17%
Timely case processing is not of sufficient concern to other (non-judicial) court staff	*23*	22	13	21	23	31
** Timely case processing is not of sufficient concern to prosecutors	*18*	26	26	32	1	37
** Timely case processing is not of sufficient concern to defense attorneys	*9*	33	39	40	37	10
Legal Environment						
** Lack of case processing goals or standards	*24*	21	13	20	17	38
Increase in legislative requirements regarding delinquency cases	*12*	30	35	31	26	27
** Increase in legislative requirements regarding non-delinquency cases	*17*	27	39	31	13	17

* Significant difference (χ^2; $p < .05$) in proportion noting problems, according to type of respondent.
** Significant difference (χ^2; $p < .01$) in proportion noting problems, according to type of respondent.
‡ Indicates the order of items according to the number of respondents noting moderate or serious problems. The item ranked first was selected by the largest number of respondents as being a moderate or serious problem, the item ranked second was selected by the next largest number of respondents, etc. Ties received equal rankings.

Resource problems ranked very high in the survey. Four of the six resource items ranked in the top ten of all problem areas. More respondents noted problems with insufficient court funds than any other item in the survey (54%). Only one respondent group failed to rank this item first—defense attorneys ranked it third, behind problems with the quality of police evidence (73%) and a lack of diversion alternatives (61%). Other resource items that ranked high included a lack of courtroom space (40%) and insufficient court staff (38%).

Caseflow Management

Poor caseflow management practices have often been cited as a major source of case processing delays (see Solomon and Somerlot, 1987). The survey examined each respondent's opinions about the extent to which caseflow management issues were problematic for their court. The survey included items on:

- case processing complexity;
- lack of established case processing procedures;
- lack of automated caseflow reports;

- inability to identify time-consuming cases early in the court process;
- lack of internal accountability for caseflow; and
- inadequate internal communication.

None of the caseflow management items were ranked very highly by respondents, suggesting that such issues do not present problems for most courts, or that most court participants are not concerned about the impact of such problems compared with other pressing issues. A number of these items, however, were highly associated with respondent dissatisfaction with case processing time (see Table 3.5 below). This suggests that while most courts did not have trouble with caseflow management issues, those that did have such troubles were very likely to be experiencing delinquency case delays.

The caseflow management problem noted most often by respondents was a lack of automated caseflow reports. Thirty percent of respondents believed this to be a moderate or serious problem in their jurisdictions (ranked 15th overall). Judges, administrators, and prosecutors were more likely to see this as a problem than were defense counsel respondents. On the other hand, defense attorneys were more likely to perceive problems with a lack of established case processing procedures, a lack of internal accountability in the court regarding case processing, and an inability to identify problem cases early in the court process.

Calendaring

A number of issues related to the calendaring of cases and the scheduling of hearings have been investigated in the research literature on case processing delays (Mahoney et al., 1988). Four items in the survey addressed these issues by asking the respondents to indicate the degree to which their court was experiencing problems due to the fact that:

- the calendar/assignment system was thought to be inefficient;
- too many court continuances were granted;
- the court lacked firm guidelines for the granting of continuances; and
- hearing schedules were not regarded as “certain” or dependable by court participants.

The calendaring problem noted most often by the respondents was that the court granted too many continuances. Overall, 38% of the respondents believed this to be either a moderate or serious problem in their court. Excessive continuances ranked seventh overall among the problems noted by respondents. Other calendaring items were believed to be serious problems by some respondents but not others. For example, more than a third of the prosecutors and defense attorneys perceived problems with inefficient case assignment systems, but only 10% of judges and 17% of administrative staff agreed. Judges were also significantly less likely than other respondents to see serious problems with a lack of guidelines governing the use of continuances.

Procedural Issues That Affect Case Flow

Several items in the survey asked the respondents to evaluate the impact of other procedural issues on their court's operations. For example, two items addressed the quality and timeliness of police investigations as they applied to the juvenile court process. One of these issues emerged as the fourth most common problem noted by respondents. More than two of every five respondents (42%) believed that the quality of evidence contained in police investigations presented either moderate or serious problems for the court. On the other hand, items related to police investigations were not particularly correlated with the respondents' dissatisfaction with delinquency case processing (see Table 3.5).

Three items in the survey addressed court functions with direct and immediate impact on the ability of the hearing officer to proceed with a scheduled hearing. Inconsistencies in the execution of these responsibilities can often result in the adjournment or continuation of a scheduled hearing due to the absence of a key individual, misunderstandings regarding previous case determinations, and/or a lack of critical case information:

- inadequate/slow "service of process" (notification of witnesses and victims of hearings);
- delays in the distribution of court orders; and
- delays in the completion of court-ordered investigations and reports.

Of these three issues, the problem most often noted by respondents was delay in the completion of investigations (ranked 10th overall). Once again, prosecutors and defense attorneys were more likely to see problems in this area than were judges and court administrators.

Staff Attitudes

Previous research on court delay has often found that the norms and expectations of those involved in the court process—i.e., the court's informal "culture"—can influence the timeliness of case processing (Church et al., 1978). When the professionals working in a court do not actively support timely case processing, researchers have found that cases are indeed handled more slowly. The survey measured this factor by asking each respondent to indicate the degree to which their court had problems due to "insufficient concerns" about timely case processing. Respondents were asked to evaluate the attitudes of judges, administrators, prosecutors, and defense attorneys.

Overall, most respondents did not believe their courts were troubled by a lack of staff concern for timely case processing. Just 15% perceived such problems with the attitudes of judges, 22% with the attitudes of administrative staff, 26% with the attitudes of prosecutors, and 33% with the attitudes of defense attorneys. When the analysis examined these factors for their relationship to dissatisfaction with case processing time, however, the attitudes of judges and administrative staff in particular appeared to be more important (See Table 3.5).

Legal Environment

Researchers investigating court delay have concluded that differences in internal court arrangements, such as the method of case calendaring or the use of continuances, cannot completely explain why some courts process cases more slowly than others. In fact, studies have found that case handling and other court operations can be strongly influenced by the court's organizational and political environment (Eisenstein and Jacob, 1977). The survey addressed environmental forces by asking respondents to assess the extent of court problems associated with legal and statutory factors in their jurisdiction. Respondents were asked to judge whether problems existed in the court due to:

- a lack of case processing standards or goals;
- an increase in legislative requirements governing delinquency cases; and
- an increase in legislative requirements related to non-delinquency cases.

Nearly one-third (30%) of respondents believed that increases in legislative requirements related to the handling of delinquency cases had caused problems in court operations (ranked 12th overall). Judges were more likely than other respondents to perceive problems with legislative requirements. The lack of standards or case processing goals was seen as a problem by 21% of respondents (ranked 24th). Defense attorneys most frequently cited the lack of standards as a problem (39%).

ORGANIZATIONAL PROBLEMS AND DISSATISFACTION WITH CASE PROCESSING TIME

In addition to analyzing the prevalence of organizational problems in the juvenile courts, the analysis examined the degree to which these items were correlated with dissatisfaction with the time needed to process delinquency cases in general. For example, 33% of the respondents who stated that their court was experiencing problems with a lack of staff were also dissatisfied with the time needed to process delinquency cases in general. In contrast, dissatisfaction with processing time was noted by just 10% of the respondents who did not believe their court was experiencing problems with lack of staff, and by 16% of those who saw only minor problems due to staff shortages. The correlation between lack of court staff and dissatisfaction with case processing time was statistically significant ($r = .4058$; $p < .0001$). *Pearson* correlation coefficients were calculated to test the association between each organizational problem and the respondents' perception of case delays in general (table 3.5).[7]

Listed in decreasing order of their association with delay problems, the top 10 survey items that were related to respondents' perceptions of delay in the handling of delinquency cases were:

1. Large backlogs of delinquency cases.
2. Insufficient concern about timely case processing among non-judicial court staff.

3. Large backlogs of non-delinquency cases.
4. Lack of internal accountability among court staff regarding caseflow management.
5. Inefficient calendar and case assignment system.
6. Insufficient court staff.
7. Insufficient concern about timely case processing among judges.
8. Lack of established case processing procedures.
9. Lack of court staff with primary responsibility for monitoring caseflow.
10. Lack of case processing goals or standards.

Of the top 10 items, four were related to court resources and workload (1, 3, 6, & 9), four were related either to the court's caseflow management system or to the procedures and standards applicable to the handling of delinquency cases (4, 5, 8, & 10), and two were related to the attitudes of court participants and the degree to which they were concerned with case processing time (2 & 7).

Some organizational problems were found to be both fairly prevalent and strongly related to perceptions of delay. For example, insufficient court staff was the sixth most prevalent problem cited by respondents and was also the sixth strongest correlate of case processing dissatisfaction. Other items addressing staffing concerns (not enough judges or hearing officers, and lack of court staff with primary responsibility for monitoring caseflow) also ranked relatively high on both measures.

A number of organizational issues, however, were not as frequently considered to be moderate or serious problems, but were highly related to perceptions of delinquency delays in courts where they were noted as problematic (e.g., large case backlogs, the attitudes of judges and other court staff toward timely case processing, inefficient calendar and case assignment system, and the absence of standards or case processing goals). These differences were most apparent when considering the organizational items related to caseflow management. For example, lack of established case processing procedures was only the 30th most frequently cited court problem (noted by 17% of all respondents) but generated the eighth strongest correlation coefficient ($r = .3994$) with delinquency case processing dissatisfaction. A lack of internal accountability regarding caseflow management was cited by 23% of respondents as a moderate to serious problem (ranked 21st), but was the fourth strongest correlate of case processing delays ($r = .4240$).

Conversely, some organizational items were frequently cited as problematic but were not highly correlated with case processing delays. For example, a lack of diversion alternatives was the third most frequently cited problem among respondents (46%). Yet, it was weakly correlated with processing time dissatisfaction ($r = .1714$). The same was true for problems with the quality of evidence in police investigations, which ranked fourth in prevalence (42%), but was ranked 32nd as a predictor of case processing delays ($r = .1637$).

TABLE 3.5
Correlation between respondents' perception of organizational/procedural problems and general dissatisfaction with delinquency case processing time.

Problem Area	Rank ‡	N	Corr. (*r*)	Signif (*p*)
Workload				
Increase in delinquency case filings	*22*	354	.2427	.000
Increase in non-delinquency case filings	*24*	310	.2282	.000
Large backlog of delinquency cases	*1*	355	.4920	.000
Large backlog of non-delinquency cases	*3*	307	.4274	.000
Resources				
Not enough judges / hearing officers	*11*	294	.3786	.000
Insufficient court staff	*6*	347	.4058	.000
Lack of court staff with primary responsibility for monitoring caseflow	*9*	341	.3971	.000
Insufficient court funds	*14*	325	.3489	.000
Lack of courtroom space	*25*	352	.2214	.000
Lack of diversion alternatives	*31*	337	.1714	.002
Caseflow Management				
Case processing is unnecessarily complex	*19*	344	.2822	.000
Lack of established case processing procedures	*8*	339	.3994	.000
Lack of automated caseflow reports	*21*	320	.2665	.000
Inability to identify time-consuming cases early in the court process	*16*	346	.3220	.000
Lack of internal accountability regarding caseflow management	*4*	324	.4240	.000
Inadequate communication within court regarding processing delays	*13*	341	.3680	.000
Calendaring				
Inefficient calendar/assignment system	*5*	340	.4102	.000
Too many court continuances granted	*12*	357	.3708	.000
Lack of guidelines governing continuances	*15*	347	.3366	.000
Hearing schedule is not regarded as "certain" by participants	*20*	350	.2747	.000
Other Procedures				
Delays in police filing of initial complaint	*29*	334	.1910	.000
Quality of evidence in police investigations	*32*	332	.1637	.003
Time consuming jury trials	*35*	180	.0977	.192
Slow service of process (hearing notification)	*18*	350	.2897	.000
Delays in distribution of court orders	*23*	348	.2289	.000
Delays in court-ordered investigations	*27*	347	.2159	.000
Counsel assignment is slow or inefficient	*28*	349	.2007	.000
Counsel reimbursement method encourages protracted case processing	*30*	289	.1846	.002
Staff Attitudes				
Timely case processing is not of sufficient concern to judges	*7*	345	.4033	.000
Timely case processing is not of sufficient concern to other (non-judicial) court staff	*2*	344	.4434	.000

(Continued)

TABLE 3.5 (cont.)

Problem Area	Rank ‡	N	Corr. (*r*)	Signif (*p*)
Timely case processing is not of sufficient concern to prosecutors	*17*	343	.3056	.000
Timely case processing is not of sufficient concern to defense attorneys	*26*	345	.2209	.000
Legal Environment				
Lack of case processing goals or standards	*10*	321	.3920	.000
Increase in legislative requirements regarding delinquency cases	*33*	329	.1273	.021
Increase in legislative requirements regarding non-delinquency cases	*34*	287	.1012	.087

‡ Indicates the order of items according to the strength of association (i.e., value of *r*). The item ranked first was most strongly correlated with respondent dissatisfaction (i.e., largest value of *r*).

This analysis suggests that while the causes of delay are multiple, juvenile courts should focus their delay reduction efforts on the specific organizational and procedural areas that are most related to difficulties with the timeliness of delinquency case processing time. The survey data suggest that a number of the most frequently cited organizational problems were only peripherally related to case processing delays. Courts seeking to reduce unwanted case processing delays may wish to begin their efforts with an investigation of the organizational problems most strongly associated with respondent perceptions of delays.

This is not to minimize the importance of the other problem areas. A wide range of organizational issues may be critical to the mission and functioning of the court, but for reasons other than timely case processing. For example, a lack of diversion alternatives (the second most frequently cited problem area in the survey) may severely limit the court's ability to intervene effectively. As the survey data suggest, however, this may not necessarily reduce the timeliness with which cases are disposed. Dispositions may not be sufficiently targeted on the characteristics of each delinquent youth, but the dispositional decisions may still be made in a timely manner.

CONCLUSION

Consistent with the increasing body of research on delays in the criminal and civil court systems, this survey of juvenile justice professionals suggests that case processing delays in juvenile courts are related to a number of organizational factors, including workloads, resources, staff attitudes, and administrative efforts to control the flow of cases. Survey items that measured these factors were found to be highly correlated with the strength of respondent dissatisfaction with case processing time. These items can be placed into two categories. Some aspects of delay can be tied to organizational issues that are highly *external*, such as workload and court resources.

Juvenile courts may have little ability to control these factors. Other aspects of delay are associated with *internal* organizational factors, including caseflow management, calendaring, and staff attitudes.

Many juvenile courts are asked to cope with expanding workloads in times of stable or even shrinking resources. The survey findings, however, suggest that juvenile justice professionals attribute case processing delays as least as much to internal as to external factors. Delays may even worsen during times of plenty. Some jurisdictions have found that adding personnel to offset an increasing workload may actually exacerbate the very organizational dynamics contributing to case processing delays (Carter Goble Associates, Inc., 1989).

Juvenile courts seeking to reduce unwanted case processing delays should be prepared to address a range of internal management practices, especially those that relate to caseflow management and the calendaring of cases. Court administrators should focus on reducing the complexity of case handling and streamlining the path by which cases reach final disposition. The entire adjudicatory and dispositional process must be more accountable and predictable, and the court should strive for greater consistency in case handling through the establishment of clear, measurable procedural guidelines. Juvenile courts should also be ready to understand and influence their organizational environments, however, so that timely case processing is a primary concern for all parties inside and outside of the court, particularly judges, court administrators, prosecutors, defense attorneys, law enforcement and service providers.

Chapter 3 Notes

1. Much of this chapter was published previously in the *Juvenile & Family Court Journal*. See "Delays in juvenile justice: Findings from a national survey," by J. Butts & G. Halemba, Vol. 45(4), 1994, pp. 31–46.

2. To examine differences between courts, one respondent from each jurisdiction was chosen as a primary respondent. Primary respondents were usually judges or chief administrators.

3. Responses of "not applicable" or "uncertain" were combined with "satisfied" and "somewhat satisfied" to create dichotomous variables in which a value of 0 indicated no dissatisfaction noted and a value of 1 indicated either "not satisfied" or "somewhat not satisfied." All dichotomous measures of dissatisfaction were constructed in this manner. Most tables presented here are arranged in summary fashion and display only the percentage of respondents expressing dissatisfaction (i.e., "not satisfied" or "somewhat not satisfied"). For each cell in these tables, the unreported corresponding percentage (i.e., the difference between the reported percentage and 100%) would indicate the proportion of respondents who were either "satisfied," "somewhat satisfied" or "uncertain" in their assessment of the time needed for case processing. On average, responses of "uncertain" or "not applicable" were given by 6% of the respondents to each question.

4. Respondents to the survey may have been more likely to express dissatisfaction with aspects of the court process over which they had the least responsibility and, therefore, the least knowledge of day-to-day administrative constraints. The authors thank Dr. Carol Burgess of the Maricopa County (Phoenix, AZ) Juvenile Court for suggesting this interpretation.

5. As was the case with dichotomous variables measuring dissatisfaction, "not applicable" or "uncertain" responses to these items were combined with responses indicating "no problem" or "minor problem" to create two-category variables with the lowest value indicating no major problems noted. All variables that measure the degree of problem perceived by respondents were constructed in this manner.

6. Some items in the questionnaire were adapted from studies of case processing delays in criminal courts, most notably studies by Mahoney and his colleagues (1988: 88) and Goerdt et al. (1989: 91).

7. Rather than using the collapsed or dichotomous version of the variables (i.e., "no dissatisfaction noted" versus "some dissatisfaction noted"), correlations were calculated with the original four-category variables. Dissatisfaction with case processing time was measured in the following categories: "Not Satisfied," "Somewhat Not Satisfied," "Somewhat Satisfied" and "Satisfied." Organizational problems were measured as: "No Problem," "Minor Problem," "Moderate Problem" or "Serious Problem." The calculation of correlation coefficients excluded respondents who indicated that they were either uncertain of their answer, or believed that a particular item did not apply to their courts.

Chapter 4
Case Processing in Three Juvenile Courts

INTRODUCTION

This chapter describes three case studies conducted in urban juvenile courts. The case studies analyzed delinquency case processing practices in each jurisdiction and examined the extent to which processing delays affected day-to-day court operations.

The three jurisdictions were Baltimore City, Maryland (which is distinct from Baltimore County), Cuyahoga County, Ohio (including the City of Cleveland), and Maricopa County, Arizona (including the City of Phoenix).

The selection of the three case study sites was based upon several factors:

- The size of the jurisdiction (i.e., population);
- The upper age of the juvenile court's legal jurisdiction and any other factors that would affect the volume of a juvenile court's delinquency caseload;
- Geographic balance;
- The availability of automated caseflow data;
- The characteristics of the case processing system itself; and
- The jurisdiction's willingness to participate in the study.

Although problems of case delay are not limited to large jurisdictions, caseflow management problems are usually more complex in large jurisdictions, making them a richer resource for studies of court operations. Furthermore, the professional staff of large courts are often more experienced at dealing with case backlogs and delay and have more insights about successful methods of managing these problems. Also, the lessons learned from studies of large courts should be transferable to the caseflow problems experienced by smaller jurisdictions.

In each of the three jurisdictions, researchers collected written documentation about the court's case handling practices and conducted on-site interviews designed to illuminate the origins, characteristics, and impact of delays in delinquency case processing. Dozens of interviews were conducted with judges, court administrators, docket managers responsible for case assignment and calendaring, prosecutors, defense attorneys, and other supervisory and line staff. The interviews focused on each jurisdiction's case processing system and the extent to which it facilitated or hindered the timely handling of delinquency cases.

Various external factors were considered, but the studies focused primarily on each court's caseflow management practices. The interviews of court personnel typically included questions such as:

> *"What specific responsibilities do you have in processing delinquency referrals?"*
>
> *"What pressures do you experience when cases become delayed?"*
>
> *"How do delays in case handling affect court staff and the juveniles involved with the court?"*
>
> *"What impact do case delays have on court operations in general?"*
>
> *"What factors do you believe contribute to case processing delays?"*

Baltimore City

The juvenile justice system in Baltimore City was selected for two reasons. First, it is one of the few cities in the United States (St. Louis is another example) that is not part of a county or any other sub-State unit of government. Baltimore City is essentially its own county, but without the typical suburban areas found in most counties. As a result, the Baltimore City juvenile court serves an intensely urban population, which gives it one of the highest case rates in the Nation and magnifies many other urban-related problems faced by large juvenile courts (table 4.1).

Second, the juvenile justice system in Baltimore has been coping with severe delay problems for the past decade. According to interviews conducted by the authors, it was once not uncommon for arrested (non-detained) juveniles to wait 6 months or more just to be contacted for an initial intake interview. More than 9 months might elapse before a court hearing could be scheduled. In the worst cases, 18 to 24 months might pass before juveniles had their first formal court hearing.

Recently, efforts to improve delinquency case processing in Baltimore have been undertaken by various agencies, including the police, the State agency responsible for intake services, the juvenile court, the State's Attorney's office, and the Public Defender's office. As a result, the Baltimore juvenile justice system is becoming more timely than it was just two or three years ago. The experiences of Baltimore may be instructive for other jurisdictions just beginning to grapple with serious juvenile justice delays.

Cuyahoga County

The Cuyahoga County Juvenile Court was selected for this study because it is representative of many urban juvenile courts facing large caseloads with limited resources. The Cuyahoga court is a service-oriented juvenile court. The court itself administers an extensive continuum of intake diversion and post-disposition services to address the needs of delinquent and unruly (incorrigible) juveniles.

TABLE 4.1
Delinquency cases disposed in three jurisdictions, 1986–1993.

		Delinquency Cases Disposed			
Baltimore City	**Population Ages 10-17**	**Non-Petitioned**	**Petitioned**	**Total**	**Total Cases per 1,000 Juveniles**
Year					
1986	81,600	3,879	4,559	8,438	103.4
1987	79,700	3,386	4,699	8,085	101.4
1988	77,900	3,236	4,105	7,341	94.2
1989	77,100	3,237	5,607	8,844	114.7
1990	70,500	2,930	4,196	7,126	101.1
1991	69,700	3,199	5,905	9,104	130.6
1992	72,300	4,645	7,586	12,231	169.2
1993	72,400	4,434	7,930	12,364	170.8
Percent Change 1986–1993	–11%	14%	74%	47%	65%
Cuyahoga County					
Year					
1986	153,200	2,555	6,866	9,421	61.5
1987	*	*	*	*	*
1988	145,500	3,207	5,577	8,784	60.4
1989	141,700	2,918	6,708	9,626	67.9
1990	142,500	3,616	7,419	11,035	77.4
1991	141,600	4,100	8,487	12,587	88.9
1992	142,300	4,485	7,398	11,883	83.5
1993	142,700	4,300	7,424	11,724	82.2
Percent Change 1986–1993	–7%	68%	8%	24%	34%
Maricopa County					
Year					
1986	211,400	11,969	5,086	17,055	80.7
1987	215,700	11,037	5,592	16,629	77.1
1988	220,800	11,265	5,961	17,226	78.0
1989	218,800	10,576	5,915	16,491	75.4
1990	225,400	12,500	7,679	20,179	89.5
1991	232,900	13,010	9,638	22,648	97.2
1992	241,800	13,521	6,720	20,241	83.7
1993	254,300	11,007	9,327	20,334	80.0
Percent Change 1986–1993	20%	–8%	83%	19%	–1%

* Data not available.

Source: *Juvenile Court Statistics* (Annual). (Snyder et al., 1990a:133–174; Snyder et al., 1990b:135–175; Snyder et al., 1990c:157–197; Snyder et al., 1992:155–197; Snyder et al., 1993:127–169; Butts et al., 1994:171–214; Butts et al., 1995:61–93; Butts et al., 1996a:59–97).

Note: The increase in Baltimore cases from 1991 to 1992 is inflated somewhat by improved reporting (i.e., reporting was more thorough after 1991).

The court has struggled to maintain control over its case processing time. Caseflow management in Cuyahoga County is a labor-intensive process. The court's ability to process most delinquency cases in a timely manner is largely the result of the vigilance of a dedicated group of staff. Their vigilance has been essential to the court's efforts to maintain efficiency in the face of steady increases in delinquency case filings, a large increase in official dependency complaints, entrenched bureaucratic procedures, autonomous courtroom staff, and inadequate information systems. The court was chosen as one of the sites for this study because it has achieved notable success in improving the timeliness of delinquency case processing despite such obstacles.

Maricopa County

The Maricopa County Juvenile Court is widely recognized as one of the most well-managed juvenile courts in the country. The court was selected for this study in part because of this reputation, but also because it is a leader in computerization. The court's Juvenile On-Line Tracking System (or JOLTS) is known by juvenile justice professionals nationwide and has inspired many other software development efforts in juvenile justice agencies. The JOLTS software allows the Maricopa court to move cases efficiently from referral to disposition and to track their progress at each stage of the process. Despite its size and ever-expanding caseload, the Maricopa County court has a long tradition of sound management and technological innovation, and has demonstrated a high degree of commitment to improving its caseflow management through automation and caseflow monitoring.

BALTIMORE CITY: LEGISLATING DELAY REDUCTION

As mentioned above, the Baltimore juvenile justice system serves an intensely urban population and handles a relatively high volume of juvenile delinquency cases. Although the juvenile population of the city decreased 11% between 1986 and 1993, the number of delinquency cases handled by the juvenile justice system increased more than 40% during that time (table 4.1).

By the early 1990s, severe caseload pressures and long-standing problems in the coordination of delinquency case processing resulted in the Baltimore juvenile justice system having some of the longest delays in the Nation. In particular, the time between the arrest of juveniles and their first contact with the juvenile justice intake process often exceeded six months. Police handling of non-detained cases often took longer than the entire court process, from intake to disposition. In the very worst cases, an arrested juvenile who was released to await court processing may not have been asked to appear for an intake interview for more than two years after his or her arrest.

In response to this situation, the Maryland legislature passed a bill in 1995 that mandated a 15-day time limit for the police to make referrals to the juvenile justice system (Senate Bill 343). A previous legislative provision required the juvenile justice intake process to be completed in no more than 25 days, a much shorter time frame than was often possible in recent years.

Although initially it was not clear exactly what the consequences would be if these deadlines were missed, most of the agencies in the Baltimore juvenile justice system were confident that the legislative requirements would help to reduce juvenile justice processing delays.

Delinquency Case Processing

The Baltimore juvenile justice system is unique in several ways. First, as noted earlier, the City is separate from the surrounding county. Second, the Baltimore City juvenile court relies heavily on referees or "Masters" to handle both its dependency and delinquency caseloads. While other juvenile courts make use of non-judicial court officers to hear some cases, the Baltimore City juvenile court relies on referees far more than the vast majority of U.S. juvenile courts (Rubin, 1991).

Finally, unlike many jurisdictions where the juvenile court's responsibility for delinquency cases begins at the moment of the police referral, the Baltimore juvenile court must wait for two other agencies to handle delinquency cases prior to any court action. The Maryland Department of Juvenile Justice (DJJ) is responsible for the juvenile justice intake process and the screening of cases for prosecution. DJJ decides how to proceed against each youth, whether to refer the case for prosecution or to handle the matter informally. If DJJ intake refers the matter for formal prosecution, screening of the charges as well as the initial filing of charges is the responsibility of the State's Attorney's Office for Baltimore City.

As recently as the 1970s, the Department of Juvenile Justice (previously known as the Department of Juvenile Services, and before that as the Juvenile Services Administration) had great discretion over the juvenile intake process. Its discretion began to be limited during the 1980s. Intake officers now have total discretion only in cases involving misdemeanors other than handgun violations. For felonies and all handgun violations, the DJJ intake worker must obtain the permission of the prosecutor's office to handle a case informally.

Discretion throughout the entire system is even more constrained in cases involving detained juveniles. Perhaps because of this reduced discretion, detention cases move far more quickly through the intake, prosecution, and dispositional process. Once a youth is detained, State law requires the juvenile court to hear the case the next business day. When DJJ makes the decision to detain a youth, it is assumed that the case will be referred for prosecution. The next court day, a DJJ intake worker (one who works in the courthouse as opposed to the DJJ offices several blocks away) will physically take the paperwork to the prosecutor's office so that charges can be filed that day. The court will then hold an "emergency arraignment," which serves as both the arraignment and the detention hearing. An adjudication hearing must be held within 30 days, with disposition required 14 days later.

The focus of attention on delinquency case processing time has been on the handling of non-detention matters. In part, this is because of their greater numbers. On average, about 80% of delinquency referrals in Baltimore do <u>not</u> involve detention.

In addition, delay problems have always been far worse in cases involving released juveniles. The Baltimore police department was apparently not troubled by the requirement that it release paperwork on detention cases almost immediately. Non-detained cases, on the other hand, were subjected to lengthy internal review prior to being sent forward for DJJ intake. DJJ also employed a less expeditious intake process in cases where the juvenile was released to await arraignment. As a result, processing delays in cases of non-detained juveniles were far more serious than in cases involving detained juveniles.

Ongoing Challenges

Prior to the enactment of the 1995 legislation, the processing of non-detained juveniles would sometimes take several months. It was not uncommon for Baltimore prosecutors to receive juvenile cases from DJJ intake in which the initial arrest had occurred more than a year before.

With the passage of the 1995 legislation, the police department was required to complete all processing of even non-detained juveniles within 15 days. DJJ is required to make intake decisions within 25 days of police referral. The prosecutor's office then has 30 days to screen the case and file charges, and by court policy an arraignment is to be held within 14 days of charges being filed.

The initial reaction to Maryland's new case processing legislation among those in the juvenile justice system was guarded enthusiasm. Officials in the juvenile court, the Department of Juvenile Justice, the State's Attorney's office, and the Public Defender's office all expressed support for the goals of the legislation. The actual impact of the legislation, however, was not as clear. (The Maryland Court of Appeals also issued a decision recently that effectively granted juveniles the right to a speedy trial.)

Most juvenile justice officials in Baltimore expect continued efforts to reduce case delays despite the new legislation. Even the provisions of the new legislation may appear to some observers to be rather lenient. Assuming all processing of non-detained juveniles is completed within the required time limits, several months will pass between a youth's arrest and his or final disposition (i.e., 15 days for police handling, 25 days for DJJ intake, 30 days for prosecutor screening, 14 days for arraignment, 30 days for adjudication, and 30 days for disposition). Thus, non-detained juveniles will still likely wait nearly 5 months between arrest and disposition.

The experiences of the Baltimore juvenile justice system point out the potentially important role that legislation (or formal court rules) can play in instigating positive changes in juvenile court case processing time, especially in jurisdictions experiencing severe delay problems. Of course, the recent changes in Baltimore also underscore the limits of formal inducements to improve case handling. Even after more aggressive legislation or court rules are enacted, the real work of reducing juvenile court delay remains to be done. Those professionals who work in the juvenile justice system must still find ways of moving cases through to final dispositions more efficiently.

CUYAHOGA COUNTY: LABOR-INTENSIVE DELAY REDUCTION

The Cuyahoga County Juvenile Court in Cleveland, Ohio is the second oldest juvenile court in the United States. The court opened its doors on June 4, 1902 when 20 juvenile males under the age of 16 appeared before the Honorable Thomas E. Callaghan, the first judge of the newly established court. Since then, the court's mandate has gradually expanded to include jurisdiction over all matters pertaining to delinquency, incorrigibility (unruliness), dependency, neglect and abuse, termination of parental rights, and juvenile traffic violations. The juvenile court is also responsible for custody, paternity and child support matters, cases in which an adult has been charged with contributing to the delinquency of a minor, and other issues involving children, such as approving a minor's right to marry or have an abortion without parental notification.

The juvenile court in Cuyahoga County is a division of the Court of Common Pleas. The main juvenile court complex is located in downtown Cleveland and houses the courtrooms, administrative offices, the detention center, and central offices for intake, probation and community services. The court leases space in a second downtown building to house supplementary programs including home detention, victim aid and restitution, traffic and child support services. A field probation office serving low-risk juveniles is also located in this second building. The juvenile court also maintains seven branch offices throughout the county that provide intake services. Field probation offices are located in five of these branch offices.

The juvenile court has six judges that are elected directly to the juvenile bench and are not subject to rotation within the Court of Common Pleas. Six magistrates assist these judges and are responsible for handling up to 60% of the jurisdiction's formally petitioned (or "official") delinquency cases.[1] Judges are responsible for reviewing the decisions and court orders of the magistrates and for determining the types of cases heard by magistrates. Typically, judges hear first and second degree felony cases with magistrates presiding over lesser felonies, misdemeanors and unruly cases.[2] Judges also generally assign certain types of dependency and custody filings to their magistrate. The court employs four additional magistrates to hear specialty dockets, such as child support, traffic and custody review. These magistrates are not assigned to a specific judge.

Juvenile Court Workload Statistics

Although Cleveland's population is half what it was in the 1950s, Cuyahoga County remains the largest county in the State, with a total population of 1.44 million and a child population (under age 18) of 332,100 (Butts et al., 1996a:79). The juvenile court has experienced a steady increase in the number and seriousness of delinquency filings in the last 10 years (table 4.2). In 1994, 12,970 delinquency cases were filed with the Cuyahoga County Juvenile Court, an increase of 21% over the number of cases in 1990.[3] The number of delinquency cases involving violent offenses increased 50% between 1990 and 1994, while drug offenses jumped 424%.

The juvenile court also experienced dramatic growth in the number of dependency, neglect and abuse actions filed during this period. Between 1990 and 1994, these case filings grew 89%. The growth in dependency, neglect and abuse actions limited the court's ability to process official delinquency cases in a timely manner.[4] Dependency, neglect and abuse cases are given priority status because of legislatively mandated case processing timelines. State legislation passed in 1989 (Senate Bill 89) required these cases to be dispositioned within 90 days of filing. Cases are to be dismissed (without prejudice) if the time limit is exceeded.

The disposition rate for official delinquency and unruly case filings declined considerably during recent years, suggesting that the juvenile court's backlog of these cases increased (table 4.3). From 1992 to 1994, the court *disposed* 21,550 official delinquency and unruly cases. This was 15% less than the 25,319 cases *filed* during the same period. This translates into an average backlog of more than 1,250 cases per year. In 1994, the difference between the number of official cases disposed and official cases filed was 1,670. During the prior three year period from 1989 to 1991, the number of dispositions kept pace with filings. From 1986 to 1988, the court officially disposed of 37% more cases than were filed. This suggests that the court had amassed a large backlog and that at least part of this backlog was disposed between 1986 and 1988.

TABLE 4.2
Cuyahoga County juvenile court workload statistics.

Court Referrals	**1990**	**1992**	**1994**	**Pct. Change 1990-94**
Delinquency, total	10,695	11,612	12,970	21%
Delinquency, official court action	6,997	7,118	7,763	11
Delinquency, violent offenses*	1,807	2,422	2,702	50
Delinquency, drug offenses	327	1,143	1,385	424
Unruly**	3,289	4,117	4,583	39
Dependency, neglect and abuse	2,094	3,641	3,968	89

* Includes homicide, assault, robbery and sex offenses.
** Status offenses including incorrigibility, curfew violations, truancy and running away from home.
Source: Cuyahoga County Juvenile Court *Annual Reports*, 1990, 1992, and 1994.

TABLE 4.3
Disposition rate for official delinquency cases and unruly cases, 1986–1994.

	1986-88	1989-91	1992-94
Official delinquency and unruly cases filed	21,109	24,593	25,319
Official delinquency/unruly dispositions	28,857	24,797	21,550
Disposition rate*	137%	101%	85%

* Rate = Number of dispositions divided by number of cases filed.
Source: Cuyahoga County Juvenile Court *Annual Report*, 1986-1994 and Chinn Planning Partnership, *Continuum of Detention Services Plan* (1994).

Local Rules for Delinquency Case Processing

Cuyahoga County has developed procedures and rules for the timing of delinquency case handling that are considerably shorter than those established by the State (table 4.4). Ohio Supreme Court Rules of Superintendence recommend that delinquency cases be disposed within six months; unruly cases are to be disposed in three months (Hamel, 1994:12–13). Cuyahoga County rules stipulate that detained cases should proceed to case disposition within a maximum of 38 calendar days from the time a youth is detained. In non-detained cases, disposition should occur within a maximum of 95 calendar days from the date the official complaint was filed with the juvenile court (116 days from date case was referred to court).

Delinquency Case Processing

The processing of delinquency cases in Cuyahoga County is a labor intensive process. Although the court has an automated information system, when contrasted with other jurisdictions (notably Maricopa County), the system in Cuyahoga County is outdated and is not sufficiently integrated into the case processing stream.[5] Still, the court has been successful in reducing case processing delays in recent years. This has been accomplished through improvements to the docketing and caseflow management system, including modifications to the manual caseflow process, reorganization of court staff to better facilitate and monitor case processing and, most importantly, staff vigilance in the monitoring of case processing activities and timelines.

Some enhancements have been made to the court's automated information system to facilitate the scheduling and tracking of hearings. However, the ability of the court to track hearings in an automated fashion has been limited by the fact that the court maintains two independent computer systems that cannot interact, necessitating duplicate and redundant data entry and data analysis. Moreover, neither information system appears to collect sufficiently comprehensive caseflow data, nor are they designed to allow for the ready development of the types of case tracking and case aging reports that are critical to maintaining continuing and effective control over caseflow.

The court's intake staff handle all incoming referrals.[6] Upon receipt of a new referral, an intake staff person completes a fact sheet that contains basic demographic and offense information on the juvenile. Data from the fact sheet are eventually entered into the court's main computer system with the appropriate system identifiers. The fact sheet is also used to log the intake decision (to divert, by-pass, or file for official action) and to generate "service of process" (written notification of relevant parties) if the case is accepted for official action and a court hearing is scheduled.

TABLE 4.4
Time frames for processing of detained and non-detained delinquency cases.

Non-Detained Cases	**Cuyahoga County Time Guidelines**	
Intake screening of referral and filing of official complaint	21 days	From date of referral to court intake. (Includes prosecutor review of the official complaint.)
Arraignment hearing	21 days	From date official complaint was filed with court.
Pre-trial hearing	14 days	From date of arraignment.
Adjudication hearing	30 days	From date of pre-trial hearing.
Disposition hearing	30 days	From date of plea/admission or adjudication.
Hearing on probation violation*	28 days	From date complaint was filed with the court.
Detained Cases		
Detention hearing/arraignment	3 days	From date youth was detained.
Intake screening of referral and filing of official complaint	1 days	From date youth was detained.
Pre-trial hearing	7 days	From date of arraignment.
Adjudication hearing	14 days	From date of Pre-Trial Hearing.
Disposition hearing	14 days	From date of plea/admission or adjudication.
Hearing on probation violation*	10 days	From date youth was detained.

* Including hearings on violations of court orders, reviews and motions.

Intake mediators are responsible for screening all delinquency referrals to determine whether a case should be diverted or set for official action. If a case is accepted for official action, the intake mediator is responsible for preparing the official petition (or "complaint") that charges the youth with delinquency. Most official felony complaints prepared by an intake mediator are forwarded to the county prosecutor's office for legal review. Attorneys assigned to the prosecutor's office make a final determination on the actual charges to be contained in the official complaint.[7] Upon completion of this review, the complaint is sent to the appropriate law enforcement representative for signature.[8]

The official complaint and accompanying case file are next routed to the "scheduling desk" in the Assignment Services unit for the scheduling of the arraignment hearing and the assignment of a judicial team (judge and magistrate). If a plea agreement is not forthcoming at arraignment, a pre-trial hearing is scheduled. Pre-trials are automatically scheduled for the following week on a specific day and time based on the day of the week of the arraignment hearing. All parties to the case are informed of the pre-trial prior to the conclusion of the arraignment hearing.

The scheduling of all subsequent hearings (i.e., adjudication and disposition hearings) is left to the discretion of the jurist. Computer terminals are available for courtroom staff to access a jurist's calendar and to schedule a subsequent hearing directly from the courtroom. Most judges use their courtroom staff to schedule future hearings in this fashion. However, most magistrates prefer to have Assignment Services schedule subsequent hearings. Overall, Assignment Services staff estimate that approximately 50% of all hearings on delinquency cases are scheduled by their office. Assignment Services anticipates that the bulk of post-arraignment hearings will be scheduled in the courtroom as jurists and their courtroom staff become more familiar with using the computer terminal and the court's scheduling software.

Assignment Services strongly encourages jurists to schedule future hearings from the courtroom. This simplifies the scheduling process in that all parties are notified of the subsequent hearing prior to leaving the courtroom and the court does not have to provide official notice to these parties. Additionally, any scheduling conflicts that arise can be resolved immediately with all parties present rather than after service has been completed.

The scheduling of a subsequent adjudication or disposition hearing by Scheduling Desk staff results in some built-in delays than can be particularly problematic if a subsequent hearing must be held at the earliest available date. The hearing officer and courtroom clerk must first complete all post-hearing processing of the case file (including the development of any court orders arising from the hearing) before releasing the file to a courtroom coordinator from Assignment Services.[9] If the just-completed hearing resulted in a court order, the courtroom coordinator will first route the case file to the Clerk's Office. There the order is "journalized" and prepared for distribution prior to the file being routed to the Scheduling Desk for the scheduling of the next hearing. This can take two to three days and sometimes longer. Furthermore, Scheduling Desk staff are unable to schedule a hearing on short notice because legal notice must be served on all parties informing them of the hearing date and time. In most instances, two weeks is the earliest that the Scheduling Desk can set a routine subsequent hearing.

Improving the Management of Caseflow

In recent years, both the judiciary and court administration became increasingly concerned with issues related to time standards, docketing time frames and caseflow management. The impetus for this increased concern was the passage of Senate Bill 89 which places strict time limits on the processing of dependency, neglect and abuse cases. The legislation required these cases to reach disposition within 90 days of filing. The bill also placed firm time requirements on the review process and the length of time a dependent, neglected or abused child may remain in temporary foster care. These mandates were enacted at a time when the juvenile court was already experiencing severe pressures to absorb the increasing number of dependency, neglect and abuse case filings.

The timeliness of delinquency case processing began to slide in the late 1980s and at least some of this was attributable to the juvenile court's anticipation of the new mandates for dependency, neglect and abuse cases. In the fall of 1990, the Administrative Judge of the juvenile court asked the court's Legal Director and Manager of Assignment Services to work with the Case Management Committee to conduct a caseflow management study and recommend methods to improve the processing of delinquency cases. While it was apparent that delinquency case processing time had increased, it was not clear how long and how often delays occurred because the court's information system was unable to provide reports that tracked case processing time.

An analysis of a small sample of randomly selected cases revealed that it took an average of 226 days (more than seven months) for official delinquency cases to proceed to final disposition (Graham and Howley, 1992). The study also revealed that much of the existing delays originated during case processing prior to the scheduling of hearings, including intake screening, prosecutor review of the official complaint, assignment of jurist and counsel, service of process, and data entry. The Director of Juvenile Court Services concluded that too many court staff were involved in the handling of each case file, and that court staff too often had complete discretion to hold a case for as long as they wished in order to complete their case processing tasks. Thus, small delays at each processing stage were resulting in considerable delays overall in scheduling hearings and ultimately disposing of cases.

In early 1991, the juvenile court implemented a revamped caseflow management system that included a number of procedural and organizational changes designed to facilitate the timely processing of delinquency cases. The monitoring of the flow of case files to and from the courtroom became a primary responsibility of Assignment Services courtroom staff. Critical caseflow management changes that were implemented included:

- A centralized processing unit was created (as part of Assignment Services) to coordinate all case processing activities once a case was scheduled for court. A courtroom coordinator was assigned to each courtroom to work with the jurist and court clerk to facilitate the flow of case files to and from the courtroom and to facilitate the timely scheduling of all future hearings.

- Empirical time frames were established for each case processing step and codified into court procedures and rules.

- The jurist assignment of delinquency cases was centralized as was responsibility for the scheduling of the arraignment hearing.

- Pre-trial hearing dates and times were tied to the date and time of the juvenile's arraignment ensuring that all parties present at the arraignment hearing were aware of the future pre-trial date.

- Jurists were encouraged to schedule all future adjudication and disposition hearings from the courtroom prior to the conclusion of the current hearing whenever possible.
- Docketing timelines were established for the scheduling of all hearing types and measures were taken to manually monitor compliance with these timelines.
- Rules were established to govern the granting of continuances with compliance to be monitored.

These changes had a dramatic impact on case processing time. A follow-up study of a similar number of randomly selected delinquency cases from a cross-section of jurists revealed that within six months the number of days to disposition had been reduced to an average of 88 days (Graham and Howley, 1992). This represented a 61% decrease in case processing time from the earlier average of 226 days. While the sample sizes used in the two studies were limited because of the time necessary to collect and analyze caseflow processing data manually, court administrators and jurists were confident that these results were fair indicators of the improvements achieved in recent years.

A critical component of these improvements was the vigilance of the courtroom coordinators and other Assignment Services staff. Each courtroom coordinator was assigned to two courtrooms and was responsible for working closely with the court clerks to facilitate the timely processing and movement of case files. Judges and administrators agreed that the courtroom coordinators should do whatever it takes to move cases. Over the years, the Assignment Services staff developed good working relationships with the judges and magistrates as evidenced by the general cooperation afforded them by jurists and their courtroom staff. This was a key element in the success of Assignment Services since the office has very little authority to require compliance with caseflow and docketing guidelines.

As of 1995, the case processing time frames promoted by Assignment Services had been codified into local court rules. The rules, however, were to serve as guidelines only. No sanctions were tied to violations. While individual courtroom coordinators continued to monitor compliance with the rules, they had no authority to hasten the processing of case files by court clerks, or to override the scheduling practices of individual courtrooms. Their success continued to depend on personal relationships and individual persistence.

Efforts to Facilitate Timely Processing of Detention Cases

In recent years, the juvenile court has taken steps to reduce the number of juveniles detained for extended periods in violation of juvenile court and/or state length of stay requirements and for those juveniles who remain in detention awaiting placement planning or placement transfer. A 1994 study indicated that between 10% and 20% of the juvenile detention population during the first two months of 1994 had been detained in excess of the 60-day limit set by internal court policy, with approximately 3% of the detained population at any one time held in excess of 90 days in violation of state statutes (Chinn Planning Partnership, 1994:19-20).[10]

In addition, up to 20% of the remaining detention population during this period were youths awaiting pre-dispositional placement planning or post-dispositional transfer to the county's Youth Development Center (YDC), the Ohio Department of Youth Services (ODYS), or to a private placement. Extended stays in detention appear to result from a number of factors (Chinn Planning Partnership, 1994:29-33):

- A lack of placement options for certain offenders (most specifically, sex offenders);
- Extensive placement referral preparation and screening; and
- Bed-space and budgetary constraints in the number of private placement options.

By the latter months of 1994, these numbers had been reduced considerably. Detention data compiled by court staff for selected weeks in August and September 1994 suggested that the number of detained juveniles in violation of length of stay limits and youth awaiting placement planning or post-dispositional transfer had been reduced by 50%.

These reductions in detention stays were the result of continuing efforts by the juvenile court to expedite the processing of detained cases including the convening of a weekly detention population meeting to staff cases that fall outside of court policy and statutory guidelines. These meetings were chaired by the Detention Center's population manager and attended by representatives from the Legal Department (Intake and Assignment Services) and Juvenile Probation in addition to staff from shelter care providers, YDC, ODYS, and court-sponsored commitment alternatives programs (boot camp and community corrections). This committee began to meet on a weekly basis in 1992. The purpose of the meetings was to:

- Expedite the screening of detained youth to determine program eligibility for placement in one of the court-sponsored commitment alternatives programs (boot camp or community corrections);
- Coordinate the post-disposition transfer of cases to placement (ODYS, YDC, and private placements) including expediting the completion of all court paperwork and placement/commitment packet materials (court orders, completion of social history and psychological assessment reports, etc.);
- Facilitate the processing of detained juveniles awaiting hearing dates and those whose hearings have been continued; and
- Monitor instances in which juveniles were detained due to probation violations and other violations of court orders (the court discourages detention in these cases unless new charges are filed).

A second Population Management Committee was established in 1991 and agreed to meet on a bi-monthly basis. This committee was chaired by the Director of Juvenile Court Services and represented a high level of commitment from the court to monitor detention cases. Committee members included the Juvenile Office Chiefs from the County Prosecutor's and Public Defender's Office, a representative from the Cuyahoga

County Department of Children and Family Services, and administrators from every court department except Human Resources. Two weeks before each meeting, Research and Information Services staff prepared a report on juveniles who had been detained for 60 days or more including home detention and shelter care cases. This report was distributed to all committee members prior to the meeting and cases were individually reviewed to see what could be done to expedite the movement of juveniles from secure detention, shelter care and home detention. The court-wide population management committee also reviewed and established court policy with regard to detention.

To facilitate the processing of detention cases, the court created a case management coordinator position. This individual worked in Assignment Services with responsibilities similar to those of the courtroom coordinators. She was responsible for overseeing and coordinating the flow of case files for all detention cases (including secure detention, home detention and shelter care). Her responsibilities included:

- On a daily basis, picking up all police reports left with detention center staff on newly detained juveniles and delivering them to Intake for expedited screening and preparation of the official complaint. This single step was thought to have increased the completion of intake screening for detention cases by a full day.

- Monitoring the files of detained juveniles to insure that the cases were screened within 72 hours, and working with Intake staff to facilitate the processing of these cases. Intake returns all case files on detained juveniles to the case management coordinator once initial screening is completed and the official complaint has been reviewed by the County Prosecutor's Office. The case management coordinator hand delivers these to the Detention/Arraignment Courtroom located in the Detention Center.

- Insuring that future court hearings on detained juveniles are set in a timely manner. The coordinator works closely with the population manager who provides a listing of detained cases for which court hearing dates have not been entered on the juvenile court's main automated system. For cases set in front of a magistrate, the case management coordinator schedules the next hearing date if this has not been accomplished in the courtroom. For cases to be heard by a judge, she delivers the case file to the judge's chambers so that the next hearing can be set by the judge's administrative staff.

- For juveniles who are not released after their initial detention hearing, working with the courtroom clerk assigned to the detention referee to insure that paperwork is completed in a timely manner. The case management coordinator types the order authorizing detention and delivers it to the assigned judge for signature.

- Facilitating the processing of all warrants and other court actions on detained juveniles that require special handling.

The concept of a case management coordinator for detention cases grew out of a pilot study conducted by Assignment Services in 1992. Of the 34 secure detention cases included in the study, half were assigned to a case management coordinator who was given responsibility for facilitating the processing of these cases. The remaining cases were permitted to proceed through normal processing. Study results were encouraging in that arraignment hearings were held on cases assigned to the case management coordinator in one-third less time than for control cases that were handled routinely (Chinn Planning Partnership, 1994:24-25).

Continuing Impediments to Timely Case Processing

Processing delays appear to have decreased considerably in the Cuyahoga County Juvenile Court during the early 1990s. The Assignment Services unit of the court conducted a number of caseflow studies that confirmed this impression. The court's success, however, was due primarily to the efforts of dedicated personnel who were willing to manually expedite and monitor case processing in an organizational environment that was not all that conducive to greater efficiency. As indicated previously, exponential growth in dependency case filings and processing requirements continues to place tremendous strains on the system and to limit the court's ability to address issues affecting the processing of delinquency cases. The court continues to be hampered in its efforts to manage caseflow. Critical factors include the following:

- Antiquated information systems that do not provide court staff with the type of caseload, case aging, or "exception" reports necessary to monitor caseflow effectively;
- Staffing and budgetary arrangements that do not encourage courtroom accountability with respect to timely case processing;
- Need for greater judicial involvement in the management of caseflow and a commitment to the timely processing of delinquency cases; and
- Inconsistencies in the enforcement of the juvenile court's policy on the granting of continuances.

1. Inadequate Information Systems

The informational capabilities of the juvenile court are severely limited. These deficiencies have reduced the ability of court staff to monitor case progress and to identify and address individual case delays in a timely fashion. The primary management information system does not meet the court's data processing and reporting needs. Data entry and retrieval, particularly in summary display and report format, are difficult if not impossible. Caseflow and case aging reports are virtually non-existent. According to the Ohio Supreme Court's recent study of caseflow management in Cuyahoga County:

> The court is unable to easily produce information that allows comparison with its time guidelines. As a result, it is very difficult to pinpoint where the caseflow management system breaks down in order to resolve problems. Data on the length of time a delinquency case takes to travel through the system [are] not available without incurring substantial staff time and effort because data must be assembled manually (Hamel, 1994:14).

Inadequacies in the court's information system and the limited support of this system by the Cuyahoga County Data Center has encouraged individual departments to develop separate automated systems. The proliferation of multiple systems on differing platforms results in numerous inefficiencies. For example, Assignment Services' case assignment and docketing systems are maintained in two separate packages on a mini-computer. Case assignment and hearing scheduling data, however, are processed by the court's primary computer system. This requires data on hearing schedules and results to be entered independently. At minimum, re-keying of data on multiple systems increases the staff time necessary to produce essential information and increases the likelihood of data-entry error. Department staff also tend to be concerned with the accuracy of their own data, but only minimally concerned with other systems. Depending on which systems they use the most, staff may occasionally make decisions based upon data that other staff know to be unreliable and/or outdated. Timely dissemination of case processing and case tracking data is difficult at best in such an environment.

2. Caseflow Accountability

Juvenile court administrators, including the Director of Juvenile Court Services, have little formal authority to require that individual jurists and their courtroom staff comply with the court's docketing and case processing directives. Local court rules are carefully worded and are only intended to serve as guidelines. No sanctions are tied to violations. Section H of Rule 20 states that "[t]he time frames set forth in this rule are case management guidelines only and a failure to follow such time frames in any individual case shall not be grounds for dismissal of the case or suppression of any evidence."

Furthermore, court administrators and individual courtroom coordinators have only limited administrative ability to require that courtroom staff comply with docketing time frames and other case processing requirements. This is particularly true of staff assigned to the judges' courtrooms. Each judge has a bailiff, assistant bailiff and clerk. These courtroom staff are hired directly by the judge, and the salaries and duties of these staff are set by the individual judges and thus differ from courtroom to courtroom. Assignment Services and the courtroom coordinators have to rely on the judge's clerk to complete the post-hearing processing of case files. These court clerks, however, also typically serve as judicial secretaries. It is not unusual for these duties to conflict (Hamel, 1994:26–27).

3. Judicial Involvement in Management of Delinquency Caseflow

The Cuyahoga County Juvenile Court judges are generally very supportive of recent court-wide initiatives to improve caseflow management and the timeliness of delinquency case processing. They are also very sensitive to case processing standards and the performance of their courtrooms. The recently implemented caseflow management system was well received by the judiciary because the system was flexible enough to allow for varying judicial needs and priorities. However, the caseflow management system may not have increased the consistency of delinquency case processing practices between courtrooms (Hamel, 1994:12–14;22–30). In general, the court lacks adequate organizational mechanisms to ensure judicial communication and cooperation on common case processing issues.

4. Inconsistencies in the Granting of Continuances

The Cuyahoga County Juvenile Court operates under a local rule that limits the granting of continuances and requires continued cases to be scheduled on a date-certain basis and at the earliest possible date from when a continuance is granted.[11] Judges and referees, however, do not consistently adhere to the policy. Some are more likely to grant continuances and, in general, allow attorneys more control over the pace of litigation.[12] Furthermore, the court's automated information system does not track continuances and no individual at the court is responsible for monitoring the frequency with which continuances are granted.

The inability of the court to implement its continuance policy contributes to delays. Not only do continuances affect the available calendar time for other cases, they create added paperwork and processing requirements for all court staff. Referee Margaret Mazza, a Cuyahoga County Juvenile Court referee known for maintaining strict control over her docket, asserted that "continuances are the kiss of death" in caseflow management and that continued cases often take up more docket time when the case finally is heard because of the likelihood that the juvenile has been referred to the court on additional charges in the interim.[13]

Conclusion

Cuyahoga County has realized considerable success in its attempts to exert more control over the pace of delinquency case processing. This success has been due largely to the efforts of dedicated staff who manually expedite the processing of delinquency cases, and it has been accomplished despite an organizational environment that is not always supportive of such efforts. Internal and external impediments to timely case processing remain, including a steady increase in case filings, new legislation that has increased the court's oversight responsibilities in dependency cases, entrenched bureaucratic procedures, autonomous courtroom staff, and an inadequate information system. Of course, many if not most juvenile courts in large, urban areas face similar challenges as they struggle to maintain control over their delinquency caseloads.

The Cuyahoga County Juvenile Court is an excellent example for other similarly situated juvenile courts. The experiences of Cuyahoga County demonstrate that significant progress can be achieved in controlling case processing delays using only the energies and talents of existing staff. On the other hand, the court is also an example of the real limits on caseflow management in courts facing a range of organizational impediments. If not remedied, such impediments can frustrate the efforts of even a dedicated and vigilant staff as they attempt to develop and nurture an effective caseflow management system.

MARICOPA COUNTY: CONTROLLING DELAYS WITH AUTOMATION

The Maricopa County Juvenile Court is one of the largest juvenile courts in the United States in one of the Nation's fastest growing urban areas. The juvenile court is a division of the Superior Court, part of a unified court system administered by the Arizona State Supreme Court. The juvenile court has original exclusive jurisdiction over all persons under the age of 18 including all matters pertaining to delinquency, incorrigibility, dependency, severance (termination of parental rights), adoptions and juvenile traffic cases. The total population of Maricopa County was 2.3 million as of 1993, including 603,800 children and youth under 18 years of age (Butts et al., 1996a:65).

The Maricopa County Juvenile Court operates two facilities located 20 miles apart. The Durango complex was built in 1976 and is the more central facility. It is located southwest of central Phoenix and serves the central and western portions of the county. A second complex, the Southeast Facility (SEF), was opened in 1990 and serves the remainder of the county. Although the presiding juvenile court judge, director of court services and court administrator are housed at the Durango complex, both facilities are self-contained units. Each facility completes its own intake procedures on new referrals (or complaints), schedules and conducts hearings on the entire range of cases before the court, operates a secure detention facility with more than 100 beds, and provides a wide range of diversion and probation services.

Six judges are assigned on a rotational basis to the juvenile court—three to each facility. The court also has 11 commissioners (similar to "referees" or "masters") who handle the bulk of the delinquency caseload (as much as 90% of all hearings). State statutes require that a judge preside over all criminal-court transfers (or "remand" hearings). Judges also hear many delinquency adjudications and dispositions. A considerable portion of the judicial workload, however, is in the neglect and abuse arena. Judges are responsible for hearing all contested dependency and termination of parental rights cases, while commissioners handle most initial and uncontested dependency hearings.

TABLE 4.5
Maricopa County juvenile court delinquency workload statistics.

	1990	1992	1994	Pct. Change 1990-94
At-risk juvenile population (Ages 8 through 17)	289,221	306,773	327,429	13%
Delinquency and incorrigibility complaints received	29,031	27,624	32,703	13
Number of juveniles involved	18,491	18,183	20,877	13
Complaints per juvenile	1.57	1.52	1.57	0
Complaints as percent of juvenile population	6.4	5.9	6.4	0
Delinquency and incorrigibility complaints petitioned and set for formal court action	8,031	9,360	9,976	24
Hearings scheduled on delinq. and incorrigibility petitions	31,460	33,720	33,510	7
Total hearings scheduled	43,846	46,037	50,775	16

Source: Maricopa County Juvenile Court, Division of Research and Planning.

Juvenile Court Workload Statistics

The delinquency workload of the Maricopa County Juvenile Court has increased steadily in recent years. Statistics for 1990 through 1994 reveal that 32,703 delinquency and incorrigibility complaints were received by the juvenile court in 1994, a 13% increase over the number received in 1990 (table 4.5).[14] This increase closely parallels other demographic trends in the county. The population of juveniles considered to be "at-risk" of delinquency in Maricopa County (youth ages 8-17) increased 13% between 1990 and 1994.[15]

During this period, the volume of complaints as a percentage of the at-risk juvenile population remained relatively constant. In 1990, 1992 and 1994, the number of delinquency and incorrigibility complaints received was equal to approximately 6% of the county's juvenile at-risk population. The average number of delinquency and incorrigibility complaints per referred juvenile also remained relatively constant during this period at 1.57 complaints per juvenile in 1990 and 1994 and 1.52 complaints per youth in 1992.

Formal court proceedings on delinquency and incorrigibility matters, however, grew at a rate faster than would be expected given population increases and a stable juvenile referral rate. The number of delinquency and incorrigibility petitions filed with the court increased at a rate almost double the increase in complaints during this five year period, reportedly due to policy changes in the County Attorney's Office.

The number of hearings scheduled on these petitions also increased, but at a rate lower than would be expected given the increase in petitions filed. In 1990, a total of 31,460 hearings on delinquency and incorrigibility petitions were scheduled. In 1994, the number of hearings on these petitions increased 7% to 33,510. Lastly, the total number of hearings scheduled by the juvenile court on all matters (including dependency, severance and adoption petitions) increased 16% from 43,846 hearings in 1990 to 50,775 hearings in 1994.

Stable Leadership

The Maricopa County Juvenile Court has long been recognized as one of the best managed juvenile courts in the nation. In 1979, it was one of the first juvenile courts to earn accreditation from the National Council of Juvenile and Family Court Judges. While 1995 was a year of transition, one of the court's trademarks for two decades has been stable and strong leadership. Only two individuals served as presiding juvenile court judge between 1978 and 1995. Judge Kimball Rose served as presiding juvenile court judge from 1978 through 1989. Judge Rose was succeeded by Judge James McDougall (1989–1995).[16] In May, 1995 Judge McDougall rotated to the Adult Division of the Superior Court and Judge John Foreman was installed as presiding judge after serving as a juvenile court judge for approximately 5 years.

In 1995 Mr. Ernesto Garcia retired as director of juvenile court services after 23 years as court director and more than 35 years with the juvenile court. Mr. Garcia developed a national reputation as a skillful administrator who was able to effectively lead the court during an extended period of growth and expansion.

In close cooperation with the judiciary, Mr. Garcia also effectively represented the needs of the juvenile court to the County Board of Commissioners. These efforts were critical in securing the funding necessary to build the SEF facility and to develop and support Maricopa County's state-of-the-art juvenile court information system, known as JOLTS (*Juvenile On-line Tracking System*). In general, the judiciary and administration of the Maricopa County Juvenile Court have long been committed to developing the organizational and technological supports necessary for sound caseflow management.

Court Automation and Caseflow Management

The Maricopa County Juvenile Court has also been a national leader in the development of automated tools to facilitate efficient case processing. For more than two decades, the court's Juvenile On-Line Tracking System has been the inspiration for numerous software development efforts throughout the Nation.[17] The system plays a central role in the day-to-day operations of the court and allows for smooth coordination of case processing between the court's organizational units within and across court facilities. The case processing needs of the County Attorney and Public Defender's Offices are also supported by the JOLTS software and to a large extent the coordination of delinquency case processing across these separate agencies is seamless.

The JOLTS software also contains sophisticated case assignment and calendaring modules and an extensive series of automated reports have been developed to assist the judiciary, court administration and line staff in monitoring performance and making the continual system adjustments necessary to expedite caseflow.

Automation facilitates caseflow management in a variety of ways in Maricopa County, including:

- Preliminary screening and routing of delinquency complaints not involving detention;
- Automated scheduling of diversion appointments and generation of appointment letters;
- Automated calendaring of court hearings;
- Assigning of delinquency cases to juvenile probation officers at court intake;
- Electronic notification of critical case events and calendar changes;
- Preparation of court documents;
- Electronic archiving of important case documents; and
- Monitoring of system performance and individual case progression.

1. Preliminary Screening and Routing of Complaints Not Involving Detention

In most juvenile courts, the bulk of the delinquency caseload consists of complaints filed by law enforcement agencies that do not result in a juvenile's detention. Nationwide, approximately 80% of all delinquency matters are handled without placing the juvenile in secure detention (Butts et al., 1996a). Delays in the processing of these cases are common because non-detained cases handled in a more relaxed fashion than complaints in which a juvenile is being held in detention.[18] In Maricopa County, for example, the paper work for delinquency complaints not involving detention are typically dropped off or mailed to the court. In detention cases, on the other hand, the matter must be screened immediately so that a petition can be filed prior to the juvenile's detention hearing.

In many courts, preliminary screening of complaints not involving detention and the initial assignment of these complaints for further processing are time consuming tasks that can take days to accomplish and often involve several different organizational units and staff. In Maricopa County, these tasks have been routinized and are accomplished automatically by JOLTS at the moment information about the complaint is entered into the system by the staff of the "Central Index" unit. JOLTS automatically evaluates the complaint against a variety of pre-defined parameters that have been incorporated into the software to guide decision-making. For example, the system automatically:

- Determines which facility (Durango or SEF) the complaint will be assigned to based on the child's zipcode.

- Determines if the compliant is eligible for diversion by examining the offenses on the complaint and the child's prior delinquent history. In Arizona, a juvenile's first two misdemeanor complaints are eligible for diversion. JOLTS will examine all charges on a complaint for eligibility and then search the database for a child's prior delinquent history. If eligible for diversion, the system grades the complaint as diversion-eligible and routes the complaint to the appropriate Intake Unit for further processing. Felony and third misdemeanor complaints are automatically routed to the Charging Bureau of the County Attorney's Office for petition screening.

- Assigns the case to a specific probation officer assigned to Intake or a specific assistant county attorney in the Charging Bureau of the County Attorney's Office based on the current caseload of the intake officer or prosecutor, respectively.

- If a youth has been previously referred to the court on a delinquency complaint and is currently on probation, JOLTS generates an automatic message notifying the assigned probation officer of the new case activity and the complaint is routed to the officer for further processing.

- If a juvenile currently on probation is detained on a new charge, JOLTS automatically generates a message notifying the probation officer that the youth is being held in the detention center.

Preliminary screening, routing and case assignment are combined into a one step process that occurs simultaneous with initial data entry. Initial case processing tasks that can take days or weeks to accomplish in many other juvenile courts are completed within minutes in the Maricopa County Juvenile Court. Complaints are routinely routed to the next processing stage within 24 hours of the receipt of the complaint by the court.

2. Automated Scheduling of Diversion Appointments and Generation of Appointment Notification Letters

Delinquency complaints eligible for diversion are routed to the appropriate Intake Unit for continued processing after Central Index has entered the complaint into the court's JOLTS database. As shown above, the court annually processes 20,000 to 30,000 complaints. The majority of these are informally "adjusted" after the juvenile has completed a specified number of community work service hours or participated in other programs provided through the court. The decision to route a complaint to Intake for diversion screening is made by the automated system. Screening of these complaints requires an Intake probation officer to conduct an initial diversion interview with the referred juvenile and parent(s) to discuss circumstances surrounding the incident, the youth's school performance, general behavior, etc. If there are no major behavioral problems and the juvenile acknowledges involvement in the alleged offense, the complaint can be informally adjusted subject to specific conditions. Conditions of adjustment generally require that the juvenile participate in a specialized education and awareness program, family or individual counseling, day treatment, restitution, or completion of community work service hours.

The Intake officer and Intake support staff rely heavily on the automated system in completing these screenings. Diversion screening tasks involving JOLTS include:

- Scheduling of the initial diversion interview using scheduling parameters built into the automated system. Intake officers typically complete 5 to 7 interviews daily. The Intake officer will examine his/her personal calendar to find an open time slot within the appropriate time frames. Once a slot is identified, the officer will schedule the interview. JOLTS will update the officer's interview calendar, post the date and time of this interview in the appropriate child file, and automatically add the information to a daily master and individual officer interview list. This is all accomplished in a matter of seconds with a limited number of keystrokes.
- The officer will direct JOLTS to generate a letter informing the child and parent(s) of the option to handle this complaint informally at the initial diversion interview as scheduled on the designated date and time. A mailing label is also generated.
- Interview cancellations are logged into the system by support staff or the Intake officer. The interview slot is freed up on the officer's calendar and these slots are used by the officer for re-scheduling interviews and second interviews in instances where a child does not show. As the slots are filled, the automated system will update the child's JOLTS file and the officer's personal calendar. JOLTS also tracks the number of times an interview has been rescheduled.
- Each day, JOLTS generates master interview calendars for each facility that are used by court receptionists to direct juveniles and their families to their scheduled interview. Immediately upon a receptionist indicating that a party has checked in, JOLTS generates an electronic message informing the Intake officer of their arrival. The system then waits for the receptionist to note that the Intake officer has met with the family. If the Intake officer does not meet with the family within a specified period of time, JOLTS sends a second reminder message to the officer. If the family continues to wait, a third message is automatically sent to the officer's supervisor or to another Intake officer who has been designated as the "Officer of the Day." If no activity is noted on the master calendar, JOLTS assumes that the family did not show up for the appointment. This permits the system to automatically track no-shows and to remind the Intake officer that another interview needs to be scheduled or that other action needs to be taken.[19]

Automation allows the Maricopa County Juvenile Court to process a large volume of diversion-eligible complaints in a very timely manner. JOLTS also plays an important part in the assignment of diversion services. Intake officers use JOLTS to enroll juveniles in specific programs or classes prior to completion of the initial diversion interview. If participation in an education and awareness program is assigned, the officer will use JOLTS to pull up a schedule of classes (including location and time), determine the class site closest to where the youth lives and the earliest day the class is held for which a slot is open. The officer will then update the class roster to reflect the youth's enrollment in the class. The JOLTS database is also automatically updated to reflect current enrollment in the class. There is no need for the child to be referred to the contracted provider for enrollment in the assigned class. Before leaving the initial interview, the child and parent(s) are informed of the date and time of the class. The family is also provided with printed confirmation of the appointment and all necessary permissions or waivers are completed. A few days before the class is held, the provider is given a roster of all juveniles expected to attend each session.

Some service providers require an application prior to enrollment. In these instances, the Intake officer will bring up a template of the provider's application and complete the application with the youth and parent(s) as part of the initial diversion interview. JOLTS automatically completes as much of the application as it can from data already maintained in the database. The remainder is provided by the officer, the juvenile, and the parent(s). The application is then immediately faxed (directly from the terminal via modem) to the provider. The JOLTS database is updated to reflect the diversion services as they are assigned.

If a juvenile is assigned to complete community work service (CWS) hours, the officer will identify the appropriate agency and set up the referral through JOLTS. The court has developed working agreements with over 500 public entities through which a juvenile can complete CWS hours. JOLTS searches the agency database and provides a list of CWS agencies that are either close to the juvenile's home address or school (using zipcode as the search criteria). The officer can obtain pertinent information on JOLTS, such as a contact person, the types of juveniles the agency accepts, the hours during which CWS activities are available, and the type of work juveniles perform. Lastly, the officer calls the provider to set up the CWS referral and the JOLTS database is automatically updated to reflect the juvenile's CWS assignment.

At the completion of the initial diversion interview, the Intake officer may use JOLTS to complete a brief summary report of the interview including presenting problems, issues and diversion services assigned. Demographic and complaint information are extracted into the report template from JOLTS while the officer provides a summary of the interview. This report is archived for later retrieval.[20]

Intake support staff track the completion of the assigned services or CWS hours through exception reports and listings provided by JOLTS. Support staff enter complaint disposition data if the juvenile completes the assigned services or CWS hours. If the juvenile does not complete the required activities during the required time frame the case is forwarded to the assigned Intake officer for further processing.

The Intake director indicated that automation improved the productivity of the court's diversion officers and has permitted the Intake unit to handle an ever-increasing workload with a minimum of additional staff. He estimated that the capabilities of JOLTS as described above reduced the time his officers spend on administrative duties and documentation and increased efficiency by 25%.

3. Automated Calendaring of Hearings

Many juvenile courts, particularly those with multiple courtrooms, struggle to maintain control over the hearing calendar. Inability to schedule hearings efficiently is often cited as a major contributor to processing delays. The scheduling of hearings is often accomplished in a haphazard fashion, resulting in repeated requests for continuances due to scheduling conflicts and inefficient use of courtrooms due to imbalances between how the calendar is partitioned and the types of hearings that actually need to be scheduled. An overabundance of hearing slots reserved for one type of hearing may limit the availability of hearing slots needed for other types of hearings. This results in the latter hearings being scheduled too far out on the calendar while the other segments of the calendar are underutilized with the courtroom sitting empty.

Over time, the Maricopa County Juvenile Court has used JOLTS to devise a very sophisticated automated calendaring system that permits the court to maintain control over the calendar and to insure that imbalances between reserved hearing slots and the scheduling needs of the court are kept to a minimum. The automated calendaring utility is used by both the Court Administrator's Office and individual courtrooms. The Court Administrator's Office is responsible for setting all advisory (initial) hearings. Court clerks assigned to individual courtrooms will, for the most part, schedule all subsequent hearings on a case. The Court Administrator's Office also assists the individual courtrooms in scheduling subsequent matters when requested.

The automated calendaring module uses a series of logical default parameters defined by the Court Administrator's Office as well as specifications provided by the user at the time of the request. The parameters guide the system in identifying prospective hearing slots. These scheduling parameters include the following:

- *Type of hearing*: Each jurist's calendar is partitioned into specific segments for various types of hearings. JOLTS will search those portions of the calendar reserved for the type of hearing requested for an available slot.

- *Hearing time frames*: JOLTS will search for a specific type of hearing slot within a designated time frame—minimum and maximum days from today's date, petition or first hearing, whichever is most appropriate.

- *Searching for earliest or latest available slot*: A default parameter directs JOLTS to search for either the earliest or latest available date. That is, JOLTS can search forwards or backwards. This parameter can be set by the user at the time of the request.

- *Searching an Individual or Master Calendar*: JOLTS can search a specific hearing officer's calendar, a calendar of a designated grouping of hearing officers, or the calendars of all hearing officers assigned to a specific facility.

- *Amount of hearing time needed*: A pre-defined time period is allotted for various hearing types (e.g., 10 minutes for routine disposition hearings, 15 minutes for adjudication hearings, etc.). The default time can be customized for individual jurists or can be set case by case. If JOLTS identifies an open hearing slot but the slot does not have the required amount of time, it will bypass it and continue to search.

- *Handling scheduling conflicts of other interested parties*: The Calendaring module simultaneously considers the court schedules of the county attorney, public defender and juvenile probation officer assigned to the case. On occasion, a scheduler may be forced to request a hearing slot that entails a time conflict. The slot will appear as requested but the potential conflicts are asterisked so that they can be discussed by the parties before a hearing time is reserved.

- *Notification of hearing changes*: All parties to a hearing are automatically notified by JOLTS through electronic mail of any changes to scheduled hearings.

After a specific hearing is requested, JOLTS will search the calendar database and provide the user with a list of available hearing slots that meet the pre-defined default parameters and hearing specifications controlled by the user. Typically, three prospective hearing slots are provided. If these slots are not satisfactory, a user can direct the system to search for additional slots that meet the requested parameters or the user can change the parameters to allow for a more expanded search. All interested parties with personal calendars maintained on the system including the jurist, county attorney, public defender and the assigned juvenile probation officer are notified via electronic mail of the newly scheduled hearing. Also, the individual calendars of these interested parties are automatically updated to reflect newly scheduled hearings.

The calendaring system can accommodate individual jurist preferences and customize their calendar accordingly. For example, a commissioner may reserve Monday mornings for a predetermined number of non-detained advisory hearings slots and Monday afternoons for a specific number of delinquency adjudication hearings. A second commissioner may reserve Monday mornings for delinquency disposition hearings and Monday afternoons for detained advisory hearings. The entire calendar is managed so that the appropriate number of hearing slots are reserved over the course of each 4-week cycle. Each jurist's four week cycle can be partitioned differently. The calendar administrator responsible for examining and coordinating the individual preferences of jurists insures that the requisite hearing coverage is provided on a court-wide basis.

At any time, JOLTS is capable of producing a summary report of how many hearing slots by type are still available per cycle. A user can obtain a screen view of a specific calendar day that displays both scheduled and available hearing slots. These reporting capabilities allow for close monitoring and adjustment of courtroom calendars to insure that the future hearing needs of the court are being met. On a weekly basis, the calendar administrator and her staff examine the availability of open hearing slots and balance these against the anticipated hearing requirements of each commissioner's caseload to determine if adjustments need to be made.[21] Adjustments may be necessary due to the utilization of additional hearing slot for continuances or because of an unanticipated increase in petition filings that places additional hearing requirements on the court (e.g., drug sweeps).

As necessary, the administrator's office will inform a commissioner (via electronic mail) of the office's intent to re-distribute available hearing slots (for example, to take some open adjudication hearing slots and re-designate then as disposition hearing slots). The office will give the commissioner time to respond to the electronic message before implementing the change.

Automated calendaring has proven to be a very powerful technological enhancement for the Maricopa County Juvenile Court that has resulted in the more efficient use and management of the court's calendar. Its impact on the timely conducting of hearings hasn't been fully realized, however, because of the relative ease with which cases can be transferred between judicial officers and lax policies regarding the granting of continuances.[22]

4. Assignment of Cases to Probation Officers

The Maricopa County Juvenile Court has a long-standing policy of assigning new cases to a specific juvenile probation officer at the very beginning of a juvenile's involvement with the court. Probation officers are assigned to new delinquency complaints either at the time a petition is filed by the County Attorney's Office or when the complaint has been routed from Central Index to Intake because JOLTS has flagged the complaint as diversion-eligible. All new delinquency complaints on juveniles currently on probation are assigned to a youth's current probation officer. The automated system plays a key role in insuring that these case assignments are made in a timely manner.[23]

When complaints are diverted to Intake for additional screening, JOLTS will assign the case to a specific intake officer based on current caseload counts and taking into account other factors such as assigning co-defendants to the same officer, reassigning a youth to the same officer if previously seen by that officer, etc. Formally petitioned complaints are assigned by JOLTS to the appropriate Investigation Unit (either Durango or SEF) based on zip code (if the youth is not currently on probation). Supervisors in the Investigation Unit review incoming cases and assign a juvenile probation officer within two days for non-detained cases and immediately for detained cases.[24] The assigned Investigation Unit officer meets with the juvenile and family prior to the initial advisory hearing and is responsible for attending all hearings on the case and the completion of the pre-disposition investigation and report (if so required by the court). For new complaints on juveniles already on probation, the currently assigned probation officer is responsible for attending all hearings on the case.

Early probation assignment ensures that trained and qualified juvenile justice personnel are responsible for facilitating each case's movement through the system. Early assignment also ensures that requests for information on the progress of a case can be directed to an accountable individual with specific knowledge of the case. Additionally, any special handling or provision of pre-disposition services is coordinated through a professional trained in such matters. Any remaining delays in the initiation of probation supervision are readily apparent to probation officers and supervisors because JOLTS has a built-in probation case management system that closely tracks client contacts and flags cases when deficiencies occur.

5. Electronic Notification

Untimely communication frequently contributes to case processing delays in juvenile courts. The Maricopa County Juvenile Court makes extensive use of electronic mail to minimize such delays. Thousands of messages are posted daily using JOLTS. The judiciary, court administration, and unit supervisors routinely communicate among themselves and staff employees through electronic mail. This further encourages the use of electronic mail among line staff who routinely check for messages from judges, court administrators and their supervisors to keep abreast of scheduled meetings, scheduling changes, management directives and individual case developments.

In addition to the routine use of electronic mail by court personnel, JOLTS automatically generates electronic messages for key case events. For example, system-generated electronic messages are automatically routed in the following instances:

- Field probation officers are automatically notified of activities regarding juveniles on their caseloads —e.g., new complaints, if a plea is accepted, if psychological assessment reports are past due, when a detainee is written up for an incident in detention, or when a warrant is issued or quashed.
- Judicial officers, county attorneys, public defenders and probation officers are automatically notified of all changes to the hearing schedule.
- Field and Intake Probation officers are automatically notified when the court receives verification that a juvenile has completed or has not shown up for a court-ordered activity (e.g., community work service, drug testing, educational class, etc.) or when payment has been made on an assessment (restitution, probation or PIC-ACT service fee, etc.).
- Field and Intake Officers are automatically notified when a due date for a payment and/or court-ordered program has passed with no indication of compliance.
- The Finance Unit is automatically notified when a juvenile in a court-funded placement is detained (i.e., so that the court does not pay the placement per diem for that youth).
- Field and Investigation Unit probation officers are automatically notified whenever a juvenile on their caseload is detained.
- After a juvenile has been in placement for 30 days, workers from the Treatment Alternatives Unit are automatically reminded to investigate funding options for continued placement.

6. Preparation of Court Documents

Word processing capabilities are fully integrated in the JOLTS software. This facilitates the automated generation of a wide variety of court documents (including petitions, court orders, and minute entries) and investigative reports (including pre-disposition reports and psychological assessments). JOLTS merges relevant child and court information into document and report templates thus reducing the amount of time necessary to complete these tasks. County attorneys utilize integrated word processing to create petitions by merging child data already maintained in the database with standard charge clauses developed by the office. Very little support staff time is needed to complete these documents.

Court clerks are able to complete minute entries using JOLTS. Minute entries contain court orders made at the hearing and include rulings that were made after a case was taken under advisement. Most minute entries are constructed by merging child, petition, and hearing data maintained in the JOLTS database with standard hearing and court order clauses. Court clerks have up to three days to complete most types of minute entries, although they are often completed within hours of the hearing. Minute entries containing warrants must be completed within 24 hours and entries containing commitment orders to the state's department of juvenile corrections must be completed in time to allow for the twice weekly transportation of juveniles to the juvenile corrections reception facility.

A considerable amount of child, family and court history information is stored in the JOLTS database. This information can be used to complete the initial sections of the pre-disposition report prepared for the court by the assigned juvenile probation officer. These initial sections provide the court with a demographic description of the child and a brief summary of all prior and pending complaints and petitions (delinquency and incorrigibility) filed with the court. The merging of JOLTS data into the report template cuts down considerably on the word processing requirements necessary to produce pre-disposition reports (by 25% or more).[25]

Delays in the submission of court reports is often a source of processing backlogs in juvenile courts (see Chapter 3). In many courts, large caseloads prevent probation officers from completing investigations and reports until just prior to the disposition hearing. In Maricopa County, probation officer have the ability to prepare their own reports without the assistance of clerical staff. The relative ease with which these reports can be completed using JOLTS as well as the high level of computer literacy among line probation staff encourages this practice.

7. Electronic Archiving of Critical Court Documents

All critical court documents and reports are electronically archived for easy retrieval from any JOLTS terminal. JOLTS stores an on-line version of the most important portions of a child's social and legal file that can be conveniently accessed and printed by all court personnel with access to a youth's court records. Important case documents external sources (i.e., documents not produced using the JOLTS word-processing utility) are routinely scanned into the system and are also archived for easy retrieval. Electronic archiving facilitates caseflow management in a number of important ways:

- The need for access to paper files is reduced considerably, diminishing the likelihood that important files may be checked out when needed or even misplaced. Electronic archiving reduces staff time spent on the management of paper records and eliminates the cancellation or continuation of hearings due to the unavailability of case files. Jurists have access to all critical case documents through terminals located in the courtroom and a hard copy of any juvenile's file can be quickly reconstructed by printing the necessary case documents archived on the system.
- Multiple individuals from different court departments can access a child's court records simultaneously without having to access the actual file or a hard copy of a document from the file. Case processing steps that may have previously been completed in sequential and laborious fashion can now be completed concurrently and quickly.
- Editing and supervisor review of court-ordered reports (e.g., pre-disposition reports) can be completed via a terminal without shuffling paperwork between court personnel (juvenile probation officer, clerical staff, and probation supervisor, etc.).

8. Monitoring of System Performance and Individual Case Progression

In Maricopa County, JOLTS provides users with a vast array of screen displays and statistical reports that facilitate effective caseload management, caseflow tracking and court-wide planning. A number of reports are generated and distributed to appropriate court staff on a regular production schedule developed by the court's Division of Research and Planning (RAPS). Other screen displays and reports can be generated without the assistance of staff from RAPS. Many of these permit a user to limit the system's search to specific types of cases (e.g., by gender, race, detention status, offense type, disposition, etc.) and/or cases falling within a specified range of calendar dates. Users also have the ability to examine caseloads and caseflow progress on a court-wide basis, by individual jurist, or by juvenile probation officer. The system's reporting capabilities give the court the capacity to track and closely monitor case activities and decisions that affect the timely processing of delinquency cases. Users have the ability to:

- Ensure that cases are assigned in an equitable manner and to closely monitor current caseloads so that they remain in relative equilibrium;
- Achieve early identification of cases with no apparent activity before the cases get lost in the shuffle and remain inactive for extensive periods of time;
- Monitor time between critical case processing stages to identify cases that are lagging so that case-specific issues can be addressed in a proactive manner;

- Identify cases with case processing inconsistencies to determine whether these inconsistencies are due to errors in data entry or faulty processing decisions;
- Monitor overall caseflow performance; and
- Analyze aggregate caseload statistics and case processing trends to support the court's short and long-term planning goals.

Most juvenile courts have at least some automated case tracking and reporting capabilities. What sets the Maricopa County Juvenile Court apart is the sophistication and flexibility of the court's automated reporting utility. Well over 100 standard listings/displays and reports are available through JOLTS and many of these are used on a daily or weekly basis by all levels of staff including court administrators, unit supervisors, line probation officers, court clerks and various other types of support staff. Research and planning staff work continually with the various levels of court personnel to expand and modify the system's reporting capabilities to provide users more comprehensive and timely information. The research and planning staff also tend to be very proactive in anticipating the needs of court staff and often independently suggest and develop new reporting capabilities for users to test.

Case "aging" reports and summary statistics are of particular interest to the court as it attempts to process cases in a timely fashion. Court rules promulgated by the Arizona Supreme Court establish benchmarks for the timely processing of delinquency (and status offense) cases. Additionally, the court has developed internal court rules and polices to compliment State rules and to guide the processing of cases not addressed by the State supreme court.

Sample Reports

Four automated reports used in Maricopa County are representative of the data that are readily available from the automated system to assist staff in the management of the court's delinquency caseload. The four types of reports include:

1. Delinquency Calendar Summary Report;
2. Delinquency Calendar Detail Report;
3. Pending Petition Summary Report; and
4. Delinquency Petition Pending 360+ Days Detail Report.

The Delinquency Calendar Summary Report (figure 4.1) is produced for general distribution to all court administrators and judicial officers on a monthly basis. The report examines how timely delinquency petitions have progressed through various hearing stages during a specified time frame.

The user provides the time frame to be examined, which can be as short as one day and as long as several years. In most instances, the report period is one month, one quarter, or one year. A second report parameter allows the user to generate separate reports for individual judicial officers. It provides users with the average number of

FIGURE 4.1
Maricopa County juvenile court center delinquency calendar summary report*
Period: 09–01–94 to 09–30–94

	Number	Average	Goal	Within Goal		Outside Goal	
Petition to advisory (detained)	223	3	2	187	84%	36	16%
Petition to advisory (not detained)	311	28	30	302	97	9	3
Advisory to adjudication (detained)	263	11	30	256	97	7	3
Advisory to adjud. (not detained)	341	24	60	328	96	13	4
Adjudication to disposition (detained)	117	24	30	110	94	7	6
Adjudication to dispo. (not detained)	276	39	45	255	92	21	8
Advisory to conclud. transfer hearing	48	29	30	48	100	0	0

* Does not includes cases in which warrants for failure to appear were issued or instances in which continuances of more than 30 days were granted by the court.

days it took for a petition to proceed through a specific processing stage, and the number and proportion of petitions that proceeded through this stage within and outside of the prescribed time limits.

For example, during September, 1994, 117 delinquency petitions involving detained juveniles had proceeded from adjudication (including pleas) through to disposition in an average of 24 days. Of these, 94% (110) reached disposition within the 30-day time limit. The remaining 6% took longer than 30 days.

A companion report (the Delinquency Calendar Detail Report) provides detailed information on all petitions processed during a specified time period (figure 4.2). This report is sorted by processing phase and the total number of days a case took to proceed through a given processing stage. This report is very useful because it identifies cases that exceeded time standards and provides the user some indication as to the reasons for the delay. The report also includes the number of continuances granted (and for how many days) during this processing phase and whether an arrest warrant (for failure to appear) was open during any part of the processing period and the number of days the warrant was open.[26]

Another very useful report generated on a monthly basis is the Pending Petition Information Report (figure 4.3). Most juvenile courts are required to generate or manually tabulate a version of the top portion of this report to submit to their appropriate state agency or commission responsible for maintaining statewide court caseload statistics. Information on petitions pending at the start and end of the time period provides an administrator with a good profile of the court's work flow.

FIGURE 4.2
Maricopa County juvenile court delinquency calendar detail report (sample output)
Period: 09–01–94 to 09–30–94

Processing Stage: Adjudication to Disposition for Detained Cases (Goal = 30 days)

File #	Petition Date	Total Goal	Goal Days	Days	Cont/ Days	Warr/ Days	First Set	End Event
1	07/09/94	Yes	20	20			09/29/94	09/29/94
2	08/15/94	Yes	23	23			09/15/94	09/15/94
3	06/24/94	Yes	25	18	1/7		09/12/94	09/19/94
4	08/03/94	Yes	28	28		Yes/9	09/17/94	09/26/94
5	07/16/94	Yes	43	27	1/16		09/06/94	09/22/94
6	07/20/94	No	51	34	1/17	Yes/1	08/23/94	09/09/94
7	06/22/94	No	56	37	1/19		08/23/94	09/13/94

FIGURE 4.3
Maricopa County juvenile court pending petition information report
Period: 09–01–94 to 09–30–94

Petition Type	Petitions Pending at Beginning of Period	Petitions Filed	Petitions Dispositioned	Petitions Pending at End of Period
Adoption	1,299	66	51	1,314
Delinquency	2,986	725	733	2,978
Dependency	3,697	77	28	3,746
Severance	730	46	29	747

Age of Pending Delinquency Petitions

	Days Delinquency Petition Pending			
Delinquent Petition Type	**0-90 Days**	**91-180 Days**	**181-360 Days**	**360+ Days**
All delinquency petitions*	1,323	401	161	201
Percent of delinq. petitions	63%	19%	8%	10%
Petitions pending disposition*	305	75	18	6
Percent pending disposition	23%	19%	11%	3%

* Excludes delinquency petitions with warrants or for juveniles over the age of 18.

Many courts are not able to generate aggregate aging statistics on their pending delinquency caseload. Caseload aging statistics are useful in determining how well a court is managing its caseflow. This report reveals that in September, 1994, 10% of all pending delinquency petitions with no open warrants had been open for more than 360 days. The majority (63%) of the court's pending delinquency petition caseload, however, consisted of relatively recent petitions that had been pending for 90 days or less. The last line of this report reveals that 23% of the most recently filed petitions had proceeded to the adjudication phase and were now awaiting disposition. A smaller portion of older cases had proceeded through adjudication and were awaiting disposition. Of the 201 oldest cases (360+ days), only 6 (3%) were awaiting disposition. This trend could suggest that problematic delays tend to appear in the earlier phases of petition processing.

A companion report (figure 4.4) provides information on delinquency petitions pending for more than 360 days. This listing includes all delinquency petitions pending for 360 days or more, including those in which warrants were issued that remain open, and open petitions in which the juvenile reached the age of majority. The report is sorted by the length of time petitions have been pending, by type of case. For example, all delayed cases pending disposition in which warrants are open are presented first (from oldest to youngest). Next, all petitions with active warrants that are held up at an earlier case processing stage are presented. Delayed cases without active warrants are presented third, and all delayed cases without active warrants and not pending disposition are provided in the last grouping. The report provides users with critical case information that can help identify reasons for delay.

FIGURE 4.4
Maricopa County juvenile court delinquency petitions pending 360+ days detail report (sample output)
Period: 09–01–94 to 09–30–94

File	Petition Date	Pend. Disp.	Warr	Cont	Futr. Hrg	Days	Age	Last Hearing Type	Last Hearing Date	Last Hearing Result	Future Hearing Type	Future Hearing Date
1	04/29/93	Yes	Yes			519	17	DISP	07/02/93	WAR		
2	05/24/93	Yes	Yes		Yes	494	17	ADJ	10/28/94	CMP	DISP	02/13/94
3	07/08/93	Yes	Yes	Yes		449	16	VOP	09/27/94	RSC	VOP	10/15/94
....												
....												
4	03/19/93		Yes			560	16	ADJ	06/21/93	WAR		
5	04/08/93		Yes		Yes	540	17	ADV	02/04/94	CMP	A/T	01/03/95
6	09/10/93		Yes	Yes	Yes	385	16	WAR	11/24/94	CMP	ADJ	01/09/95
...												

Studies and Experimentation

The staff of the Maricopa County Juvenile Court have been highly conscious of the need to examine the organizational dynamics and external factors that impede and facilitate caseflow. In 1981, the research and planning division of the court conducted an analysis of case processing time, calendar goals and judicial officer needs. The study recommended additional judicial officers and the implementation of certain procedural changes. This was followed by a second, more comprehensive study in 1984 that found case processing time frames had improved somewhat since 1981 but consistently fell below the standards set by the Court Calendar Goals established in 1981 (Burgess and McCarthy, 1984).

The 1984 study included a detailed analysis of the court's caseload (new filings and backlogs), available resources (the number and availability of hearing officers), and procedures, as well as how each of these affected case processing times for all types of cases handled by the court. The study recommended the development of monthly case monitoring reports for all case processing stages for which time standards had already been enacted and the establishment of additional calendaring goals. The study led to many of the automated calendaring enhancements and the development of the monitoring reports discussed above.

In January of 1991, the presiding judge appointed a Caseflow Management Task Force to continue the court's review of its calendaring practices and to develop recommendations that would serve as the foundation for the implementation of a new case management system. Subcommittees were formed for each of the court's major case dockets. A sixth subcommittee was charged with reviewing the court's various calendaring approaches including a comparison of master, individual and team calendaring.

The final report of the task force and subcommittees was presented in May, 1992. The report contained specific recommendations for case processing time frames and policies and procedures for a new calendaring system. The Delinquency Subcommittee developed flowcharts for the tracking of case processing events necessary to complete seven different case types from start to finish. The flow charts reflected streamlined procedures. Unnecessary steps were eliminated with considerable emphasis placed on the automation of procedures. The process proposed by the Delinquency Subcommittee was designed to accommodate the "normal" case. The report anticipated that 80% of all delinquency cases would fall within proposed time frames.

The Calendaring Subcommittee recommended the adoption of a team calendar system that would give jurists direct responsibility for hearing scheduling. The subcommittee believed an individual calendar system would reduce conflicts among parties, increase the predictability of hearings, reduce continuances and courtroom "dead time," and generally enhance caseflow management. The subcommittee recommended that cases be assigned to judicial officers based on geographic considerations. The subcommittee believed its recommendations would foster the development of a team concept even with the individual calendar system since the county attorney, public defender, and probation officer would all be assigned to cases in similar fashion.

The presiding juvenile court judge accepted the recommendations of the Caseflow Management Task Force with only minor revisions and established an on-going Calendar/Caseflow Advisory Oversight Committee to monitor the implementation of a caseflow management system and to serve as a continuing advisory group for the maintenance of the system. The oversight committee agreed to meet on a monthly basis with its membership to include the presiding juvenile court judge, the chief deputy juvenile county attorney, the chief deputy juvenile public defender, the head commissioner, the director of juvenile court services, the court/calendar administrator, the juvenile court clerk services administrator, a representative of Arizona's public child welfare agency (the Department of Economic Security), and the chairperson of the Juvenile Practice Committee.

Research and Planning staff worked closely with the oversight committee in redesigning and developing additional case tracking and aging reports. Certain recommended changes to delinquency case processing were modified after being found difficult to implement in their original form. Changes were made to the judicial case assignment and calendaring system to further foster case continuity and case processing accountability.

CONCLUSION

Automation has not completely eliminated case processing delays in Maricopa County. Delays in the processing of delinquency cases still occur, sometimes in violation of court rules and polices. While automated calendaring has resulted in more efficient use of the court's delinquency calendar, continuances are still problematic and the court continues to take steps to firm up its policies regarding continuances. The court's ability to track and monitor caseflow also does not automatically lead to timely case processing. As of 1995, the court was again updating its automated case tracking and reporting utilities so that court personnel would be more apt to use the system to monitor case movement.

The consistent improvement of caseflow management in Maricopa County, however, illustrates the potential of automation to strengthen the day-to-day operations of juvenile courts. Comprehensive and flexible information systems allow for better coordination and monitoring of case processing among all organizational units of the court. While automation is not a panacea, it is an essential tool for any court wishing to tackle the wide range of internal and external issues that affect the timing of delinquency dispositions. The Maricopa County Juvenile Court has used its automated information tools to infuse the entire court system with greater efficiency and accountability.

Chapter 4 Notes

1. The court has recently revamped its jurist assignment system to create six teams with each magistrate being assigned to a specific judge. Previously, three magistrates were randomly assigned to delinquency cases. Their orders on a specific case would be reviewed by the judge appointed to the case. A fourth magistrate was responsible for hearing all delinquency arraignments.

2. There are no statutory limitations to the types of delinquency cases a magistrate may preside over. There are statutory provisions, however, requiring that a judge preside over abortion by-pass cases and adult cases in which the alleged charge is contributing to the delinquency of a minor.

3. Unlike the analysis in Table 4.1 which uses the unit of count preferred by Juvenile Court Statistics ("cases disposed"), this analysis presents counts of case filings. Thus, the measures vary slightly.

4. Although unruly referrals also grew during this period, this increase had less impact on court workloads because unruly filings are generally diverted to a private provider without substantive screening.

5. Of course, Maricopa County also employs considerably more staff to maintain its automated system.

6. Referrals involving non-detained juveniles are filed with court intake at either the main court building or at one of the seven branch offices. Police referrals on detained juveniles are filed with staff at the court's detention facility at the time the youth is detained and are routed to court intake in the main court building for screening. The juvenile court has a "case management coordinator" who is responsible for facilitating the court processing of detention cases. To facilitate screening of these cases, the case management coordinator picks up police reports from the juvenile detention facility and delivers them to Intake.

7. The prosecutor's office is responsible for confirming probable cause, deciding whether to initiate criminal court transfer proceedings (or "bindover"), deciding on property forfeiture motions and reviewing the praecipe for sufficiency. Reviews are not generally conducted on misdemeanor and lesser (third and fourth degree) felony complaints (Hamel, 1994).

8. Intake screening of delinquency referrals on detained juveniles (including those placed in shelter care or on home detention) must be completed within 72 hours. This includes time for the prosecutor's office to complete the legal review of the official petition. For delinquency referrals on juveniles not detained at the time of arrest, the Intake Unit has up to 21 days to complete case screening. This includes the 72 hours provided for the prosecutor's legal review.

9. A courtroom coordinator from Assignment Services is assigned to each courtroom.

10. Ohio statutes limit the amount of time a juvenile may be detained in secure detention to a period not exceeding 90 days. Local juvenile court policy limits detention stays to 60 days.

11. Local Court Rule #10 states that "[n]o case will be continued on the day of the trial or hearing except for good cause shown, which cause was not known to the party or counsel prior to the day of the trial or hearing and provided that the party and/or counsel have used diligence to be ready for trial and notified or made diligent efforts to notify the opposing party or counsel as soon as they became aware of the necessity to request a postponement. This rule may not be waived by consent of counsel."

12. The recent report from the Ohio Supreme Court came to similar conclusions regarding implementation of the court's continuation policy and the influence of attorneys on the pace of litigation (Hamel, 1994:22–24).

13. According to Referee Mazza, a lenient jurist might continue 60% of their cases on any given day, and then increase the number of cases set for the docket in order to adjust for anticipated continuances, which just "feeds the problem."

14. Unlike the analysis in Table 4.1 which uses the unit of count preferred by Juvenile Court Statistics ("cases disposed"), this analysis presents counts of complaints received. In addition, the data provided for this analysis include cases of "incorrigibility," which are not included in Table 4.1. Thus, the two caseload measures vary considerably.

15. Matters involving children under the age of 8 are not considered to be delinquency complaints in Arizona.

16. Judge Rose was later installed as Presiding Superior Court Judge and in this capacity continued to provide leadership and support to the juvenile court. Judge Rose served as Presiding Superior Court Judge until 1995.

17. Modified versions of JOLTS have been installed in a number of juvenile courts, including courts in Fulton and Clayton County Georgia (Atlanta), Wayne County Michigan (Detroit), and Pima County Arizona (Tucson).

18. Most States require detention hearings within 24 to 48 hours.

19. JOLTS also tracks when parties check in for court hearings.

20. A hard copy of the report is also placed in the juvenile's paper file.

21. The Court Administrator's Office does not schedule the judges' calendars. However, commissioners preside over 90% of all hearings on delinquency matters.

22. The authors' interviews suggested that the vast majority of requests for continuances are granted. One court administrator indicated that an estimated 97% of all such requests were approved.

23. JOLTS is also used to assign delinquency cases to prosecutors from the County Attorney's Office.

24. The assignment of petitioned cases to juvenile probation officers in the Investigation Unit can also be accomplished directly through JOLTS without supervisor involvement based on assignment parameters maintained by unit supervisors.

However, supervisors and court administration prefer that assignment of these cases be more individualized via manual review.

25. Interview data suggest that 25% understates the savings from both the probation officers who no longer have to dictate specific items and for typists who no longer have to transcribe these dictations. JOLTS automatically provides a narrative on each referral as part of the production of the pre-disposition report. Dictating and transcribing these narratives was once very time consuming especially for juveniles with extensive delinquency histories.

26. Arizona Supreme Court Rule 6.1, subsection G permits the time elapsed during certain types of continuances to be excluded from the calculation of time limits. The data provided in the goal days column of the Delinquency Calendar Detail Report subtracts the number continuance days from the total number of days found in the preceding column.

Chapter 5
National Trends in Case Processing Time

INTRODUCTION

The number of law violations handled by U.S. juvenile courts has grown considerably in recent years.[1] Between 1985 and 1994, the Nation's total delinquency caseload increased 41% while the number of cases involving person offenses grew 93% (Butts et al., 1996b). Concern about the speed of the juvenile court process has also increased in the past decade. It may still be true that the average juvenile court case is handled more quickly than the typical criminal court case, but the degree of difference appears to be getting smaller.

For example, a 1989 study by the National Center for State Courts examined felony disposition times in 26 metropolitan trial courts. The median time between case initiation and final disposition (plea, verdict, or dismissal) ranged from 22 to 233 days (Goerdt et al., 1989:64). Nine (35%) of the jurisdictions had median disposition times in excess of 100 days. The *average* median was 86 days. In comparison, a study using data from the National Juvenile Court Data Archive examined case processing time for delinquency cases handled in 1992 by juvenile courts in 24 large counties (Butts and Halemba, 1994). For formally petitioned delinquency cases, the median time to disposition ranged from 36 to 171 days, and ten (42%) of the jurisdictions had medians greater than 100 days.[2] The *average* median among the juvenile courts was 91 days, five days longer than the average median of the criminal courts. Of course, juvenile court dispositions typically include placement and supervision decisions which are similar to criminal sentencing. If sentencing days were added to the criminal court data described above, the average processing time for criminal court cases would certainly increase. Still, the rate at which juvenile and criminal courts handle their caseloads is more similar than previously believed.

This chapter examines national patterns in the timing of delinquency case processing from 1985 through 1994. It explores the extent to which case processing time varied by the size of the jurisdiction in which the court was located, the rate at which cases were formally petitioned and adjudicated by the court, the composition of the court's delinquency caseload, and the use of secure detention prior to disposition. The analysis employs a database constructed from automated case records collected by the National Juvenile Court Data Archive, a project of the National Center for Juvenile Justice.[3] The database includes nearly 3 million delinquency cases handled between 1985 and 1994 in 17 different States.

THE JUVENILE COURT PROCESS

Measuring variations in the timing of juvenile court case processing can be a complex task.[4] The case handling practices of juvenile courts vary greatly between jurisdictions, and the courts themselves may be organized quite differently depending on State law. As of 1990, 28 States and the District of Columbia placed exclusive jurisdiction over delinquent juveniles in a general trial court or an equivalent specialized court at the highest trial level;[5] three States placed juvenile jurisdiction in a state-wide inferior court;[6] and 20 States placed it in a combination of courts (Szymanski, 1990).[7] Most States give juvenile courts legal jurisdiction over cases involving delinquency, neglect, and status offense proceedings. Many juvenile courts also have jurisdiction over adoptions, terminations of parental rights, interstate compact matters, emancipation, and consent (i.e., to marry, enlist in the armed services, be employed, etc.). Occasionally, juvenile courts may even have jurisdiction over traffic violations and child support matters.

In addition to differences in structure and organization, juvenile courts across the U.S. also vary considerably in their responsibilities and activities. Compared to adult courts, the juvenile court process is highly individualized and multifaceted. Juvenile courts focus on more than just the legal process leading to the final disposition of a case. Their decisions consider the rights and welfare of the individual juvenile and the juvenile's family, as well as the role of other agencies involved with the family such as the educational and child welfare systems. A juvenile court's adjudicatory process usually incorporates information about the youth's welfare, the family's situation, the court's prior involvement with both the youth and the family, and the youth's history of adjustment in previous placements or program settings.

Some juvenile courts focus exclusively on the adjudication process. Juveniles brought before such courts will be referred to other agencies following disposition. These courts are likely to have few employees—a judge, perhaps a court reporter and a clerk—and their case handling procedures are relatively uncomplicated. Other juvenile courts provide a full array of pre-trial and post-dispositional services with large professional staffs. Juvenile courts in more than half of the States administer their own probation services and many are responsible for detention and intake as well (Torbet, 1990). These full-service courts function as social welfare agencies, residential treatment providers, correctional facilities, and collection agencies. They require more complicated and time consuming procedures.

Jurisdictions also vary in the degree to which law enforcement agencies divert youths from the juvenile justice system. If the police send virtually all delinquency referrals forward for court handling, the juvenile court must contend with a more diverse population of youth. This would require the juvenile court intake unit to employ more aggressive case screening practices before any formal court actions are considered. Prosecutors may also have differing authority and involvement at the point of intake, which could affect the relative use of various alternatives to juvenile court action.

Many matters referred to the juvenile court are resolved without official action. In recent years, half of the delinquency cases referred to U.S. juvenile courts were handled without formal petitions or judicial hearings (Butts et al., 1996b). A juvenile involved in an unofficial (or informal) case may agree to some type of service or sanction, such as voluntary probation or community service, but no charges or petitions are filed in the case. Because informal cases are completed faster than formally charged matters, the extent to which a court relies on informal handling for delinquency cases will affect its overall case processing time.

Case Processing Stages

In order to study delinquency case processing across many different jurisdictions, it is necessary to impose a standard definition of the various steps involved in the juvenile justice process. The National Juvenile Court Data Archive developed a generic model of juvenile justice processing precisely for this purpose.[8] The Archive's generic model is used to restructure juvenile court data files from different jurisdictions so that the handling of delinquency cases can be tracked through the same basic steps. The model recognizes that certain processing steps are common to all juvenile justice systems, regardless of terminology, the jurisdictional configuration of the court, or the allocation of service delivery responsibilities. All juvenile justice systems must have some version of intake, a pre-trial procedure in which charges are delineated, an adjudication process which establishes the facts of a case, and a dispositional process which imposes sanctions. While no single jurisdiction may use these terms in exactly this manner, the Archive restructures the processing of all delinquency cases into the same basic sequence. (See the box on the following page.)

By examining the time between the first and last stages of this generic juvenile justice process, the following analysis explores the extent of variation in case processing time for delinquency cases in juvenile courts throughout the United States. Specifically, the study investigates how case processing times may have changed since 1985, whether case processing is slower or faster in smaller versus larger jurisdictions, in cases that involve secure detention versus those that do not, and in cases that are formally petitioned and formally adjudicated versus those that are dismissed or disposed with voluntary sanctions.

SOURCE OF DATA

This study relies on data files contributed voluntarily to the National Juvenile Court Data Archive by juvenile courts and juvenile justice agencies throughout the United States. Each year, the Archive collects more than 700,000 computerized juvenile court case records that describe approximately half of the delinquency cases handled by juvenile courts nationwide. This information is used to generate the national estimates of delinquency cases reported in the annual *Juvenile Court Statistics* series (e.g., Butts et al., 1996b).

Unlike traditional research data files that are collected for a unique purpose, the data files contributed to the Archive are usually extracted from automated information systems used to support court operations. As a result, the information is not always

Generic Model of Juvenile Justice Case Processing

Intake → *Petition Decision* → *Adjudication* → *Disposition*

Intake. Upon referral from a law enforcement agency or any other source (schools, etc.), delinquency cases are screened by an intake department, often within the juvenile court or the prosecutor's office. This intake department may decide to dismiss the case for lack of legal sufficiency or to resolve the matter informally. Informal (or nonpetitioned) dispositions may include a voluntary referral to a social service agency, informal probation, or the voluntary payment of fines or restitution. In cases where no further actions are taken, this intake decision is considered to be the case's final disposition.

Petition Decision. If the intake department decides that a case should be handled formally within the juvenile court, a petition is filed and the case moves to the adjudicatory stage, usually by placing it on the court calendar (or docket) to await an adjudication hearing. A small number of petitions may be dismissed before an adjudication hearing is held.[9]

Adjudication. At an adjudication hearing, a youth may be adjudicated as a delinquent and the case would then proceed to a disposition hearing. If, on the other hand, the case results in a failure to adjudicate (analogous to an acquittal), the petition would be dismissed and the case would be considered disposed at that point. The case may also be "continued" in contemplation of dismissal. The court may recommend that the youth take some action prior to a dismissal, such as paying restitution or voluntarily attending drug counseling. Such a case would not be considered complete until dismissed.

Disposition. At a disposition hearing, the juvenile court determines the most appropriate sanction for an adjudicated youth. The court's options typically include commitment to an institution, placement in a group home or other residential facility, probation (either regular or intensive), referral to an outside agency (for drug treatment, mental health services, etc.), the imposition of fines, a period of community service, or restitution payments.

uniform across jurisdictions. Juvenile courts collect and organize their data using their own definitions and coding categories. In addition, much of the information that would be of interest to researchers is typically not available in automated data files (e.g., social service histories, family background, co-defendant information, etc.), and the detail available in some data files may not be contained in others. Even when similar data elements are available, they may have inconsistent definitions or overlapping coding categories. Still, the limited amount of information that is available from an automated system tends to be highly accurate because it is the same data used to conduct the daily business of the court.

Study Sample

Of the 1,500 jurisdictions that regularly contribute case-level data files to the Archive, some are able to submit only basic information about the youth involved in each case (e.g., age, sex, race, and offense). Many jurisdictions, however, are able to contribute more detailed records with multiple indicators of court activity, including the calendar dates of case processing events. During the period from 1985 to 1994, detailed data with case processing dates were contributed annually by juvenile courts in 17 States: Alabama, Arizona, Connecticut, Florida, Hawaii, Maryland, Minnesota, Mississippi, Missouri, Montana, Nebraska, North Dakota, Ohio, Pennsylvania, South Carolina, Utah, and Wisconsin. In some of these States (e.g., Utah and Pennsylvania), case records were available from every jurisdiction in the State. In others, records were available from only a sub-set of jurisdictions, ranging from just one large county (e.g., Ohio) to nearly all counties (e.g., Wisconsin).

Some individual jurisdictions were excluded from the study sample for one or more reasons. Individual counties were included in the final sample only if all of the following conditions were met:

1) Detailed records were available for every year between 1985 and 1994;
2) The total population of the jurisdiction was 20,000 or more as of 1990;[10]
3) The jurisdiction disposed at least 30 formally-processed delinquency cases in each year from 1985 through 1994; and
4) Accurate dates of referral and dates of disposition were recorded in at least 90% of the delinquency case records in every year from 1985 through 1994.[11]

Altogether, 267 counties met all four criteria. As of the 1990 Census, these counties contained 22% of the U.S. population. A majority (153) of the jurisdictions had total populations between 20,000 and 100,000, while 81 had populations between 100,000 and 400,000, and 33 counties had populations greater than 400,000.

RESULTS

Together, the jurisdictions in the study sample handled 2.9 million delinquency cases between 1985 and 1994. Their combined annual caseload increased 57% between 1985 and 1994, from 237,509 to 372,055 cases per year (table 5.1). The characteristics of the delinquency cases processed by the sample jurisdictions were very similar to the characteristics of delinquency cases handled nationwide, according to the national estimates presented in *Juvenile Court Statistics 1994* (Butts et al., 1996b). For example, 16% of the cases handled by the sample jurisdictions in 1994 involved the use of secure detention at some point between referral and disposition, compared with 20% nationally.[12] About half of all cases were processed formally in 1994, both nationally and in the study sample. While the sample jurisdictions adjudicated 33% of their delinquency cases in 1994, adjudications occurred in 32% of delinquency cases nationwide. The profile of offenses and dispositions among the cases processed by sample jurisdictions were also similar to those of delinquency cases nationwide. Cases in which the most serious charge was an offense against a person accounted for approximately one-fifth of all cases in both the study sample and the national estimates. Out-of-home placement was ordered in 10% of sample cases as well as all cases nationwide. The comparability of the sample data with national delinquency caseloads was evident in both 1985 and 1994.

Time From Referral to Disposition

The number of days between referral and disposition was calculated for every delinquency case handled by the sample jurisdictions from 1985 through 1994 (table 5.2). In 1985, 23% of the delinquency cases disposed by the sample jurisdictions had disposition times exceeding 90 days. By 1994, this percentage had increased to 31%. The median time to disposition for all cases in 1994 was 54 days, an increase of 26% from 1985. (The median is the preferred measure of central tendency in a study of case processing time because, unlike an average, the median is not affected by a small number of cases with extreme values).

Disposition time appeared to be related to jurisdiction size. In 1994, the median time to disposition for cases from large counties was 59 days, compared with 46 days in midsize jurisdictions, and 34 days in small jurisdictions. In the largest counties, 35% of all delinquency cases required more than 90 days to reach disposition, compared with 19% of cases from the smallest counties. Similar differences in the disposition times of small versus large jurisdictions were apparent in 1985.

In 1994, the median disposition time for cases involving secure detention was 52 days, compared with 57 days for cases that did not involve detention. There was very little difference in the timing of 1985 case processing according to whether detention was involved. It is important to recognize that the measure of detention in this analysis is simply whether or not detention was used at any point prior to disposition of a case. It does not specify the amount of time a youth spent in detention, nor does it control for the point in case processing when a youth was detained.

TABLE 5.1
Characteristics of delinquency cases handled in 1985 and 1994 by juvenile courts in 267 U.S. counties, compared with national delinquency estimates.

	1985			1994		
	Study Sample		Nat'l Est.	Study Sample		Nat'l Est.
Total Delinquency Cases	237,509	100%	100%	372,055	100%	100%
Pre-Disposition Detention						
Cases not involving detention	121,350	81%	80%	188,764	84%	80%
Cases involving detention	29,389	19	20	35,124	16	20
Juvenile Court Handling						
Informal (non-petitioned cases)	105,790	45%	55%	152,156	41%	45%
Formal (petitioned cases)	131,719	55	45	219,899	59	55
Juvenile Court Adjudication						
Not adjudicated	132,168	65%	70%	247,793	67%	68%
Adjudicated	70,034	35	30	124,158	33	32
Most Serious Charge						
Person (robbery, assault, etc.)	41,497	17%	16%	81,274	22%	21%
Property (burglary, larceny, etc.)	145,952	61	60	196,027	53	52
Drug (sales, possession, etc.)	13,602	6	7	28,134	8	8
Public order (vandalism, weapons)	36,458	15	18	66,620	18	19
Most Restrictive Disposition						
Placed out of the home	21,888	9%	9%	37,571	10%	10%
Probation or other supervision	83,825	35	37	126,000	34	35
Fine, restitution, other services	52,999	22	15	76,869	21	18
Dismissed or released	78,797	33	39	131,615	35	37
County Population in 1990						
Small: Under 100,000	26,302	11%	*NA*	49,502	13%	*NA*
Midsize: 100,000 to 400,000	50,663	21	*NA*	81,028	22	*NA*
Large: Over 400,000	160,544	68	*NA*	241,525	65	*NA*

Notes: Detail may not add to total because of missing data for some variables. Percentages may not add to 100% due to rounding.

Source: All data are from the National Juvenile Court Data Archive, National Center for Juvenile Justice, Pittsburgh, Pennsylvania. National estimates are from *Juvenile Court Statistics 1994* (Butts et al., 1996b). Study sample includes all delinquency cases disposed in 267 counties with populations greater than 20,000 in 17 States: Alabama, Arizona, Connecticut, Florida, Hawaii, Maryland, Minnesota, Mississippi, Missouri, Montana, Nebraska, North Dakota, Ohio, Pennsylvania, South Carolina, Utah, and Wisconsin. In 1990, these counties contained 22% of the U.S. population.

TABLE 5.2
Days elapsed between referral and final disposition for delinquency cases handled in 1985 and 1994 by juvenile courts in 267 U.S. counties.

	Number of Cases		Median Days to Disposition		Percent of Cases Over 90 Days	
	1985	1994	1985	1994	1985	1994
Total Delinquency Cases	237,509	372,055	43	54	23%	31%
Small county (under 100,00)	26,302	49,502	28	34	14	19
Midsize county	50,663	81,028	34	46	18	26
Large county (over 400,00)	160,544	241,525	49	59	27	35
No use of detention	121,350	188,764	43	57	23	34
Detention used	29,389	35,124	44	52	21	29
Informal (non-petitioned)	105,790	152,156	23	28	11	18
Formal (petitioned)	131,719	219,899	64	72	34	40
Formal Cases						
Small county	16,368	32,427	41	46	19	24
Midsize county	27,528	48,134	53	58	27	32
Large county	87,823	139,338	73	84	39	47
No use of detention	53,662	94,750	69	82	35	45
Detention used	23,888	29,342	49	58	23	32
Not adjudicated	45,298	95,671	67	77	35	44
Adjudicated	70,034	124,158	60	69	32	38
Person offense	25,723	49,881	75	82	41	46
Property offense	79,068	111,098	64	73	34	41
Drug offense	7,110	18,969	67	77	33	43
Public order offense	19,818	39,951	47	56	27	31
Adjudicated Cases						
Placed out of the home	18,253	35,262	51	62	28	34
Probation supervision	39,570	69,550	63	70	33	38
Fine, restitution, etc.	9,622	14,986	59	72	32	41
Dismissed or released	2,589	4,360	90	79	50	45

Notes: Detail may not add to totals because of missing data for some variables.

Source: Data stored in the National Juvenile Court Data Archive, National Center for Juvenile Justice, Pittsburgh, Pennsylvania (See Table 5.1 notes).

In both 1985 and 1994, formally charged cases had substantially longer disposition times than cases handled informally. The median processing time for formal cases was 72 days in 1994, and two of every five formal cases required more than 90 days to reach disposition. Informally handled cases, on the other hand, had a median disposition time of 28 days in 1994, with only 18% taking more than 90 days to conclude. Formally charged cases in large jurisdictions took even longer to dispose. The median disposition time for petitioned delinquency cases from the largest 33 counties was 84 days in 1994; nearly half (47%) had disposition times of more than 90 days.

The impact of juvenile court efforts to accelerate the disposition of detention cases was pronounced among formally petitioned cases. When secure detention was used at some point in the processing of formally charged cases, the median disposition time was 58 days in 1994. In cases where detention was never used, the median time from referral to disposition was 82 days.

One of the longer median disposition times was for formally charged delinquency cases in which the juvenile was never adjudicated (77 days in 1994). More than two of every five (44%) of these cases in 1994 had disposition times in excess of 90 days. In part, this may reflect the use of court continuances in cases that are held open pending a juvenile's completion of voluntary sanctions, a practice used in many juvenile courts with large caseloads.

Disposition times varied somewhat according to the most serious offense involved in a case, with formally charged person offense cases having the longest median disposition time in both 1985 (75 days) and 1994 (82 days). Public order offense cases had the shortest median time (47 days in 1985, and 56 days in 1994). The type of disposition ordered for formally adjudicated cases also appeared to be associated with length of case processing. Adjudicated delinquency cases resulting in dismissal or release orders were handled more slowly than those ending in other dispositions, although the number of dismissed or released cases was relatively small. Of the four major types of court dispositions, out-of-home placement cases had the shortest processing time in both 1985 and 1994.

Case Completion Rates

Another technique that can be used to examine case processing time is to plot the cumulative disposition rate in a continuous fashion, producing a visual representation of what proportion of all cases were completed at any increment of processing time—30 days, 60 days, 90 days, etc. Compared with analyses of central tendency (i.e., mean and median), analyzing the cumulative disposition rate often produces a more detailed understanding of case processing time (e.g., Grossman et al., 1981).

Substantial differences in the timing of formal and informal delinquency cases were apparent when depicted in graphic form (figure 5.1). The disposition rate for informal cases handled by the sample courts was very rapid in the first few weeks following referral. In 1994 more than half (53%) of all informal cases were completed

FIGURE 5.1
Rate of disposition for 1994 delinquency cases processed by juvenile courts in 267 sample counties, by manner of handling.

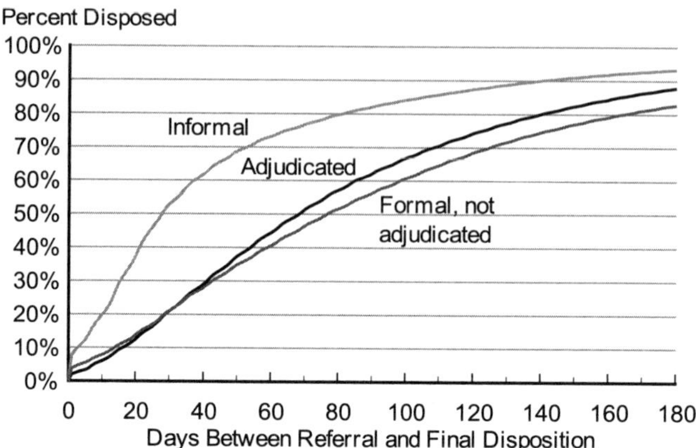

Notes: Analysis based on informally handled cases (n=152,156), formally petitioned cases which were not adjudicated (n=95,671), and adjudicated cases (n=124,158).

Source: Data stored in the National Juvenile Court Data Archive, National Center for Juvenile Justice, Pittsburgh, Pennsylvania (see Table 5.1 notes).

FIGURE 5.2
Rate of disposition for 1994 delinquency cases processed by juvenile courts in 267 sample counties, by size of county population.

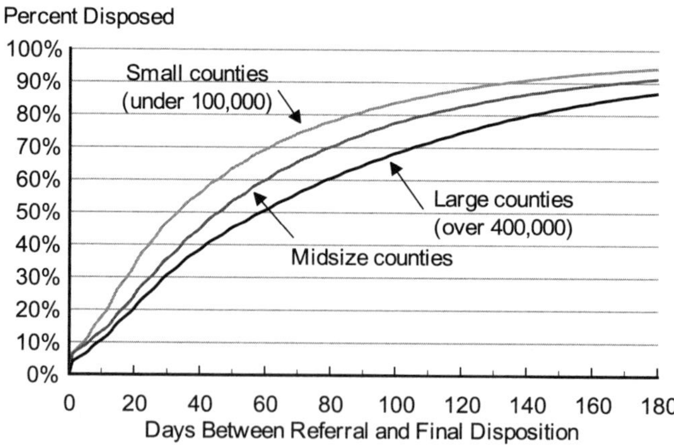

Notes: Analysis based on all delinquency cases from small counties (n=49,502), cases from midsized counties (n=81,028) and large counties (n=241,525).

Source: Data stored in the National Juvenile Court Data Archive, National Center for Juvenile Justice, Pittsburgh, Pennsylvania (see Table 5.1 notes).

within 30 days of referral. On the other hand, fewer than one-quarter (21%) of formally petitioned cases were disposed within 30 days. Even after 120 days, 26% of formally adjudicated cases had yet to reach disposition. The same was true for 31% of formally-charged, non-adjudicated cases.

Graphic analysis also revealed substantial differences in case processing time according to the size of jurisdictions (figure 5.2). In 1994 delinquency cases from the largest jurisdictions (those with more than 400,000 residents) took considerably longer to reach disposition. Four months or 120 days after referral, 25% of all delinquency cases from the largest jurisdictions were still short of final disposition. The smallest jurisdictions in the study, or those with between 20,000 and 100,000 total residents, appeared to move cases to disposition more quickly. In these jurisdictions, 81% of all delinquency cases were disposed within 90 days.

Changes in Case Processing Time

As shown above, the median time to disposition increased for nearly all types of delinquency cases between 1985 and 1994. Overall, the median time to disposition for cases from the sample jurisdictions increased 26%, from 43 days in 1985 to 54 days in 1994. Pronounced increases were also seen in formally processed cases, which had a median of 72 days in 1994 compared with 64 days in 1985. Comparing the timing of formally petitioned cases only, the disposition time for cases from large counties (populations over 400,000) increased somewhat more than those from smaller counties. The median disposition time for formally processed cases from large counties grew 15% between 1985 and 1994, from 73 days to 84 days, while the median for cases from smaller counties (under 100,000 population) grew 12%, from 41 to 46 days.

Increases in disposition time varied according to the most serious offense involved in a delinquency case.[13] In all four of the major categories of delinquency offenses, cases from large counties had longer median disposition times (figure 5.3). In some instances, however, the relative growth in disposition time was greater among cases from midsize or small counties. For example, formally processed person offense cases from large jurisdictions had a median disposition time of 90 days in 1994, up 8% from 1985 (83 days). Cases from midsize jurisdictions, however, increased relatively more between 1985 and 1994, from 58 to 70 days, or a change of 21%. Person offense cases from small jurisdictions had a median disposition time of 56 days in 1995, up 14% from 1985 when the median was 49 days.

In many offense categories, changes in delinquency case processing time exhibited two distinct patterns. For many types of cases, median disposition times increased between 1985 and 1990 and then declined between 1990 and 1992. The median time to disposition for property offense cases, for example, fell 4 to 6 days in all three population groups between 1990 and 1992. Between 1992 and 1994, however, the median time to disposition increased considerably in all three population groups.

FIGURE 5.3
Median days to disposition for formally processed delinquency cases in 267 sample counties 1985-1994, by offense and population.

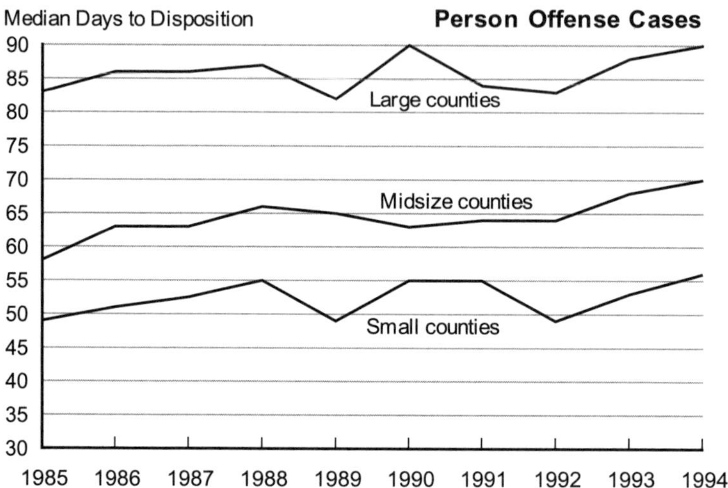

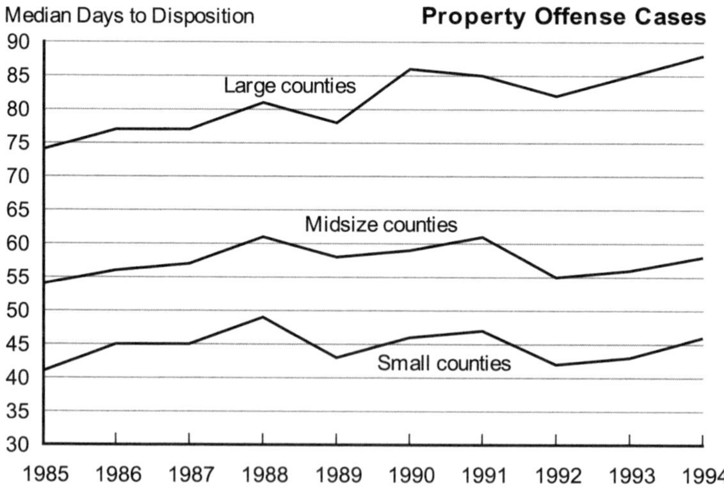

Source: Data stored in the National Juvenile Court Data Archive, National Center for Juvenile Justice, Pittsburgh, Pennsylvania (see Table 5.1 notes).

FIGURE 5.3 (cont.)

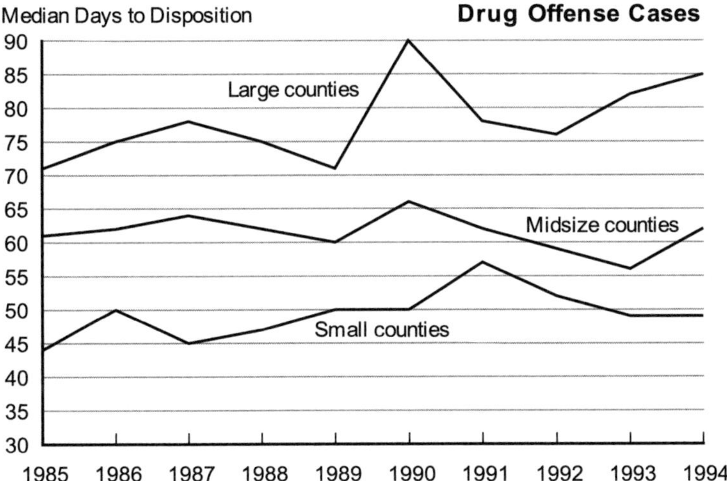

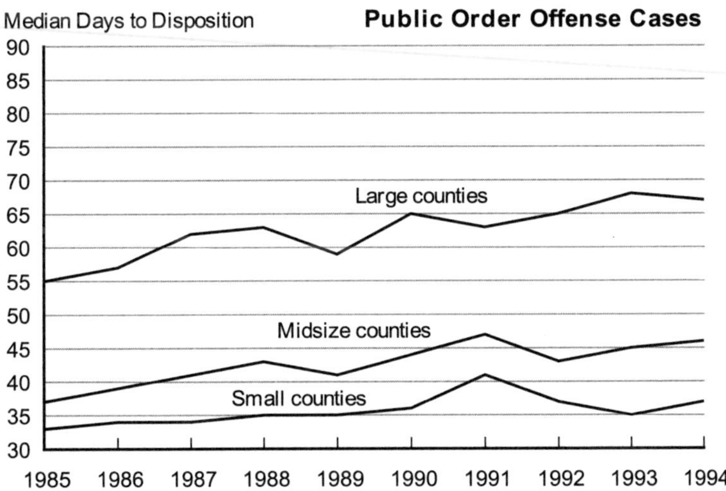

Source: Data stored in the National Juvenile Court Data Archive, National Center for Juvenile Justice, Pittsburgh, Pennsylvania (see Table 5.1 notes).

Jurisdictional Differences in Case Processing Time

Large jurisdictions are over-represented in the preceding analyses due to the size of their caseloads. In fact, 67% of all formally petitioned delinquency cases in this study were handled by the 33 largest counties among the sample of 267 jurisdictions. Thus, the measures presented above may reflect the nature of case processing in a relatively small number of jurisdictions. In order to understand jurisdictional variations in case processing time it is helpful to reduce the disproportionate influence of large counties.

An entirely different method may be used to examine jurisdiction-level differences in case processing time. Rather than analyzing cases, this method analyzes jurisdictions by constructing aggregate case processing measures for each county.[14] Using the original data file, a *jurisdiction-level* data file was constructed that contained aggregate measures of case processing time for each county in the study, independently of the number of cases disposed. For example, a single aggregate measure for median days to disposition was calculated for each jurisdiction whether that measure summarized the processing of 100 cases or 1,000 cases. County-aggregate variables included the total number of formally handled delinquency cases, the number of cases that were detained, adjudicated, etc. Aggregate measures of case processing time included the mean and median days from referral to disposition for all cases, the percentage of all cases that required more than 90 days to complete, the mean and median days for detained cases, adjudicated cases, and so on. Using these aggregate measures, the analysis was able to explore jurisdictional differences in case processing time while controlling for caseload size.

Among all sample jurisdictions, the median disposition time for petitioned delinquency cases ranged from 1 day to 218 days. The *average median* was 67 days (table 5.3). Jurisdictions with the largest populations had the highest average median. Among all counties with populations greater than 200,000, the average median disposition time for petitioned cases was 85 days, compared with an average of 68 days for counties between 60,000 and 200,000 in population, and 55 days for counties with populations under 60,000. In all categories except adjudicated and detained cases, the average median processing time increased consistently with county population.

TABLE 5.3
Average median disposition time (in days) for 1994 cases disposed in sample counties, by case type, 1994 population, and 1994 caseload.

	Formally Petitioned Delinquency Cases				
				Adjudicated Cases	
	Total	Non-adjud	Adjudicated	Released	Detained
All counties (n=267)	67	73	69	77	55
County Population in 1994					
Small: Under 60,000 (n=101)	55	60	59	70	56
Midsize: 60–200,000 (n=100)	68	72	70	74	49
Large: Over 200,000 (n=66)	85	95	83	88	63
Cases disposed in 1994					
Under 200 cases (n=104)	65	73	67	75	52
200–500 cases (n=95)	61	63	65	70	55
Over 500 cases (n=68)	79	88	77	88	62

Note: Each measure represents the average of the median case processing times for counties in that category. In other words, while the median disposition time for petitioned cases ranged from 1 to 218 days among the 267 sample jurisdictions, the *average* county median was 67 days.

Source: Data stored in the National Juvenile Court Data Archive, National Center for Juvenile Justice, Pittsburgh, Pennsylvania (see Table 5.1 notes).

A different pattern was found when median disposition times were analyzed according to the number of petitioned delinquency cases disposed by the sample jurisdictions. Although the pattern was again not entirely uniform, the average median disposition time for petitioned delinquency cases was greatest in jurisdictions with the largest caseloads (over 500 formally handled cases per year), while the next longest disposition times were generally found among the jurisdictions with the smallest caseloads (under 200 cases per year).

The relationship between processing time and the size of jurisdictions—both in terms of population and caseload—generally suggests that processing delays were more problematic in larger jurisdictions. However, it is possible that the differences shown in Table 5.3 were due to random variations or the influence of a few jurisdictions with unusual disposition times. One way to examine this possibility was to portray the association between population size and case processing time for every jurisdiction in the study.

The relationship between jurisdiction size and case processing time was examined by plotting the median case processing time for formally handled cases in each jurisdiction against the total population of that jurisdiction (figure 5.4). The correlation between jurisdiction size and median disposition time was apparent, but relatively weak. There was considerable variation in median processing time regardless of population, and some of the longest case processing times were seen in relatively small jurisdictions.

Clearly, a jurisdiction's median case processing time for delinquency cases is more than simply a reflection of its size or the relative burden of its caseload. Many factors affect case processing time. Other factors that have been identified by research on criminal court case processing include the severity of the court's caseload, the proportion of all cases that result in formal charges and conviction, and the characteristics of the jurisdiction itself—size and demographic composition, legal structure, etc. (see Chapter 2).

FIGURE 5.4
Median days to disposition for formal delinquency cases disposed in 1994, by county population in 1994.

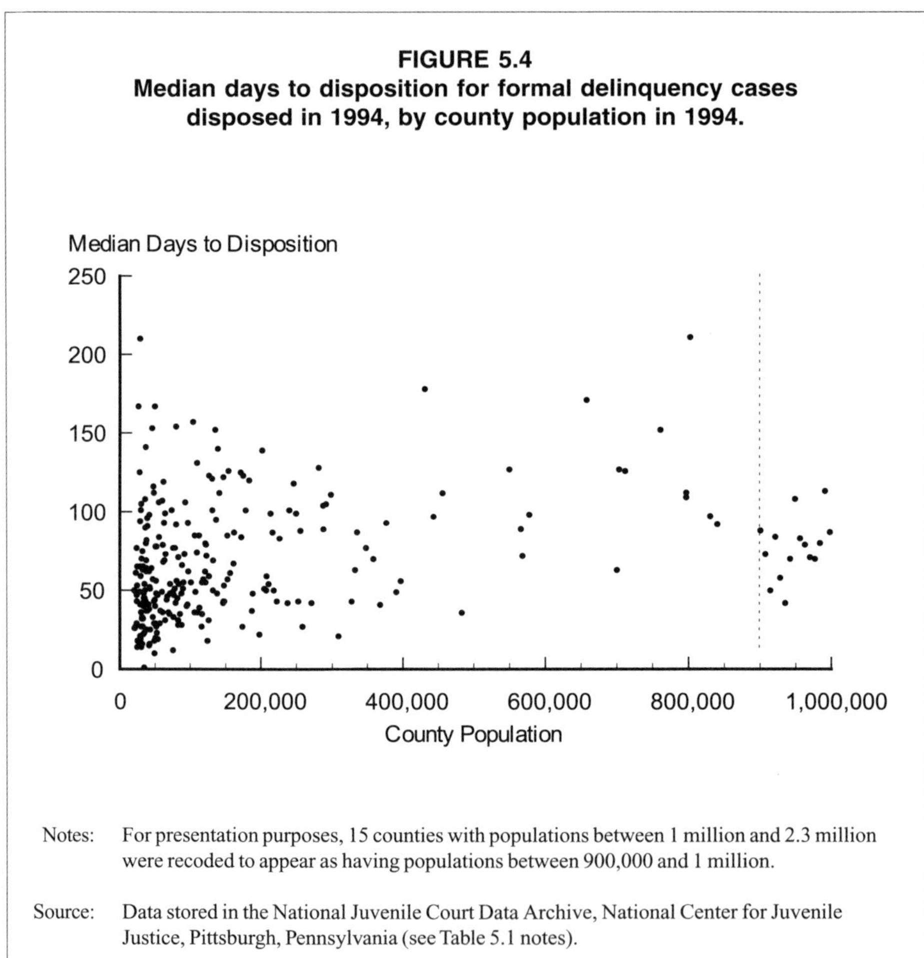

Notes: For presentation purposes, 15 counties with populations between 1 million and 2.3 million were recoded to appear as having populations between 900,000 and 1 million.

Source: Data stored in the National Juvenile Court Data Archive, National Center for Juvenile Justice, Pittsburgh, Pennsylvania (see Table 5.1 notes).

Characteristics of Delinquency Caseloads

As shown in Chapter 2, researchers studying justice delays have often shared the assumption that court processing time is longer in jurisdictions with more serious caseloads. In other words, as the proportion of cases involving serious charges or severe dispositions increases, so too should the time required to process all of the court's cases. This assumption was examined by categorizing the sample jurisdictions according to the seriousness of their delinquency caseloads in 1994—e.g., the proportion of formal delinquency cases that involved a person offense as the most serious charge, the proportion of cases that involved a drug offense as the most serious charge, the proportion of cases that resulted in out-of-home placement rather than probation or other dispositions, and the proportion of formal cases that were adjudicated by the court. The sample jurisdictions were divided roughly into thirds according to each of these factors.

For example, in 100 jurisdictions person offense cases accounted for fewer than 17% of all formal delinquency cases, while they made up between 17% and 24% of all cases in 88 jurisdictions, and 25% or more of all cases in 79 jurisdictions (table 5.4). The average median disposition times of these three groups varied as expected. In 1994, the average median was 78 days among jurisdictions where person offense cases accounted for a large proportion of all formal cases, compared with an average median of 56 days in jurisdictions where person offense cases were a smaller component of the caseload. In addition, changes in disposition time were greater between 1985 and 1994 among the jurisdictions with higher proportions of person offense cases.

An even stronger association between caseload severity and disposition time was found when the analysis examined jurisdictions according to the relative proportion of drug offenses in their caseloads. In jurisdictions with the most drug offense cases (8% or more), the average median disposition time was 80 days, up 36% from 1985. In jurisdictions with the fewest drug offense cases, on the other hand, the average median disposition time was 59 days, an increase of just 13% from 1985.

The association between disposition time and out-of-home placement was also in the expected direction but not as strong. The average median disposition time for formal delinquency cases was 69 days among the 87 jurisdictions where out-of-home placement cases accounted for 18% or more of all formal cases, compared with 64 days among jurisdictions where placement cases were 9% or less of the caseload.

The relationship between disposition time and the use of adjudication by the sample jurisdictions was in the opposite direction. The average median disposition time was lowest (58 days in 1994) among the jurisdictions with the highest proportion of adjudications (those where 80% or more of all formally-handled delinquency cases were adjudicated). This finding, however, was consistent with analyses that have found disposition times decrease as the relative proportion of adjudications in a jurisdiction grow (Butts, 1997). Such a finding suggests that in courts where adjudications become frequent and routine, most of the court's screening of cases occurs at the point of petitioning rather than adjudication, and the court's deliberations at the adjudication stage are less involved and less time-consuming. On the other hand, the percentage increase in the average median disposition time between 1985 and 1994 was greatest (35%) in jurisdictions with the highest rates of adjudication.

TABLE 5.4
Average median disposition time in 1985 and 1994, by characteristics of formal delinquency caseload in 1994.

Formal Delinquency Caseload in 1994	Counties	Average Median 1985	Average Median 1994	Percent Change
Total	n=**267**	**54**	**67**	**24%**
Proportion involving person offenses				
Under 17%	n=100	48	56	17
17% – 24%	n=88	58	74	28
25% or more	n=79	58	78	34
Proportion involving drug offenses				
Under 4%	n=93	52	59	13
4% – 7%	n=92	53	65	23
8% or more	n=82	59	80	36
Proportion placed out of home				
Under 10%	n=85	57	64	12
10% – 17%	n=95	53	69	30
18% or more	n=87	53	69	30
Proportion adjudicated				
Under 55%	n=86	57	64	12
55% – 79%	n=99	60	79	32
80% or more	n=82	43	58	35

Note: Average median is the average of the median processing times of a group of counties.

Source: Data stored in the National Juvenile Court Data Archive, National Center for Juvenile Justice, Pittsburgh, Pennsylvania (see Table 5.1 notes).

Changes in Court Workload

Court workload is often presumed to affect case processing time. The study was able to examine this factor in part by comparing changes in average median case processing time among sample jurisdictions according to whether their delinquency caseloads increased between 1985 and 1994. Overall, the average median disposition time of sample jurisdictions increased 24% between 1985 and 1994, from 54 to 67 days. Among jurisdictions that experienced increases of 50% or more in the size of their delinquency caseloads, the average median disposition time grew 109%, from 44 to 92 days (table 5.5). Among jurisdictions with declining caseloads, on the other hand, the average median processing time fell 35%, from 66 to 43 days. This relationship was found among both large and small counties. In all three population groups, disposition times increased far more in jurisdictions where caseloads increased substantially between 1985 and 1994.

Of course, this analysis is suggestive only. Without more information about court resources (e.g., number of judges, courtrooms, and support staff), it is not possible to draw firm conclusions about the relationship between caseload changes, court workload, and disposition time. Still, the clear association between growing delinquency caseloads and aggregate patterns in disposition time supports the common assumption that caseload pressures lead to case processing delays.

TABLE 5.5
Average median disposition time in 1985 and 1994, by population, by percentage change in formal delinquency caseloads from 1985 to 1994.

	Caseload Change: 1985 to 1994	Counties	Average Median 1985	Average Median 1994	Percent Change
All Jurisdictions	Decreased	n=79	66	43	-35
	Up 1%–49%	n=103	53	65	23
	Up 50% or more	n=85	44	92	109
Small Jurisdictions	Decreased	n=39	57	34	-40
	Up 1%–49%	n=29	42	52	24
	Up 50% or more	n=33	31	83	168
Midsize Jurisdictions	Decreased	n=28	76	49	-36
	Up 1%–49%	n=40	50	62	24
	Up 50% or more	n=32	47	91	94
Large Jurisdictions	Decreased	n=12	74	59	-20
	Up 1%–49%	n=34	66	80	21
	Up 50% or more	n=20	63	110	75

Note: Average median is the average of the median processing times of a group of counties. See Table 5.3 for definitions of county population size in 1994.

Source: Data stored in the National Juvenile Court Data Archive, National Center for Juvenile Justice, Pittsburgh, Pennsylvania (see Table 5.1 notes).

State Legislation and Court Rules

Finally, the analysis considered the extent to which juvenile courts in the sample counties were operating under legislation or court rules that mandated time frames for the disposition of delinquency cases. As of 1992, approximately half of the states in the country used some form of legislation or court rules to regulate delinquency case processing time in their juvenile courts (see Chapter 1). In 31 States, there were formal deadlines for holding adjudication hearings in delinquency cases. In 25 States, there were time limits for when juvenile court dispositional hearings must begin or be concluded. Some States regulated the timing of the juvenile court process for detained juveniles only. Others had timelines for both detained and non-detained cases.

A dichotomous measure was created to distinguish sample jurisdictions in which "minor" versus "major" time controls had been established as of 1992. The measure indicated whether statutes or State court rules had been implemented in 1992 to regulate the timing of 1) adjudications or 2) dispositions, for 3) detained cases or 4) non-detained cases. If more than two such provisions had been enacted, the jurisdiction was considered to have implemented "major" time controls.[15]

Of the sample jurisdictions, 107 (40%) were in States that had imposed "major" controls over the timing of delinquency case processing (table 5.6). Jurisdictions with major controls appeared to have smaller increases, or even decreases, in median case processing times between 1990 and 1994, while jurisdictions with only minor controls saw their case processing times increase.[16] Among jurisdictions with major controls, for example, the average median time to disposition for all formal delinquency cases was 60 days in 1994, compared with 72 days among jurisdictions with either no controls or only minor controls on case processing time. While jurisdictions with minor controls experienced an increase in their average median processing time between 1990 and 1994 (from 61 to 72 days), jurisdictions with major controls exhibited no increase during the same time period. For formally-handled, non-adjudicated cases, the average median of jurisdictions with minor controls increased from 69 days in 1990 to 84 days in 1994. Among jurisdictions with major controls, on the other hand, the average median for non-adjudicated cases decreased from 63 to 57 days in the same 5-year period.

When the analysis controlled for county population, the association between State controls and delinquency case processing time was less clear. Among midsize counties, for example, the association between State controls and average median disposition time was consistent, but changes in disposition time between 1990 and 1994 seemed to favor jurisdictions without major controls. Among large counties, differences in case processing times for adjudicated cases were opposite from what would be expected if State controls were actually effective in reducing delinquency case processing time.

Again, the lack of more detailed measures of regulatory efforts by the sample jurisdictions suggests caution in interpreting these patterns. At a minimum, however, the analysis indicates that the use of State court rules and legislation may be related to the overall timing of juvenile court case processing in some jurisdictions and for some types of delinquency cases. Additional analysis is needed to clarify the impact of statutory controls on juvenile court operations and the handling of individual cases.

TABLE 5.6
Average median disposition time in 1990 and 1994, by population, by State controls on case processing time as of 1992.

	State Controls on Processing Time	Counties	Average Median 1990	Average Median 1994	Percent Change
All Jurisdictions					
Total formal cases	Minor	n=160	61	72	18%
	Major	n=107	60	60	0
Non-adjudicated cases	Minor	n=157	69	84	22
	Major	n=105	63	57	-10
Adjudicated cases	Minor	n=160	61	72	18
	Major	n=106	61	65	7
Small Jurisdictions					
Total formal cases	Minor	n=49	47	70	49
	Major	n=52	50	41	-18
Non-adjudicated cases	Minor	n=49	59	83	41
	Major	n=51	56	38	-32
Adjudicated cases	Minor	n=49	58	69	19
	Major	n=51	52	48	-8
Midsize Jurisdictions					
Total formal cases	Minor	n=73	64	69	8
	Major	n=27	56	64	14
Non-adjudicated cases	Minor	n=70	70	77	10
	Major	n=27	52	58	12
Adjudicated cases	Minor	n=73	66	70	6
	Major	n=27	59	69	17
Large Jurisdictions					
Total formal cases	Minor	n=38	71	81	14
	Major	n=28	81	91	12
Non-adjudicated cases	Minor	n=38	80	98	23
	Major	n=27	86	92	7
Adjudicated cases	Minor	n=38	70	77	10
	Major	n=28	79	90	14

Note: Average median is the average of the median processing times of a group of counties. Comparison of time periods is restricted to 1990 and 1994 because data on State controls were available for 1992 only. See Table 5.3 for definition of county size.

Source: Data stored in the National Juvenile Court Data Archive, National Center for Juvenile Justice, Pittsburgh, Pennsylvania (see Table 5.1 notes).

CONCLUSION

The results of this study indicate that delinquency case processing time has increased in the past decade. Overall, the median disposition time for delinquency cases handled by the 267 jurisdictions in this study jumped 26% between 1985 and 1994, from 43 days to 54 days. Median disposition time for formally processed cases from large counties grew 20%, from 49 days to 59 days, while the median for small counties grew 21%, from 28 to 34 days. The largest relative increase in disposition time was for cases in midsize counties (those between 100,000 and 400,000 in total population). In these jurisdictions, the median disposition time climbed from 34 days in 1985 to 46 days in 1994, an increase of 35%.

The timing of juvenile court dispositions is at least partly related to the size of jurisdictions. After all, court delay is a bureaucratic phenomenon. Large jurisdictions with more burdensome caseloads are more likely than small jurisdictions to have problems with case processing delays. This study found that jurisdictions which experienced substantial increases in delinquency caseloads had far greater increases in disposition time. Caseload pressures, it would appear, do contribute to increased processing delays.

However, the study also suggests that there is considerable variation in case processing time after the population of a jurisdiction and changes in its juvenile court caseload are taken into account. Other factors that appear to be related to delay problems in juvenile courts include the severity of the offenses charged against juveniles in the court's caseload, the rate at which the court uses out-of-home placement and formal adjudication for delinquency cases, and the enactment of State statutes or court rules to control case processing time. Future research on juvenile court processing time should focus on clarifying the role these factors play in reducing or exacerbating delay.

Most importantly, the results of this study support the contention that juvenile court and criminal court processing times are far more similar than once believed. Delinquency cases handled by the Nation's juvenile courts often take as long to resolve as cases tried in the criminal courts. Moreover, many of the juvenile court disposition times analyzed in this study exceed even the most lenient time frames established during the past two decades by professional juvenile justice standards (see Chapter 1).

Clearly, delays in the juvenile justice system deserve the attention of researchers and policy makers who in the past have focused exclusively on delay in the adult courts. A decade ago, one researcher found that there was "essentially no literature on the delay of juvenile justice" (A.R. Mahoney, 1985:37). More recent reviews of the literature also found very few publications dealing with the timing of the juvenile court process (see Chapter 2). Barry Mahoney and his colleagues once acknowledged that researchers usually study civil and criminal court delays because delay problems have been more visible in trial courts. They noted, however, that "in terms of the human costs of protracted litigation, the impacts [of delay] may be greatest in some of the lower visibility courts such as those dealing with juvenile and domestic relations cases" (Mahoney et al., 1988:210). At the very least, this study provides even greater impetus for researchers to begin to explore the "human costs" of delay in the juvenile justice system.

Chapter 5 Notes

1. Some of the introductory material in this chapter was adapted from an article by the same author. See Butts, J.A. (1997, forthcoming). "Necessarily relative: Is juvenile justice speedy enough?" *Crime and Delinquency*, Vol. 43, No. 1.

2. Three jurisdictions were in both the NCJJ and NCSC studies (Allegheny County, Pennsylvania, Cuyahoga County, Ohio, and Maricopa County, Arizona). In two of these jurisdictions, the median disposition time for felony cases exceeded that of formally handled delinquency cases by just 5 and 11 days. In the third jurisdiction, the adult median was 61 days greater than the juvenile court median.

3. For a more complete description of the National Juvenile Court Data Archive and its contents, see any recent *Juvenile Court Statistics* report.

4. Portions of this section were adapted from Design Principles for Juvenile Court Information Systems, (Torbet et al., 1991).

5. Alaska, Arizona, Arkansas, California, Connecticut, DC, Florida, Hawaii, Idaho, Illinois, Iowa, Kansas, Minnesota, Missouri, Montana, New Jersey, Nevada, North Dakota, Ohio, Oklahoma, Pennsylvania, Rhode Island, South Dakota, Utah, Washington, West Virginia, Wisconsin, and Wyoming.

6. Delaware, New York, and South Carolina.

7. Alabama, Colorado, Georgia, Indiana, Kentucky, Louisiana, Maine, Maryland, Massachusetts, Michigan, Mississippi, Nebraska, New Hampshire, New Mexico, North Carolina, Oregon, Tennessee, Texas, Vermont, and Virginia.

8. These descriptions of case processing stages are adapted from *Juvenile Court Statistics* (Butts et al., 1996b).

9. This analysis excludes all cases which do not involve juvenile court adjudication hearings because a youth was transferred to criminal court instead. Criminal court transfers account for less than 1% of all cases referred to U.S. juvenile courts (Butts et al., 1996b).

10. In order to eliminate very small counties that handled only a few cases per year, jurisdictions under 20,000 in total population were deleted from the data file before analysis. The removal of these small counties reduced the study's initial database of delinquency cases by just 5%.

11. If fewer than 10% of the case records from any one jurisdiction contained errors in these two date fields, the erroneous records were deleted from the database. If 10% or more of the records contained date errors, the entire jurisdiction was removed from the database.

12. A youth may be placed in a detention facility at different points as a case progresses through the juvenile justice system. In this study, a case involving detention refers only to those instances in which a youth was placed in a restrictive facility under court authority while awaiting the outcome of the court process.

13. Detailed comparisons of the processing times of sample jurisdictions are based on formally petitioned cases only because the jurisdictions in the study were known to vary in the extent to which they relied on their juvenile courts to handle informal (i.e., less serious) delinquency matters. The treatment of formally petitioned delinquency cases was more consistently reported among the sample jurisdictions.

14. This method has been used before with data from the National Juvenile Court Data Archive to analyze the influence of poverty and race on juvenile justice decision making (Sampson and Laub, 1993).

15. This reflects the use of legislation and State court rules only. Local court rules may also be used to set case processing standards.

16. The comparison is restricted to the 5-year period from 1990 to 1994 because data on statutory controls were available for 1992 only.

Chapter 6
Implications and Conclusions

> Case processing time is not just a procedural or organizational issue. It has important implications for the theory of juvenile justice and the role of the court in creating change in troublesome youths. Given the importance of time in a child's life, court delay may have implications for juveniles that are both quantitatively and qualitatively different than its implications for adults (Anne Rankin Mahoney, 1985:54).

Speed has always been a critical ingredient in the efforts of the justice system to secure the safety of the community and protect the rights of the accused. In recent years, the speed of case processing has also become a concern in the juvenile justice system, particularly as the philosophy of juvenile justice has begun to reflect the adult system's emphasis on holding offenders accountable for their behavior by imposing sanctions that provide "just deserts." On the other hand, it could be argued that timeliness in case processing should be valued in the juvenile justice system regardless of philosophy. In order to achieve the multiple and diverse goals of the juvenile justice process, the system's response to delinquent youth should begin and conclude as quickly as possible, in keeping with established principles of fairness and due process.

Delays in the juvenile justice process may be particularly critical because adolescents are thought to experience the passage of time in an accelerated fashion and may fail to properly associate delayed dispositions with the delinquent behavior that prompted the court to act. Unwanted delays also increase the likelihood that an active delinquent may be charged with a new offense before the court has fully responded to the initial incident. Most importantly, the jurisdictional authority of the juvenile justice system is time-limited. Every day of delay means one less day available to prevent young offenders from becoming adult criminals.

CRITICAL MOMENTS

Delays can occur at any point in the juvenile justice process—from arrest, to referral, intake, adjudication, disposition, and sanctioning. Processing delays can be aggravated by the actions of police, court intake, probation agencies, courtroom staff, attorneys, judges, placement facilities, service providers, or virtually any individual or organization involved in the juvenile justice system. Jurisdictions seeking to control or reduce delays in juvenile justice should examine the efficiency of their case handling procedures at every step from arrest to final disposition.

In terms of the juvenile justice system's impact on the behavior of young offenders, one of the most critical delays in case processing may be the time between a youth's initial contact with law enforcement and his or her first appearance in court. Young (and especially inexperienced) offenders are often most amenable to court intervention during the time of uncertainty immediately following an arrest. The anxiety produced by the justice system is likely to be highest at first contact and then gradually diminish as the days of waiting turn into months. The overall impact of the process may be enhanced by scheduling a youth's first court appearance as soon as possible after arrest. Law enforcement agencies should recognize the special characteristics of adolescents and streamline their procedures to hasten initial court referrals in cases involving young offenders. Juvenile and family courts in general should be more attentive to the role of the first appearance.

Even if the legal goals of the first appearance are relatively trivial, officials may want to consider maximizing the bureaucratic formality of a juvenile's first court contact. Because the adult system is regularly portrayed in television dramas, many people know the difference between a bail hearing and sentencing. The juvenile court and its accompanying terminology, however, are largely unknown to the public. Juveniles and their families often do not completely comprehend the exact purposes of their numerous court appearances. A rapid first appearance with an imposing atmosphere might be a cost-effective method of enhancing the overall impact of the court process.

Another critical processing point in the juvenile justice system is the time between the decision to divert a youth for informal handling and the actual implementation of voluntary services or sanctions. Juvenile courts typically pay less attention to the efficiency of case processing in non-petitioned or unofficial cases because such cases are perceived to be less serious than formally charged cases. However, the young and first-time offenders that are typically handled informally by juvenile courts may be highly amenable to services and sanctions. The juvenile justice system should not waste the opportunity to influence the future behavior of young offenders simply because their current behavior does not yet appear serious when compared with other cases. Even when juveniles are to receive only minor supervision or make a single restitution payment, intake workers and court staff should make every effort to implement the case plan in a timely fashion.

Significant processing delays may also occur at the point of charging, when the prosecutor's office reviews a case and considers what charges to include in a formal allegation of delinquency. Investigatory and evidentiary tasks (e.g., lab tests in drug cases) may take several days or weeks to complete. Meanwhile, court action is postponed and the youth may nurture the hope that the juvenile justice system will have a minimal reaction to his or her offense. Prosecutors should ensure that such procedures are as streamlined as possible so that young offenders do not respond to the negative effects of delay.

Of course, the most time-consuming aspect of the juvenile justice process is the coordination and conduct of the various court hearings involved in delinquency matters—preliminary hearings, criminal court transfer hearings, detention, adjudication, disposition, and review hearings. In many jurisdictions, the scheduling of these hearings is at the heart of most delay problems. Because court hearings require the presence of multiple parties, simple calendaring problems often result in continuances and costly delays. Courts should make every attempt to simplify the scheduling of hearings. When sufficient resources are available, automated information systems should be employed to identify and resolve calendar conflicts.

An often-neglected choke point in the juvenile justice process is the time between a court's final disposition in a case and the implementation of services or sanctions. Post-dispositional delays can be very aggravating to those within the juvenile justice system. After weeks of interviews, investigations, and court hearings, it can be quite frustrating to reach a final disposition and then wait still longer for a youth to begin performing community service or be placed in a treatment facility. Delays following court disposition are often caused by the procedures of agencies external to the court. Reducing these delays, therefore, may require extra effort because the case handling preferences of several organizations must be accommodated. Any initiative to control unwanted delays in the juvenile justice system, however, should include a post-dispositional component.

REDUCING DELAY

Beyond everyday management efforts, the methods most commonly used to combat juvenile justice delays are: 1) statutes, 2) administrative rules, and 3) professional standards. Research on delay reduction programs indicates that the impact of statutes, rules, and standards may be limited if they are not supported by other efforts. However, they can help to establish an expectation throughout the juvenile justice system that delinquency cases should proceed as quickly as possible.

Court administrators may sometimes advocate the use of statutes and administrative rules rather than standards in the belief that the greater legal authority of statutes and rules will ensure timely case handling, especially if they include dismissal sanctions for cases not disposed within required deadlines. In addition, juvenile justice officials may prefer statutes and rules because they assume (or hope) that legislative enactment of case processing goals will be followed by the resources required to meet the requirements.

Voluntary standards, however, should continue to be an essential element in reducing unwanted juvenile justice delays. Nearly half of the States have no legislation or State court rules to regulate delinquency case processing time in their juvenile courts. Some of the States that do regulate delinquency case processing time do so only in cases involving detained juveniles. Thus, voluntary standards may be the only case processing goals that exist in many jurisdictions.

Formal case processing goals help to establish consensus about the level of performance expected of people working in the juvenile justice system. Voluntary guidelines and standards can establish this consensus just as effectively as statutes and rules, provided the entire organization and its leadership (especially the judiciary) are clearly committed to the goals.

Voluntary standards are also easier to implement than statutes and rules, since they derive their authority from consensus rather than the threat of legal sanctions. As with statutes and rules, standards help to express and reinforce a commitment to reducing unnecessary case delays, provide clear goals for case handling, and support the development of procedures for monitoring caseload status and tracking the progress of individual cases.

Juvenile Justice Standards

Several national organizations have developed standards for delinquency case processing. The development of these standards and guidelines reflects a growing awareness of the importance of juvenile court delay among legal professionals and policy makers. Of course, the impact of voluntary standards on actual case processing time may be limited. This is especially true if the time frames suggested by the standards are considerably faster than the pace at which many juvenile courts are able to process their delinquency caseloads.

According to this study, case processing time in many jurisdictions already exceeds the recommendations of existing professional standards. The median time between referral and disposition for petitioned delinquency cases currently exceeds 60 days in many jurisdictions. In the largest jurisdictions, nearly half of all formally petitioned cases have disposition times in excess of 90 days.

In order to be more useful and to achieve lasting reductions in unwanted case processing delays, professional standards for the juvenile justice system may need to be reconceptualized. For example, existing juvenile justice standards tend to focus on the total time between court referral (or arrest) and either adjudication or final disposition. Future case processing standards for the juvenile justice system should focus on each of the separate components of juvenile justice processing. In other words, there should be separate standards for intake, pre-trial hearings, adjudication, etc. To be comprehensive, standards should also include non-court activities (e.g., police processing and post-dispositional tasks).

In addition, many of the current standards (as well most statutes and court rules) are inflexible and simplistic. They often impose a single time goal, or at best they offer two goals, one for detained cases and one for youth released to await disposition. Future standards should be stated in terms of staged, cumulative targets. In other words, standards should call for a certain proportion of cases to be disposed within 30 days, another proportion to completed within 60 days, etc. This approach would allow for exceptions and encourage ongoing tracking of case processing time. In sum, any effort to develop new juvenile justice standards should focus on component-based standards, provide for graduated time goals, and apply to the entire system, both pre-referral and post-disposition.

Rather than issuing a single time target, case processing standards could be based upon a grid of discrete time goals (figure 6.1). For example, the standards might recommend that law enforcement agencies complete their screening of juvenile arrests and make court referrals within 7 days for 75% of all non-detained cases, and no more than 10 days in 98% of all non-detained cases. In cases involving detained juveniles, however, law enforcement agencies could be encouraged to complete 98% of court referrals within one day.

Although the hypothetical goals shown in Figure 6.1 are expressed individually for each of the various processing components, overall goals are suggested by the sum of all components. For example, in 75% of all cases involving formally handled, non-detained juveniles, the process of referral, intake, and charging should be completed in 21 days. All court hearings through the disposition should be completed within 24 days of charging. Thus, a court's overall target would be for 75% of all formally handled, non-detained cases to reach disposition within 45 days.

FIGURE 6.1
Fictitious example of comprehensive, component-based, graduated case processing time standards for juvenile justice agencies.

	Case Processing Time Goals		
Informal / Diverted Cases	**75% of all cases to be completed in…**	**90% of all cases to be completed in…**	**98% of all cases to be completed in…**
Police report and referral	7 days	8 days	10 days
Intake screening	7 days	14 days	15 days
Diversion plan/disposition	3 days	6 days	10 days
Implement disposition	4 days	7 days	25 days
Total days to implementation	21 days	35 days	60 days
Formal / Non-Detained Cases			
Police report and referral	7 days	8 days	10 days
Intake screening	7 days	14 days	15 days
Filing of charges	7 days	10 days	10 days
Pre-adjudicatory hearings	5 days	14 days	14 days
Adjudication	10 days	10 days	21 days
Disposition	9 days	14 days	20 days
Implement disposition	15 days	20 days	30 days
Total days to adjudication	36 days	56 days	70 days
Total days to disposition	45 days	70 days	90 days
Total days to implementation	60 days	90 days	120 days
Formal / Detained Cases			
Police report and referral	1 days	1 days	1 days
Intake screening	1 days	1 days	1 days
Filing of charges	3 days	7 days	10 days
Pre-adjudicatory hearings	3 days	5 days	7 days
Adjudication	7 days	21 days	30 days
Disposition	5 days	10 days	21 days
Implement disposition	10 days	45 days	50 days
Total days to adjudication	15 days	35 days	49 days
Total days to disposition	20 days	45 days	70 days
Total days to implementation	30 days	90 days	120 days

The Federal Role

Whatever their exact configuration, juvenile justice standards should be developed at the State and local level rather than being imposed from the Federal level. A Federal agency such as OJJDP could provide guidelines for local agencies on how to fill in a grid of standards such as the one shown in Figure 6.1, but the development of the case processing goals themselves should reflect each jurisdiction's local priorities and conditions.

Practice Orientation

A new approach is needed for evaluating the efficiency of delinquency case processing. This new approach should be developed in an organizationally-sensitive and empirically-based fashion, and should be rooted in detailed analyses of court practices rather than an idealized and possibly unrealistic vision of how courts *should* operate. As Anne Rankin Mahoney advised, the application of time standards in the juvenile justice system should be informed by an intimate understanding of the juvenile court and its unique task environment:

> Before standards for juvenile cases are widely adopted, issues of time in juvenile court should be considered carefully and data collected on the extent to which delay occurs in juvenile justice systems. Time may have a different meaning in juvenile courts than it does in adult courts, and an uncritical application of time standards and delay reduction procedures to juvenile courts may be inappropriate (Mahoney, 1985:37).

The development of guidelines for delinquency case processing—whether mandatory or voluntary—should begin with an awareness of what constitutes effective juvenile court practice. Rather than starting out with an arbitrary goal of reaching all dispositions in 90 or 120 days, courts should first determine how much time is actually required for a quality intake procedure, how much for a thorough preliminary hearing, how much for an adjudicatory hearing, etc. These various time requirements (and the resource requirements they suggest) could then be compiled into a comprehensive body of case processing guidelines. Such a process would be similar to the method used to develop the "resource guidelines" for juvenile court handling of child abuse and neglect cases recently published by the National Council of Juvenile and Family Court Judges (1995). State and federal policy makers should consider funding projects to develop similar "model systems" for delinquency case processing.

Caseflow Management

No matter how well designed they may be, statutes, rules, and standards will never be able to eliminate all unwanted delays in the juvenile court's handling of delinquency cases. In order to control delay, it is necessary to confront the organizational arrangements that often perpetuate delay. The research literature supports an organizational approach to delay reduction (see Chapter 2). The "bread and butter" of any organizational effort to control delay is the re-engineering of court operations through an effective caseflow management system.

Since the 1970s, court administrators and researchers have come to believe that an aggressive caseflow management system is the best method of reversing the political, bureaucratic, and personal incentives that are often conducive to delay problems. Caseflow management encourages the juvenile justice system to control delay not with rules and sanctions but with the active oversight of each case using direct and frequent consultation between court managers, judges, and the bar.

> The court... must make necessary organizational adjustments related to delays, in cooperation with court and agency staff. The court must design explicit processes to ensure timely hearings and must make sure they are implemented by all judges and administrative staff (National Council of Juvenile and Family Court Judges, 1995:20).

The American Bar Association once described some of the essential characteristics of effective caseflow management systems (Solomon and Somerlot, 1987:7–31):

- To succeed, a caseflow management system must have the commitment and leadership of judges, especially the chief or presiding judge.
- Caseflow management systems should be developed and implemented with active participation from the bar.
- Caseflow management systems should ensure that the court plays an early and active role in managing the progress of each case to the point of disposition.
- Courts must establish control over the use of continuances, with clear policies for when hearings may be postponed. Dates for hearings should be clearly stated and credible, and the caseflow management system should ensure that they occur with certainty.
- Caseflow management systems should incorporate several types of standards: 1) "overall time" standards related to case disposition, 2) "intermediate time" standards controlling the time between major case events, and 3) "system management" standards related to issues such as continuances.
- Caseflow management should be backed up by an information system capable of tracking individual case progress and providing regular measurement of performance.

Most of the issues involved in juvenile court caseflow management would be similar to the issues faced by criminal and civil courts. Thus, the American Bar Association's recommendations for effective caseflow management are applicable as well to the juvenile justice system.

However, caseflow management in the juvenile court must also contend with the unique characteristics of adolescent offenders and the juvenile court process. As mentioned earlier in this study, for example, juvenile courts may find it helpful to "track" delinquency cases according to the goals of intervention rather than simply case complexity as in the criminal courts. Instead of reserving an accelerated case processing track only for detained youth or those charged with serious offenses, juvenile courts may also want to devise a rapid processing track for young, first-time offenders. The goal of caseflow management in these less serious cases would be not only a speedy disposition, but also an immediate first appearance before a judge or magistrate.

Treatment-oriented case tracking is only one issue which suggests that caseflow management systems should be designed especially for the juvenile court. To date, most of the research development efforts in caseflow management have completely ignored the juvenile justice system. Rather than simply importing conventional management technologies into a juvenile justice environment, policy makers, administrators, and researchers should begin to collaborate in designing caseflow management systems that are more suitable for the juvenile court and more attuned to the special needs of the adolescent offenders involved in the juvenile justice system.

CONCLUSION

Juvenile justice professionals have been aware of the importance of delinquency case processing time for several decades. During the 1970s and 1980s, several national associations and government commissions issued time standards for juvenile court proceedings. State and local governments have also tried to establish guidelines for delinquency case processing time. About half of the States have implemented at least some statutory time limits on the handling of delinquency cases. Other States have attempted to use court rules to designate the maximum delay permitted in delinquency cases.

Federal policy makers have also called on the juvenile justice system to handle young offenders with greater efficiency. In 1993 the U.S. Department of Justice's Office of Juvenile Justice and Delinquency Prevention issued a "comprehensive strategy" for dealing with serious, violent, and chronic juvenile offenders. One of the founding principles of this strategy was the use of "immediate interventions" that attempt to correct delinquent behavior as soon as possible and thereby prevent juveniles from becoming even further involved with the juvenile justice system (Wilson and Howell, 1993:19).

Compared with other aspects of juvenile justice policy, however, processing delays have not been a very prominent concern among researchers, practitioners, or elected officials. Very few studies have even considered the causes and consequences of delayed delinquency cases, and virtually no literature exists on the relative effectiveness of various delay reduction techniques. This study is offered as a beginning. The purpose of the study was to generate a foundation of information and analysis that would inform future debates about the effectiveness of the juvenile court and increase awareness of the role of case processing time in the court's efforts to reduce the social impacts of juvenile crime. It is hoped that the results of this study will provide a starting point for future efforts to address the problem of delays in the juvenile justice system.

REFERENCES

Aldrich, Howard E.
1979 *Organizations and Environments*. Englewood Cliffs, NJ: Prentice-Hall.

Aldrich, Howard E., and Jeffrey Pfeffer
1976 Environments of organizations. *Annual Review of Sociology 2*:79–105.

Banfield, Laura, and C.D. Anderson
1968 Continuances in Cook County criminal courts. *University of Chicago Law Review 35*:256.

Bernard, Thomas J.
1992 *The Cycle of Juvenile Justice*. New York, NY: Oxford University Press.

Berzensky, M.D.
1978 Formal reasoning in adolescence: An alternative view. *Adolescence 13*:279–290.

Blumberg, Abraham S.
1967 *Criminal Justice*. Chicago, IL: Quadrangle Books.

Bortner, M.A.
1982 Inside a Juvenile Court: The Tarnished Ideal of Individualized Justice. New York, NY: New York University Press.

Bridges, G.S.
1982 The Speedy Trial Act of 1974: Effects on delays in federal criminal litigation. *Journal of Criminal Law & Criminology 73*:50–73.

Burgess, Carol A.
1982 Recidivism of Juvenile Burglars: A Perceptual View of Specific Deterrence. Tucson, AZ: University of Arizona, Doctoral Dissertation.

Burgess, Carol, and William McCarthy
1984 *Court Calendaring Goals: 1983 Case Processing*. Phoenix: Maricopa County Juvenile Court Center.

Bureau of Justice Assistance
1993 *Differentiated Case Management: Program Brief*. Washington, DC: Bureau of Justice Assistance, U.S. Department of Justice.

Butts, Jeffrey A.
1996a *Offenders in Juvenile Court, 1993* (Update on Statistics). Washington, D.C.: Office of Juvenile Justice and Delinquency Prevention, U.S. Department of Justice.

Butts, Jeffrey A.
1996b Speedy trial in the juvenile court. *American Journal of Criminal Law 23*(3)515–560.

Butts, Jeffrey A.
1997 (forthcoming) Necessarily relative: Is juvenile justice speedy enough? *Crime & Delinquency 43*(1).

Butts, Jeffrey, and Richard Gable
1992 *Juvenile Detention in Cook County and the Feasibility of Alternatives.* Pittsburgh, PA: National Center for Juvenile Justice.

Butts, Jeffrey A., and Gregory J. Halemba
1994 Delays in juvenile justice: Findings from a national survey. *Juvenile & Family Court Journal 45*(4):31–46.

Butts, Jeffrey A., Howard N. Snyder, Terrence A. Finnegan, Anne L. Aughenbaugh, Nancy J. Tierney, Dennis Sullivan, Rowen S. Poole, Melissa H. Sickmund, and Eileen C. Poe
1994 *Juvenile Court Statistics 1991.* Washington, D.C.: Office of Juvenile Justice and Delinquency Prevention, U.S. Department of Justice.

Butts, Jeffrey A., Howard N. Snyder, Terrence A. Finnegan, Anne L. Aughenbaugh, Nancy J. Tierney, Dennis Sullivan, and Rowen S. Poole
1995 *Juvenile Court Statistics 1992.* Washington, D.C.: Office of Juvenile Justice and Delinquency Prevention, U.S. Department of Justice.

Butts, Jeffrey A., Howard N. Snyder, Terrence A. Finnegan, Anne L. Aughenbaugh, and Rowen S. Poole
1996a *Juvenile Court Statistics 1993.* Washington, D.C.: Office of Juvenile Justice and Delinquency Prevention, U.S. Department of Justice.

Butts, Jeffrey A., Howard N. Snyder, Terrence A. Finnegan, Anne L. Aughenbaugh, and Rowen S. Poole
1996b (forthcoming) *Juvenile Court Statistics 1994.* Washington, D.C.: Office of Juvenile Justice and Delinquency Prevention, U.S. Department of Justice.

Campbell, W.J.
1973 Delays in criminal cases: Before the Conference of Metropolitan Chief Judges of the Federal Judicial Center. *Federal Rules Decisions 55*:230.

Cannavale, Frank J., and William D. Falcon
1976 *Witness Cooperation.* Lexington, MA: Lexington Books.

Carter Goble and Associates, Inc.
1989 *State of Hawaii Judicial System: An Operational Analysis of the First Circuit Family Court.* Author.

Chinn Planning Partnership
1994 *Continuum of Detention Services Plan.* Cleveland, OH: Author.

Chapper, Joy A., and Roger A. Hanson
1988 Taking the delay out of criminal appeals - Three jurisdictions take three different approaches. *Judges' Journal 27*:7–9, 44–47.

Church, Thomas W. Jr.
1981 Who sets the pace of litigation in urban trial courts? *Judicature 65*:76–85.

Church, Thomas W. Jr.
1982 The "old and the new" conventional wisdom of court delay. *Justice System Journal 7*:395–412.

Church, Thomas Jr. et al.
1978 *Justice Delayed: The Pace of Litigation in Urban Trial Courts.* Williamsburg, VA: The National Center for State Courts.

Church, Thomas W. Jr, and Milton Heumann
1992 *Speedy Disposition: Monetary Incentives and Policy Reform in Criminal Courts*. Albany, NY: State University of New York Press.

Chused, Richard H.
1973 The juvenile court process: A study of three New Jersey counties. *Rutgers Law Review*, *26*:488.

Choper, Jesse H.
1984 Consequences of Supreme Court decisions upholding individual constitutional rights. *Michigan Law Review 83*:1.

Clarke, D.S., and J.H. Merryman
1976 Measuring the duration of judicial and administrative proceedings. *Michigan Law Review 75*:100–105.

Dale, Michael J.
1992 The 1992 survey of Florida law. *Nova Law Review 17*:335.

Doyle, John F.
1978 Comparing court productivity. *Judicature 61*:416–421.

Eisenstein, James, and Herbert Jacob
1977 *Felony Justice: An Organizational Analysis of Criminal Courts*. Boston: Little, Brown & Co.

Elkind, David
1966 Conceptual orientation shifts in childhood and adolescence. *Child Development 37*: 493–498.

Emery, F.E. and E.L. Trist
1965 The causal texture of organizational environments. *Human Relations 18*:21–31.

Feeley, Malcolm M.
1983 *Court Reform on Trial: Why Simple Solutions Fail*. New York, NY: Basic Books.

Feeley, Malcolm M.
1992 *The Process is the Punishment: Handling Cases in a Lower Criminal Court*. New York: Sage.

Feld, Barry C.
1991 Justice by geography: Urban, suburban, and rural variations in juvenile justice administration. *Journal of Criminal Law & Criminology 82*: 156–210.

Feld, Barry C.
1993a Juvenile (in)justice and the criminal court alternative. *Crime and Delinquency 39*:403–424.

Feld, Barry C.
1993b *Justice for Children: The Right to Counsel and the Juvenile Courts*. Boston: Northeastern University Press.

Flanders, Steven
1977 *Case Management and Court Management in United States District Courts*. Washington, D.C.: Federal Judicial Center.

Flanders, Steven
1978 Case management in federal courts: Some controversies and some results. *The Justice System Journal 4*:147–165.

Flanders, Steven
1980 Modeling court delay. *Law & Policy Quarterly 2*:305–320.

Fleming, Macklin
1973 The law's delay: The dragon slain Friday breathes fire again Monday. *Public Interest 32*:13–33.

Flicker, Barbara D.
1982 *Standards for Juvenile Justice: A Summary and Analysis, 2nd edition.* Cambridge, MA: Ballinger Publishing Company.

Foschio, Leslie G.
1973 Empirical research and the problem of court delay. In *Reducing Court Delay*. Washington, D.C.: National Institute of Law Enforcement and Criminal Justice, Law Enforcement Assistance Administration, U.S. Department of Justice.

Frank, J.P.
1969 *American Law: The Case for Radical Reform.* New York, NY: Macmillan Company.

Frase, Richard S.
1976 Speedy Trial Act of 1974. *University of Chicago Law Review 43*:667–723.

Galanter, Marc
1974 Why the 'haves' come out ahead: Speculations on the limits of legal change. *Law & Society Review 9*:95.

Gallagher, J.M., and I.C. Moppe
1976 Cognitive development and learning. In J. F. Adams (Ed.), *Understanding Adolescence*. 3rd Edition. Boston, MA: Allyn and Bacon.

Garner, Joel H.
1987 Delay reduction in the federal courts: Rule 50(b) and the Federal Speedy Trial Act of 1974. *Journal of Quantitative Criminology 3*:229–250.

Gillespie, Robert W.
1977 *Judicial Productivity and Court Delay: An Exploratory Analysis of the Federal District Courts.* Washington, D.C.: National Institute of Law Enforcement and Criminal Justice, Law Enforcement Assistance Administration, U.S. Department of Justice.

Goerdt, John, Chris Lomvardias, Geoff Gallas, and Barry Mahoney
1989 *Examining Court Delay: The Pace of Litigation in 26 Urban Trial Courts, 1987.* Williamsburg, VA: National Center for State Courts.

Good, Dale W.
1980 Court reform: Do critics understand the issues? *Judicature 63*:365–375.

Gordon, Simeon E.
1978 Measurement of court delay. *Justice System Journal 3*:322–327.

Graham, Richard T., and John Howley
1992 Cuyahoga County develops more efficient case management system. *Juvenile Justice Digest 20*, 6.

Grau, Charles W., and Arlene Sheskin
1982 Ruling out delay: The impact of Ohio's rules of superintendence. *Judicature 66*:109–121.

Grisso, Thomas
1996 Society's retributive response to juvenile violence: A developmental perspective. *Law and Human Behavior 20*: 229–247.

Grossman, Joel B., Herbert M. Kritzer, Kristin Bumiller, and Stephen McDougal
1981 Measuring the pace of civil litigation in federal and state courts. *Judicature 65*:86–113.

Hagan, John, and Marjorie S. Zatz
1985 The social organization of criminal justice processing: An event-history analysis. *Social Science Research 14*:103–125.

Hamel, Cherstin M.
1994 *Cuyahoga County Court of Common Pleas, Juvenile Division: Case Management Review—Final Report.* Columbus, OH: Supreme Court of Ohio.

Hausner, Jack, and Michael Seidel
1979 *An Analysis of Case Processing Time in the District of Columbia Superior Court.* Washington, D.C.: Institute for Law Social Research.

Haynes, H. Paul
1973 Reducing court delay. *In Reducing Court Delay.* Washington, D.C.: National Institute of Law Enforcement and Criminal Justice, Law Enforcement Assistance Administration, U.S. Department of Justice.

Heumann, Milton
1978 *Plea Bargaining: The Experiences of Prosecutors, Judges, and Defense Attorneys.* Chicago, IL: University of Chicago Press.

Heumann, Milton, and Thomas W. Church
1990 Criminal justice reform, monetary incentives, and policy evaluation. *Law & Policy 12*:81–102.

Hewitt, William E., Geoff Gallas, and Barry Mahoney
1990 *Courts That Succeed: Six Profiles of Successful Courts.* Williamsburg, VA: National Center for State Courts.

Holten, N. Gary, and Lawson L. Lamar
1991 *The Criminal Courts: Structures, Personnel, and Processes.* New York, NY: McGraw-Hill.

Inhelder, Barbara, and Jean Piaget
1958 *The Growth of Logical Thinking From Childhood to Adolescence.* New York, NY: Basic Books.

IJA/ABA, Institute of Judicial Administration-American Bar Association
1980a Standards relating to interim status. In *Juvenile Justice Standards Series.* Cambridge, MA: Author.

IJA/ABA, Institute of Judicial Administration-American Bar Association
1980b Standards relating to pretrial court procecures. In *Juvenile Justice Standards Series*. Cambridge, MA: Author.

IJA/ABA, Institute of Judicial Administration-American Bar Association
1980c Standards relating to court organization and administration. In *Juvenile Justice Standards Series*. Cambridge, MA: Author.

Jacob, Herbert
1983 Courts as organizations. In Keith O. Boyum, and Lynn Mather (Eds.), *Empirical Theories About Courts*. New York, NY: Longman, Inc.

Katz, L.R., L.P. Litwin, and R.H. Bamberger
1972 *Justice is the Crime: Pretrial Delay in Felony Cases*. Cleveland, OH: Case Western Reserve University Press.

Lawyers Conference Task Force on Reduction of Litigation Cost and Delay
1986 *Defeating Delay: Developing and Implementing a Court Delay Reduction Program*. Chicago, IL: American Bar Association.

Lemert, Edwin M.
1967 Legislating change in the juvenile court. *Wisconsin Law Review* 421.

Levin, A. Leo, and E.W. Woolley
1961 *Dispatch and Delay: A Field Study of Judicial Administration in Pennsylvania*. Philadelphia, PA: Institute of Legal Research, University of Pennsylvania Law School.

Levin, Martin A.
1975 Delay in five criminal courts. *Journal of Legal Studies 4*:83–131.

Luskin, Mary Lee
1978 Building a theory of case processing time. *Judicature 62*:115–127.

Luskin, Mary Lee, and Robert C. Luskin
1986 Why so fast, why so slow?: Explaining case processing time. *Journal of Criminal Law & Criminology 77*:190–214.

Luskin, Mary Lee, and Robert C. Luskin
1987 Case processing times in three courts. *Law & Policy 9*:207–232.

Mahoney, Anne Rankin
1985 Time and process in juvenile court. *The Justice System Journal 10*:37–55.

Mahoney, Anne Rankin
1987 *Juvenile Justice in Context*. Boston, MA: Northeastern University Press.

Mahoney, Barry et al.
1988 *Changing Times in Trial Courts: Caseflow Management and Delay Reduction in Urban Trial Courts*. Williamsburg, VA: National Center for State Courts.

March, James G., and Herbert A. Simon
1958 *Organizations*. New York, NY: John Wiley and Sons, Inc.

Marvell, Thomas B., and Mary Lee Luskin
1991 Impact of speedy trial laws in Connecticut and North Carolina. *Justice System Journal 14*:343–357.

Mather, Lynn M.
1979 *Plea Bargaining or Trial? The Process of Criminal Case Disposition.* Lexington, MA: Lexington.

Mayo, Elton
1949 *The Social Problems of an Industrial Civilization.* Boston, MA: Harvard University, Graduate School of Business Administration.

Mays, G. Larry, and William A. Taggart
1986 Court delay: Policy implications for court managers. *Criminal Justice Policy Review 1*:198–210.

McCarthy, Francis Barry
1994 The serious offender and juvenile court reform: The case for prosecutorial waiver of juvenile court jurisdiction. *Saint Louis University Law Journal 38*:629–671.

McGarrell, Edmund F.
1993 Trends in racial disproportionality in juvenile court processing: 1985–1989. *Crime and Delinquency 39*(1):29–48.

Meyer, John W., and Brian Rowan
1977 Institutionalized organizations: Formal structure as myth and ceremony. *American Journal of Sociology 83*(2):440–463.

Miller, R.S.
1966 A program for the elimination of the hardships of litigation delay. *Ohio State Law Journal 27*:406.

Misner, R.
1979 Delay, docmentation and the Speedy Trial Act. *Journal of Criminal Law and Criminology 70*:214–234.

Mohr, Lawrence B.
1976 Organizations, decisions and courts. *Law and Society Review 10*:621–642.

Morse, Wayne L., and Ronald H. Beattie
1932 Survey of the Administration of Criminal Justice in Oregon. *Oregon Law Review 11.*

Nagel, Stuart, Marian Neef, and Nancy Munshaw
1978 Bringing management science to the courts to reduce delay. *Judicature 62*:128–143.

National Conference of State Trial Judges
1985 *Standards Relating to Court Delay Reduction.* Chicago, IL: American Bar Association.

National Council of Juvenile and Family Court Judges
1995 *Resource Guidelines: Improving Court Practice in Child Abuse & Neglect Cases.* Reno, NV: Author.

Neubauer, David W.
1974 *Criminal Justice in Middle America.* Morristown, NJ: General Learning Press.

Neubauer, David W., and John Paul Ryan
1982 Criminal courts and the delivery of speedy justice: the influence of case and defendant characteristics. *The Justice System Journal 7*:213–235.

Neubauer, David W. et al.
1981 *Managing the Pace of Justice: An Evaluation of LEAA's Court Delay Reduction Program.* Washington, D.C.: National Institute of Justice, U.S. Department of Justice.

Nimmer, Raymond
1976 A slightly moveable object: A case study in judicial reform in the criminal justice process: The omnibus hearing. *The Denver Law Journal 48*:206–230.

OJJDP, Office of Juvenile Justice and Delinquency Prevention
1980 *Standards for the Administration of Juvenile Justice: Report of the National Advisory Committee for Juvenile Justice and Delinquency Prevention.* Washington, D.C.: Office of Juvenile Justice and Delinquency Prevention, U.S. Department of Justice.

Packer, Herbert L.
1968 *The Limits of the Criminal Sanction.* Stanford, CA: Stanford University Press.

Partridge, A.J.
1980 *Legislative History of Title I of the Speedy Trial Act of 1974.* Washington, DC: Federal Judicial Center.

Pfeffer, Jeffrey, and Gerald R. Salancik
1978 *The External Control of Organizations.* New York, NY: Harper & Row.

Piaget, Jean
1971 The theory of stages in cognitive development. In D. Green (Ed.), *Measurement and Piaget.* New York, NY: McGraw-Hill.

Piaget, Jean
1972 Intellectual evolution from adolescence to adulthood. *Human Development 15*:1012.

Piaget, Jean, and Barbara Inhelder
1969 *The Psychology of the Child.* New York, NY: Basic Books.

Posner, Richard A.
1973 An economic approach to legal procedure and judicial administration. *Journal of Legal Studies 2*:399–458.

Pound, Roscoe, and Felix Frankfurter
1922 *Criminal Justice in Cleveland: Reports of the Cleveland Foundation Survey of the Administration of Criminal Justice in Cleveland, Ohio.* Cleveland, OH: The Cleveland Foundation (reprinted in 1968 by Patterson Smith, Montclair, NJ.).

President's Commission on Law Enforcement and Administration of Justice
1967 *Task Force Report: The Courts.* Washington, D.C.: Author.

Raine, J.W., and M.J. Wilson
1993 Organizational culture and the scheduling of court appearances. *Journal of Law and Society 20*:237–255.

Rhodes, W.M.
1976 The economics of criminal courts: A theoretical and empirical investigation. *Journal of Legal Studies 5*:319–320.

Roethlisberger, F.J., and William J. Dickson
1939 *Management and the Worker*. Cambridge, MA: Harvard University Press.

Rosenberg, Maurice
1965 Court congestion: Status, causes and proposed remedies. In Harry Jones (Ed.), *The Courts, the Public, and the Law Explosion*. Englewood Cliffs, NJ: Prentice-Hall.

Rosenberg, Maurice, and Michael I. Sovern
1959 Delay and the dynamics of personal injury litigation. *Columbia Law Review 59*:1115–1189.

Rosett, Arthur, and Donald R. Cressey
1976 *Justice by Consent: Bargains in the American Courthouse*. Philadelphia, PA: Lippincott.

Rothman, David J.
1980 *Conscience and Convenience: The Asylum and its Alternatives in Progressive America*. Glenview, IL: Scott, Foresman and Company.

Rubin, H. Ted
1991 *Baltimore City Juvenile Court: A Review of Organization and Process*. Denver, CO: Institute for Court Management of the National Center for State Courts.

Ryan, John Paul
1978 Management science in the real world of courts. *Judicature 62*:144–146.

Ryan, John Paul, Marcia J. Lipetz, Mary Lee Luskin, and David W. Neubauer
1981 Analyzing court delay-reduction programs: Why do some succeed? *Judicature 65*:58–75.

Saari, David
1982 *American Court Management*. Westport, CT: Quorum Books.

Sampson, Robert J., and John H. Laub
1993 Structural variations in juvenile court processing: Inequality, the underclass, and social control. *Law and Society Review 27*(2):285–311.

Sanborn, Joseph B. Jr.
1993 The right to a public jury trial: A need for today's juvenile court. *Judicature 76*:230–238.

Sarat, Austin
1978 Understanding trial courts: A critique of social science approaches. *Judicature 61*:318-326.

Shine, James, and Dwight Price
1992 Prosecutors and juvenile justice: New roles and perspectives. In I.M. Schwartz (Ed.), *Juvenile Justice and Public Policy: Toward a National Agenda*. New York, NY: Lexington Books.

Skolnick, Jerome H.
1967 Social control in the adversary system. *Journal of Conflict Resolution 11*:52.

Snyder, Howard N.
1988 *Court Careers of Juvenile Offenders.* Pittsburgh, PA: National Center for Juvenile Justice.

Snyder, Howard N., Terrence A. Finnegan, Ellen H. Nimick, Melissa Sickmund, Dennis P. Sullivan, and Nancy J. Tierney
1990a *Juvenile Court Statistics 1986.* Washington, D.C.: Office of Juvenile Justice and Delinquency Prevention, U.S. Department of Justice.

Snyder, Howard N., Terrence A. Finnegan, Ellen H. Nimick, Melissa Sickmund, Dennis P. Sullivan, and Nancy J. Tierney
1990b *Juvenile Court Statistics 1987.* Washington, D.C.: Office of Juvenile Justice and Delinquency Prevention, U.S. Department of Justice.

Snyder, Howard N., Terrence A. Finnegan, Ellen H. Nimick, Melissa Sickmund, Dennis P. Sullivan, and Nancy J. Tierney
1990c *Juvenile Court Statistics 1988.* Washington, D.C.: Office of Juvenile Justice and Delinquency Prevention, U.S. Department of Justice.

Snyder, Howard N., Melissa Sickmund, Ellen H. Nimick, Terrence A. Finnegan, Dennis P. Sullivan, Rowen S. Poole, and Nancy J. Tierney
1992 *Juvenile Court Statistics 1989.* Washington, D.C.: Office of Juvenile Justice and Delinquency Prevention, U.S. Department of Justice.

Snyder, Howard N., Jeffrey A. Butts, Terrence A. Finnegan, Ellen H. Nimick, Nancy J. Tierney, Dennis P. Sullivan, Rowen S. Poole, and Melissa H. Sickmund
1993 *Juvenile Court Statistics 1990.* Washington, D.C.: Office of Juvenile Justice and Delinquency Prevention, U.S. Department of Justice.

Snyder, Howard, and Melissa Sickmund
1995 *Juvenile Offenders and Victims: A National Report.* Washington, DC: Office of Juvenile Justice and Delinquency Prevention, U.S. Department of Justice.

Snyder, Howard, Melissa Sickmund, and Eileen Poe-Yamagata
1996 *Juvenile Offenders and Victims: 1996 Update on Violence.* Washington, DC: Office of Juvenile Justice and Delinquency Prevention, U.S. Department of Justice.

Solomon, Maureen, and Douglas K. Somerlot
1987 *Caseflow Management in the Trial Court: Now and for the Future.* Chicago, IL: Lawyers Conference Task Force on Reduction of Litigation Cost and Delay, Judicial Administration Division, American Bar Association.

Swigert, Victoria Lynn, and Ronald A. Farrell
1980 Speedy Trial and the legal process. *Law and Human Behavior 4*:135–145.

Szymanski, Linda A.
1990 *Courts Exercising Family Court Jurisdiction.* Pittsburgh, PA: National Center for Juvenile Justice.

Szymanski, Linda A.
1993 *Juvenile's Right to a Jury Trial in a Delinquency Hearing* (1992 Update). Pittsburgh, PA: National Center for Juvenile Justice.

Szymanski, Linda A.
1994 *Juvenile Court Case Processing Time: A Statute, Court Rule, and Case Law Analysis.* Pittsburgh, PA: National Center for Juvenile Justice.

Taylor, Frederick W.
1911 *Principles of Scientific Management.* New York, NY: Harper.

Torbet, Patricia M.
1990 *Organization and Administration of Juvenile Services: Probation, Aftercare and Delinquent Institutions.* Pittsburgh, PA: National Center for Juvenile Justice.

Torbet, Patricia M. et al.
1991 *Design Principles for Juvenile Court Information Systems.* Pittsburgh, PA: National Center for Juvenile Justice.

Trist, E.L., and K.W. Bamforth
1951 Some social and psychological consequences of the longwall method of coal-getting. *Human Relations 4*:3–38.

Trotter, Joseph A., Jr., and Caroline S. Cooper
1982 State trial court delay: Efforts at reform. *American University Law Review 31*:213–236.

Wice, Paul
1978 *Criminal Lawyers; An Endangered Species.* Beverly Hills, CA: Sage Publications.

Wildhorn, Sorrel et al.
1977 *Indicators of Justice.* Lexington, MA: Lexington Books.

Wilson, Charles H. Jr
1972 Delay and congestion in the criminal courts. *Florida Bar Association Journal 46*:88–92.

Wilson, John J., and James C. Howell
1993 *Comprehensive Strategy for Serious, Violent, and Chronic Juvenile Offenders: Program Summary.* Washington, D.C.: Office of Juvenile Justice and Delinquency Prevention, U.S. Department of Justice.

Zatz, Marjorie S.
1982 Dynamic modeling of criminal processing histories. In John Hagan (Ed.), *Quantitative Criminology: Innovations and Applications.* Beverly Hills, CA: Sage Publications.

Zatz, Marjorie S., and Alan J. Lizotte
1985 The timing of court processing: Towards linking theory and method. *Criminology 23*:313–335.

Zeisel, Hans, Harry Kalven, and Bernard Buchholz
1959 *Delay in the Court.* Boston, MA: Little, Brown.

Zimring, Franklin E.
1991 The treatment of hard cases in American juvenile justice: In defense of discretionary waiver. *Notre Dame Journal of Law, Ethics & Public Policy 5*:267–280.

CASES CITED

Arkansas v. McCann, 853, S.W. 2d, 886 (1993).

Barker v. Wingo, 407 U.S. 514 (1972).

D.A.L. v. Florida, 456 So.2d 1333 (1984).

E.R. v. Florida, 617 So.2d 1149 (1993).

Hedgepeth v. U.S., 365 F.2d 952 (1966).

Illinois v. A.J., T.M., L.R. and J.R., 135 Ill.App.3d 494, 481 N.E.2d 1060 (1985).

Illinois v. M.A., 132 Ill.App.3d 444, 477 N.E.2d 27 (1985).

In re Eric C., 124 N.H. 222, 469 A.2d 1305 (1983).

In re Gault, 387 U.S. 1, 87 S.Ct. 1428 (1967).

In re Juan V., 160 A.D.2d 303, 553 N.Y.S.2d 397 (1990).

In re Winship, 397 U.S. 358, 90 S.Ct. 1068 (1970).

In the Interest of M.A., 483 So.2d 511 (1986).

In the Interest of T.K., 731 P.2d 887, 11 Kan.App.2d 632 (1987).

In the Matter of J.D.P., 410 N.W.2d 1 (1987).

In the Matter of James H., 597 N.Y.S.2d 53 (1993).

In the Matter of Jessie C., 154 Misc.2d 103, 583 N.Y.S.2d 1011 (1992).

In the Matter of Jose R., 598 N.Y.S.2d 243 (1993).

In the Matter of J.V., 127 Misc.2d 780, 487 N.Y.S.2d 304 (1985).

In the Matter of Lydell J. and Taseem D., 154 Misc.2d 94, 583 N.Y.S.2d 1007 (1992).

In the Matter of Nicole D., 154 Misc.2d 378, 584 N.Y.S.2d 403 (1992).

In the Matter of Oranchank, 120 Misc.2d 319, 466 N.Y.S.2d 172 (1983).

In the Matter of Robert S., 152 Misc.2d 975, 579 N.Y.S.2d 851 (1991).

In the Matter of Shannon FF, 189 A.D.2d 420, 596 N.Y.S.2d 219 (1993).

In the Matter of Steven C., 129 Misc.2d 946, 494 N.Y.S.2d 658 (1985).

J.J.S. v. Florida, 440 So.2d 465 (1983).

J.T. v. Florida, 601 So.2d 283 (1992).

Kent v. United States, 383 U.S. 541 (1966).

Klopfer v. North Carolina, 386 U.S. 213, 223 (1967).

McKeiver v. Pennsylvania, 403 U.S. 528 (1971).

R.J.A. v. Foster, 603 So.2d 1167 (1992).

Schall v. Martin, 467 U.S. 253 (1984).

Shanks v. Cianca, 491 So.2d 1267 (1986).

Smith v. United States, 360 U.S. 1 (1959).

Solomon v. Mancusi, 412 F.2d 88, 2d Cir. (1969).

State of Washington v. Adamski, 761 P.2d 621 (1988).

State of Washington v. Day, 734 P.2d 491 (1987).

State of Washington v. Smith, 734 P.2d 491 (1987).

T.C. v. State of Florida, 540 So.2d 937 (1989).

APPENDIX

U.S. Counties Surveyed by the *Delays in Juvenile Justice Sanctions Project*

COUNTY	1990 POPULATION
Alabama	
Baldwin	98,280
Mobile	378,643
Arizona	
Maricopa	2,122,101
Mohave	93,497
Pima	666,880
California	
Alameda	1,279,182
Kern	543,477
Monterey	355,660
Riverside	1,170,413
San Bernardino	1,418,380
San Diego	2,498,016
San Francisco	723,959
San Mateo	649,623
Santa Clara	1,497,577
Sonoma	388,222
Ventura	669,016
Colorado	
Boulder	225,339
Connecticut	
Hartford	851,783
District Of Columbia	606,900
Delaware	
New Castle	441,946
Florida	
Dade	1,937,094
Duvall	672,971
Hillsborough	834,054
Orange	677,491
Pinellas	851,659
Polk	405,382
Seminole	287,529
Volusia	370,712

COUNTY	1990 POPULATION
Georgia	
Gwinnett	352,910
Warren	6,078
Hawaii	
Honolulu	836,231
Illinois	
Alexander	10,626
Carroll	16,805
Cook	5,105,067
Lake	516,418
Indiana	
Marion	797,159
Iowa	
Scott	150,979
Kansas	
Barber	5,874
Pratt	9,702
Kentucky	
Letcher	27,000
Pike	72,583
Louisiana (Parishes)	
E. Baton Rouge	380,105
Jefferson	448,306
Orleans	496,938
St. Tammany	144,508
Union	20,690
Massachusetts	
Bristol	506,325
Hampden	456,310
Middlesex	1,398,468
Plymouth	435,276
Suffolk	663,906
Maryland	
Baltimore	692,134
Charles	101,154

COUNTY	1990 POPULATION
Maryland (contnued)	
Frederick	150,208
Prince George's	729,268
Michigan	
Genesee	430,459
Oakland	1,083,592
Tuscola	55,498
Wayne	2,111,687
Minnesota	
Hennepin	1,032,431
Ramsey	485,765
Missouri	
Boone	112,379
Jackson	633,232
St. Louis City	396,685
Mississippi	
Tate	21,432
North Carolina	
Guilford	347,420
Mecklenburg	511,433
Wake	423,380
North Dakota	
Kidder	3,332
Richland	18,148
Nebraska	
Douglas	416,444
New Jersey	
Bergen	825,380
Camden	502,824
Essex	778,206
Middlesex	671,780
Monmouth	553,124
Morris	421,353
Somerset	240,279
New Mexico	
Bernalillo	480,577
Nevada	
Clark	741,459
Elko	33,530

COUNTY	1990 POPULATION
New York	
Erie	968,532
Jefferson	110,943
Monroe	713,968
Onondaga	468,973
Suffolk	1,321,864
Ohio	
Cuyahoga	1,412,140
Hamilton	866,228
Stark	367,585
Trumbull	227,813
Pennsylvania	
Clearfield	78,097
Delaware	547,651
Philadelphia	1,585,577
Westmoreland	370,321
York	339,574
Rhode Island	
Providence	596,270
South Carolina	
Aiken	120,940
Berkeley	128,776
Cherokee	44,506
Chesterfield	38,577
Orangeburg	84,803
Pickens	93,894
Richland	285,720
Tennessee	
Knox	335,749
Montgomery	100,498
Rutherford	118,570
Sumner	103,281
Weakley	31,972
Texas	
Austin	19,832
Brazoria	191,707
Burleson	13,625
Ector	118,934
Henderson	58,543
Jeff Davis	1,946
Potter	97,874
Travis	576,407

COUNTY	1990 POPULATION
Utah	
Salt Lake City	725,956
Virginia	
Bristol City	18,426
Northampton	13,061
Petersburg City	38,386
Washington	
Pierce	586,203
Snohomish	465,642
Spokane	361,364
Wisconsin	
Milwaukee	959,275
Waukesha	304,715
West Virginia	
Calhoun	7,885
Wyoming	
Sublette	4,843